D1830497

THE

HINDOOS AS THEY ARE

Owing to the antiquity and rarity of this book, certain pages are regrettably absent, and readability is compromised due to the blurring of the original text. If you possess any insights regarding the availability of these missing sections, kindly inform us. Your assistance is crucial in ensuring the completion of this significant work for the benefit of future generations.

THE

HINDOOS AS THEY ARE

A DESCRIPTION OF THE MANNERS, CUSTOMS

AND

INNER LIFE OF HINDOO SOCIETY

IN BENGAL.

BY

SHIB CHUNDER BOSE.

GYAN

Published by

Gyan Publishing House
5, Ansari Road
Daryaganj, New Delhi-110002
Phone: 011-47034999, 9811692060
E-mail: books@gyanbooks.com

Distribution Network
gyanbooks.com
India, USA, Canada, UK, Australia

© Publisher

All rights reserved. No part of this work may be reproduced, stored, adapted, or transmitted in any form or by any means, electronic, mechanical, photocopying, micro-filming, recording or otherwise, or translated in any language, without the prior written permission of the copyright owner and the publisher.

ISBN: 978-93-6208-295-4 (PB)
First Published, 1881

2nd Impression 2024

Printed at: Gyan Press, Delhi.

The book is sold subject to the condition that it shall not, by way of trade or otherwise, be lent, resold, hired out, or otherwise circulated without the prior publisher's written consent.

THE HINDOOS AS THEY ARE
Author: SHIB CHUNDER BOSE

THE
HINDOOS AS THEY ARE

A DESCRIPTION OF THE MANNERS, CUSTOMS
AND
INNER LIFE OF HINDOO SOCIETY
IN BENGAL.

SHIB CHUNDER BOSE

WITH A PREFATORY NOTE BY

THE REV. W. HASTIE, B. D.,
PRINCIPAL OF THE GENERAL ASSEMBLY'S INSTITUTION, CALCUTTA.

London:
EDWARD STANFORD, 55, CHARING CROSS.
Calcutta:
W. NEWMAN & Co., 3, DALHOUSIE SQUARE.
1881.

CONTENTS.

Page.

PREFATORY NOTE. i

INTRODUCTION. iii

I. THE HINDOO HOUSEHOLD 1

II. THE BIRTH OF A HINDOO 22

III. THE HINDOO SCHOOL-BOY 30

IV. VOWS OF HINDOO GIRLS 35

V. MARRIAGE CEREMONIES 41

VI. THE BROTHER FESTIVAL 90

VII. THE SON-IN-LAW FESTIVAL 92

VIII. THE DOORGA POOJAH FESTIVAL 93

IX. THE KALI POOJAH FESTIVAL 136

X. THE SARASWATI POOJAH 151

XI. THE FESTIVAL OF CAKES 155

XII. THE HOLI FESTIVAL 159

XIII. CASTE 165

XIV. A BRAHMIN 180

XV. THE BENGALEE BABOO 191

XVI. THE KOBIRAJ, OR NATIVE PHYSICIAN 209

XVII. HINDOO FEMALES 216

XVIII. POLYGAMY 227

XIX. HINDOO WIDOWS 237

XX. SICKNESS, DEATH, AND SHRAD OR FUNERAL CEREMONIES 246

XXI. SUTTEE, OR THE IMMOLATION OF HINDOO WIDOWS . 272

XXII. THE ADMIRED STORY OF SABITRI BRATA, OR THE WONDERFUL TRIUMPH OF EXALTED CHASTITY . 280

APPENDIX 293

PREFATORY NOTE.

Babu Shib Chunder Bose is an enlightened Bengali, of matured conviction and character, who, having received the stirring impulse of Western culture and thought during the early period of Dr. Duff's work in the General Assembly's Institution, has continued faithful to it through all these long and changeful years. His extended and varied experience, his careful habit of observation and contrast, his large store of general reading and information, and his rare sobriety and earnestness of judgment, eminently qualify him for lifting the veil from the inner domestic life of his countrymen, and giving such an account of their social and religious observances as may prove intelligible and instructive to general English readers. In the sketches which he has now produced we are presented with the first-fruits of "the harvest of a quiet eye" that has long meditatively watched the strange ongoings of this ancient society, and penetrated with living insight into the springs and tendency of its startling changes.

Although I had no special claim to any right of judgment upon the present phases of Hindu life, the writer took me early into his confidence, and from the apparent quality and sincerity of his work I had no hesitation in encouraging him to persevere, recommending him, however, to leave historical speculation to others and to confine himself to a faithful delineation of facts within his own experience. While his manuscripts were passing through my hands, I took pains to verify his descriptions by frequent reference to younger educated natives, who, in all cases, confirmed the accuracy and reliability of the details. The book will stand on its own merits with English readers, whose happily increasing interest in the forms and movements of Hindu life at this transitional period when the picturesque institutions and habits of thousands of years are visibly and irrevocably passing away, should gladly welcome its fresh and opportune representations. And all who, viewing without regret the decay of the old order and animated by the faith of nobler possibilities than it has ever achieved, are actually engaged in the great work of religious regeneration and social reform in India, should find much in these truthful but saddening sketches to intensify their sympathies and give definite direction and guidance to their best efforts.

W. HASTIE.

THE GENERAL ASSEMBLY'S INSTITUTION,
23rd March, 1881.

INTRODUCTION.

In presenting the following volume to the Public, I am conscious of the very great disadvantage I labor under in attempting to communicate my thoughts through the medium of a language differing from my mother-tongue both in the forms of construction and in the methods of expression. My appeal to the indulgence of the public is based on the ground of my work being true to its name. It professes to be a simple, but faithful, delineation of the present state of Hindoo society in Bengal, and especially in Calcutta, the Athens of Hindoosthan. I cannot promise any thing thrilling or sensational. My principal object is to give as much information as possible regarding the moral, intellectual, social and domestic economy of my countrymen and countrywomen. The interest attaching to the information and facts furnished will greatly depend on the spirit in which they may be received. To such of my readers as feel a genuine interest in a true reflection of the present state of society in this country, passing from a condition of almost impenetrable darkness to that of marvellous light, through the general and rapid diffusion of western knowledge, I do not think the details I have given will be found dull or dry. Not a few of the facts stated will, I fear, prove painfully interesting to those who are cognisant of the many incrusted defects and deficiencies still lurking in our social system. But if we carefully look at it we shall doubtless discover that it is not all darkness and clouds, "it has its crimson dawns, its rosy sunsets." The multitudinous phases of Hindoo life, though sadly revolting and repulsive in many respects, have nevertheless some redeeming features, revealing radiant glimpses of simpleand innocent joys. In discussing the various social questions in their purely earthly aspects and relationships, it may be I have treated some of them inadequately and superficially, but in so doing I claim the merit of a humble endeavour after perfect honesty. I have in no wise exaggerated, but have simply followed the golden maxim of "nothing ex tenuate nor set down aught in malice."

The men of the land, and not the land of the men, form the subject matter of my work. My attention has long been directed to the domestic, social, moral, intellectual and religious condition of the Hindoos. The deep researches of European savants have from time to time thrown a flood of light on the learning and antiquities of India. We have every reason to admire the great truthfulness and accuracy of their observations in many respects. As foreigners, however, they were naturally constrained to pay but a subordinate attention to the peculiar domestic and social economy of the Natives. The idea of attempting a sketch of the inner life and habits of the Hindoos in this age, was originally suggested to the writer by the Revd. Drs. Duff and Charles—two Christian philanthropists, whose names are deservedly enshrined in the grateful memory of the Hindoo community of Bengal, the great centre of their educational and religious achievements. It was cordially approved by that high-minded statesman, Sir Charles Theophilus, afterwards Lord Metcalfe, who practically taught the Indian Public what a writer in the "*Nineteenth Century*" so aptly calls the great Trinity of liberty,—freedom of speech, freedom of trade, and freedom of religion.

To supply this desideratum, and not merely to gratify the natural curiosity to know the inner life of the Hindoos, but to do something in the line of social amelioration by "bringing the stagnant waters of Eastern life into contact with the quickening stream of European progress," have been the chief aim of the following pages. Should a liberal Public, here as well as in Europe and America, vouchsafe its countenance to this my first literary enterprise, I purpose to continue my humble labor in the same sphere, extending my observation, if advisable, to a picture of the social life of Upper, Western and Southern India. The vastness of the subject is one great difficulty. It will open to all civilized and philanthropic nations a wide and yet unexplored field for the exercise of their thoughts and sympathies.

To Europeans, and more especially to Englishmen, who have for more than a century and a half, been the great and beneficent arbiters under Providence of the destiny of this vast empire, a correct knowledge of the domestic and social institutions of the Hindoos, is of the most vital importance, being essentially indispensable to a right understanding of the existing wants, wishes, feelings and sentiments, condition and progress of the subject race. Many erroneous ideas concerning the singular customs and observances of the people of India still prevail in Europe and America. They are partly due to defective observation, and partly to the prejudices of men whose minds are too pre-occupied to properly understand and appreciate the peculiar phases of character, manners and usages among nations other than their own. Such men are unfortunately led to associate the Natives "with ways that are dark and tricks that are vain." To remove the mass of misconception yet prevailing in some quarters by placing before the general reader a true and comprehensive knowledge of the daily life of a people, who occupy such a huge spot on the earth's surface, and whose numbers are counted by hundreds of millions, is indeed an important step towards the solution of a great social problem, and towards the removal of the gulf that divides the sons of the soil from the English rulers of the country. The tendency of close and constant intercourse is to promote an identity of interests between the two races. As a Native, the author may be allowed to have had the facilities requisite for acquiring a clear idea of the manners and customs of his countrymen, which may counterbalance in some degree the drawbacks and deficiencies naturally experienced by him on the score of language.

The Rev. W. Hastie, B. D., Principal of the General Assembly's Institution, and Mr. J. B. Knight, C. I. E., have laid me under great and lasting obligations by their kind suggestions and encouragement. I have particularly to thank the former for the prefatory note which he has written in response to my special request.

SHIB CHUNDER BOSE.

I.

THE HINDOO HOUSEHOLD.

IT is my intention in the following pages to endeavour to convey to the mind of the European reader some distinct idea of the present manners and customs, usages and institutions of my Hindoo countrymen, illustrative of their peculiar domestic and social habits and the *inner* life of our society, the minutiæ of which can never be sufficiently accessible to Europeans. "It is in the domestic circle that manners are best seen, where restraint is thrown aside, and no external authority controls the freedom of expression."

I shall begin with a general account of the normal Hindoo household, as at once the living centre and meeting point of the various elements of our society. But as it is impossible to describe the manifold gradations of social condition in a single sketch, I shall draw from the domestic arrangements of a family of one of the higher castes and provided with a convenient share of worldly prosperity. Only the principal elements in the group can now be alluded to, and some of them will be described with greater detail in separate sketches.

The family domicile of a Hindoo is, to all intents and purposes, a regular sanctum, not easily accessible to the outside world. Its peculiar construction, its tortuous passages, its small compartments and special apportionment, obviously indicate the prevalence of a taste "cabined, cribbed, confined," and preclude the admittance of free ventilation and free intercourse. The annals of history have long since established the fact that the close confinement system which exists in Bengal, was mainly owing to the oppressions of the Moslem conquerors, and more recently to the inroads of the Pindaree marauders, commonly termed *Burghees*, the tales of whose depredations are still listened to with gaping mouths and terrified interest.

The gradual consolidation of the British power having established on a firm basis the security of life and property, the people are beginning to avail themselves of an improved mode of habitation, affording better facilities of accommodation and a wider range of the comforts and conveniences of life. From time out of mind there has existed in the country a sort of domestic and social economy, bearing a close resemblance to the old patriarchal system, recognising the principle of a common father or ruler of a family, who exercises parental control over all. The system of a joint Hindoo family* partaking of the same food, living under the same roof from generation to generation, breathing the same atmosphere, and worshipping the same god, is decidedly a traditional inheritance which the particular structure of Hindoo society has long reared and fostered. This side of the subject will be enlarged upon in its proper place.

A few words about the respective position and duties of the principal members of a Hindoo household will be in place at the outset. I shall, therefore, begin with the *Kartá* or male head, who, as the term imports, exercises supreme control over the whole family, so that no domestic affair of any importance may be undertaken without his consent or knowledge. The financial management, almost entirely regulated by his superior judgment, seldom or never exceeds the available means at his disposal. The honor, dignity and reputation of the family wholly depend on his prudence and wisdom, weighted by age and matured by experience.

* The late Dr. Jackson, who was the family physician of the great Native millionaire,—Baboo Ashutosh Dey—seeing the very large number of men and women who resided in his family dwelling house, very facetiously remarked that the mansion was a small colony. A similar remark was made by Dr. Duff when he happened to see the numerous members of the Dutt family in Nimtollah, West of the Free Church Institution. If all the hildren and adults, male and female, of the family now, are counted, the actual number would, if I am not mistaken, come up to near 500 persons, perhaps more.

His own individual happiness is identified with that of the other members of the household. There is a proverbial expression among the Natives, teaching that the counsel of the aged should be accepted for all the practical purposes of life (except in a few unhappy instances to be noticed hereafter) and the rule exerts a healthy influence on the domestic circle. As the supreme Head he has not only to look after the secular wants of the family but likewise to watch the spiritual needs of all the members, checking irregularities by the sound discipline of earnest admonition. In accordance with the usual consequences of a patriarchal system, a respectable Hindoo is often obliged to support a certain number of hangers-on, more or less related to him by kinship. A brother, an uncle, a nephew, a brother-in-law, etc., with their families, are not unfrequently placed in this humiliating position, notwithstanding the currency of the trite apothegm,—which says, "it is better to be dependent on another for *food* than to live in his *house*." This saying is to be supplemented by another which runs thus: "*Luckhee*, the goddess of prosperity, always commands a numerous train." The proper significance of these phrases is but too practically understood and felt by those who have been unfortunate enough to come under their exemplification.

Next in point of importance in the category of the domestic circle is his wife, the *Ghinni*, or the female Head, whose position is a responsible one, and whose duties are alike manifold and arduous. She has to look after the victualling department, report to her husband or sons the exact state of the stores,* order what is wanted, account for the extra consumption of victuals, adopt the necessary precaution against

* Natives are always provident enough to lay in a month's supply of articles which are not of a perishable nature. In the Upper and Central Provinces, they generally provide a twelve-months' requirements at the harvest season when prices are moderate. They are thus enabled to husband their resources in the most economical manner possible.

being robbed, see that everyone is duly fed, and that the rite of hospitality is extended to the poor and helpless, watch that the rules of purity are practically observed in every department of the household, and make daily arrangements as to what meals are to be prepared for the day. The study of domestic economy engages her attention from the moment she undertakes the varied duties in the inner department of a household, the proper management of which, is, to her, a congenial occupation, becoming her sex, her position, her habitude, her taste. Independent of these domestic charges which are enough to absorb her mind, she has other duties to discharge, which shall be indicated hereafter.

The next chief constituents in the body of the household, are the daughters and daughters-in-law, whose relative positions and duties demand a separate notice. Viewed from their close relationship it is reasonable to conclude that they should bear the kindliest feelings to each other and evince a tender regard for mutual happiness, returning love for love and sympathy for sympathy. But, as elsewhere, unhappily, such is the depravity of human nature that the operation of antagonistic influences arising from dissimilar idiosyncracies, embitters some of the sweetest enjoyments of life. In the majority of cases, a *nanad*, the sister of the husband, though allied to another family, is nevertheless solicitous to minister to the domestic felicity of her *vaja* or the wife of his brother, but unhappily her intent is often misconstrued, and the sincerity of her motive questioned. Instead of an unclouded cordiality subsisting between them, the generous affection of the one is but ill-requited by the other. Hence, an unaccountable coldness commonly springs up between them which materially subtracts from the growth of domestic felicity. Shame on us that a vast amount of ignorance and prejudice yet renders us incapable of appreciating the highest end of the social state.

When the several female members of a household meet together, enlivened by the company of their neighbours and friends (such visits being few and far between), these first object of inquiry is generally the amount of ornaments possessed, their workmanship, their value. Few things please them better than a conversation on this subject, which from the absence of mental culture, almost wholly monopolizes their mind, despite the natural tendency of human intellect to a progressive development. If not thus absorbed, the time is usually frittered away by sundry petty frivolous inquiries of a purely domestic character. On matters of the most vital importance their notions are as crude and irrational as they are absurd and childish.* Except in isolated instances, their bearing towards each other is generally marked by suavity, and kindliness of manners which has a tendency to draw closer the bond of union between them all.

* The following scene will clearly illustrate the point. At an assembly of some females on a festive occasion, among other current topics of the day, the conversation turned on the religion of the *Sahib logues* (Europeans). Impelled by a sense of duty and justice no less than by the convictions of conscience, I admired the disinterested exertions of the Christian Missionaries in endeavouring to spread among our benighted countrymen the benefits of a good education as well as the blessings of a good religion. Fearlessly encountering all the dangers of the deep, which, happily for the cause of human advancement, have now been greatly minimized, renouncing all the pleasures of the world, and fortifying their minds against persecution, suffering and reproach, they come, not only among us but travel through the most uncongenial climes "to preach Christ." The remarkable disinterestedness and self-denial of some of these Missionaries is a bright reality, to appreciate which is to appreciate Christianity. Before the propagation of the religion of Christ, said I, the most admired form of goodness was centred in patriotism or the love of one's own country, but Jesus brought with him a new era of philanthrophy, the main pervading principle of which is a spirit of martyrdom in the cause of mankind. Can we find traces of such catholicism in our Hindoo Shaster? The universal fatherhood of God and brotherhood of man is only practically enunciated in the religion of Christ. The females were all struck with the noble, sublime, yet humble, forgiving and disinterested virtues of the religion of the *Sahib logues*. But a pert young female, quite unschooled by experience and too much wedded to wordly attractions, rather thoughtlessly replied that "the act of giving education is a good thing in its own way, so far as it affords a means of earning money, but why do the *Padrees* (Missionaries) strive to convert our Hindoo boys, and thereby compel them to forsake their parents to whom they owe their being? What advantage do they gain by such conversions? This is not good. Brahmo religion does not demand any such sacrifice. Why do the heads of the *Padrees* ache for this purpose? They ought to give all their money to us, poor women, that we may buy ornaments therewith." Such is the low, grovelling idea they generally have of Christianity. It is useless to argue with them, simply because their minds are completely saturated with deep-rooted prejudice, and narrow, debased, selfish views.

It is on such occasions that the amiable loveliness of human nature, is displayed,—brightening, for a time, at least the otherwise dark region of a Hindoo zenana and cheering the hearts of its inmates. In a thickly populated city like Calcutta, with its broad roads and dense crowds at all hours of the day, without a closed conveyance, either a palkee or a carriage, no married female is permitted to leave the house even for a single moment, for that of her sister, perhaps some three doors from her own. So great is the privacy, and punctiliousnesss with which female honor is guarded in the East. The sanction of the male or female head must, as a standing rule of female etiquette, be obtained before any one is at liberty to go out even to return a friendly or ceremonious visit. The reader may form an idea as to the tenacity with which the close zenana system in a respectable family is enforced, from the circumstance of a young *Bahou* or daughter-in-law (the rules being not so strict in the case of a daughter) being set down as immodest and unmannerly, if she were accidently seen to tread the outer or male compartment of the house. If she but chance to articulate a word or a phrase so as to reach the ear of a male outside, she is severely censured, and steps are instantly taken, to teach her better manners for the future. Even the *Ghinni*, or female Head, does not escape censure for a like offence. With such scrupulous pertinacity is the privacy of the *inner* life of the Hindoo society observed. A social line of demarcation is drawn around the zenana which a genteel Hindoo female is told and taught never to overstep, either in her conversation or bearing Woe be to the day when she is incautiously led to move beyond her sphere, which, for all the practical purposes of life, is closely hemmed in by a ring of miserable seclusion, illustrating the scornful lines of the poet :

"Let Eastern tyrants from the light of heaven
Seclude their bosom slaves."

A few advanced Hindoos, more especially the Brahmos, who have received the benefits of an enlightened education, are making strenuous efforts to ameliorate the degraded condition of their wives and sisters (the mothers being too old and conservative to acquiesce in the spirit of modern innovation) and bring them to the front, if possible, by ignoring the rules of orthodoxy. But it is the firm belief of such as have been schooled by experience and observation, that the time is yet far distant when this bold, sweeping, social revolution shall be brought about with the general consensus of the people at large. The moral tone of Native society must be immensely raised, its manners and customs entirely remodelled, and its traditional institutions and prescriptive usages thoroughly purified before the consummation of so desirable an object can be successfully effected.

A Hindoo girl, even after marriage, enjoys greater liberty and is treated with more indulgence at her father's house than at her father-in-law's. The cause of this is obvious. From the very period of her birth, she is nurtured by her mother, aunts, sisters and other female relatives, no less than by her father, uncle, brothers and other male members of the family, all of whom naturally continue to bear her the same love and affection throughout her after life. A mother hugs her more tenderly, caresses her more fondly, hangs about her more affectionately, feels greater sympathy in her joy and sorrow, and watches more carefully how she grows up in health to her present state, than a mother-in-law. Whether she is eating, talking or playing, her mother's care never ceases. Should maternal admonition fail to produce the desired effect, as it does in a few isolated instances, the usual threat of sending her to her father-in-law's, acts as the most wholesome corrective.

The social relaxations of Hindoo females have a very limited range. Some delight in reading the Mahábhárat, the

Ramayán, tales, romances, etc, while others are fond of needle-work, playing at cards, or listening to stories of a puerile description. Though they seldom come out of their houses, except under permissive sanction, yet their stock of gossip is almost inexhaustible. They are generally lively and loquacious, and the chief passion of their life is for the acquisition of ornaments. They possess a retentive memory, seldom forgetting what they once hear. Fond of hyperboles, the sober realities of life have little attraction for their minds. Their social tone is neither so pure nor so elevated as becomes a polished, refined community. It is almost needless to add, that their familiar conversation is not characterised by that chaste, dignified language, which constitutes the prominent feature of a people far advanced in the van of civilization. Objectionable modes of expression generally pass muster among them, simply because they labor under the great disadvantage of the national barrenness of intellect and the acknowledged poverty of colloquial literature.

It is a well-known fact that Hindoo males and females do not take their meals together. Both squat down on the floor at the time of eating. Except in the case of little girls, it is held highly unbecoming in a grown up female to be seen eating by a male member of the family. As a rule, women take their meals after the men have finished theirs. There is a popular belief that women take a longer time to eat than men. Of the perfection of the culinary art, the former are better judges than the latter. They chat and eat leisurely because they have no offices to go to, nor any definite occupation to engage their minds in. A Hindoo writer has said, that commonly speaking, they eat more and digest more readily than men. Naturally modest, they take their meals without any complaint, though sometimes they are served with food not of the very best description. The choicest part of the food is offered in the first instance to the males and the residue is kept for the females.) A woman is religiously forbidden to taste of anything in the shape of eatables before it is given to a man. Simple in taste, diet and habits, but shut up in a state of close confinement, and leading a monotonous life, scarcely cheered by a ray of light, they are necessarily not receptive of large communications of truth.

The children form an important link in the great chain of the domestic circle. When sporting about in childhood they have commonly spare persons, light brown skins, high foreheads beaming with intelligence, large dark eyes, with aquiline noses, small thin-lipped mouths, and dark soft hair. The fairness of their complexion is generally sallowed by exposure to the sun in the earliest stage of childhood.

(The child grows up under the fostering care of its parents amidst all the surroundings of the family domicile. As it advances in years the mother endeavours, according to her very limited capacity, to instil into its mind the rude elements of knowledge. From the incipient stage of early infancy when his mind is rendered susceptible of culture and expansion, crude and imperfect religious ideas largely leavened with superstition, are communicated to him, which subsequently mould his character in an undesirable manner. His early affections and moral principles are most entirely influenced by the impressions he receives at the maternal fount, and he seldom comes in contact with the outer world. He is taught to pay divine homage to all the idols that are worshipped at stated periods of the year, and his indistinct ideas grow into deep convictions, the pernicious influence of which can only afterwards be effaced by the blessings of western knowledge. In the villages "*chánaka sloaka*" or elementary lessons are still given as a sort of moral exercise. The mother from want of adequate capacity or culture is unfit to engraft on the youthful mind the higher divine truths, to teach the child how to look on men, how to feel for them, how to bear with them, how to be true, honest, manly, and how to "look beneath the outward to the spiritual, immortal and divine." Solid, practical wisdom, however, is often extracted from the most commonplace experiences, even by untutored minds.

"Honor thy father and thy mother," is the first scriptural commandment with promise, the importance and excellence of which is early impressed on the mind of a Hindoo child by wise, discreet parents. And Hindoos are honorably distinguished by their affections for their parents, and continue to be so even in the maturer years of their life.

In the case of a girl, even the most elementary sort of instruction is neglected except that she occasionally studies the Bengallee primer,—an innovation which the spirit of the times countenances. When of proper age, she is sent to a female school where she pursues her studies until finally withdrawn therefrom after her marriage.) As a rational being she may continue to evince a natural desire and aptitude for intellectual progress and to carry it on by home study according to her taste and position in life. A few have made astonishing progress, despite certain formidable obstacles which an abnormal state of society inevitably interposes. The traditional bugbear of becoming a widow if she were to learn to read and write has happily passed away, not only in the great centres of education but likewise in several parts of the rural districts, where, to all appearances, females are just beginning, as it were, to assert their right to the improvement of their minds. This is certainly an unerring presage, foreshadowing the advent of national regeneration in the fullness of time. Many families being well-to-do in the world engage a Christian governess*

* The following incident will doubtless contribute not a little to the amusement of the reader. One day a governess was giving instructions in needle-work to a young married girl of thirteen years of age. She, (the girl) was industriously plying the needle, when lo! an aged female cook from the house of her husband suddenly appeared before her, and simply enquired of her how she was. The shy girl, overpowered by a sense of shame, dropped down her veil almost to the ground, and not only stopped work but likewise ceased to talk to

both for elementary instruction as well as for needle-work, the latter being an accomplishment which even the most matronly ladies have now taken a great liking for. The introduction of this art of tasteful production has, in a great measure, superseded the idle, unprofitable gossip of the day, driving away ennui and slothfulness at the same time.

In almost every respectable Hindu household there is a tutelar god, chiefly made of stone and metal after one of the images of Krishna, set up on a gold or silver throne with silver umbrella and silver utensils dedicated to its service. Every, morning and evening it is worshipped by the hereditary *Purohit*, or priest, who visits the house for the purpose twice a day, and who, as the name implies, is the *first* in all religious ceremonies, second to none but the *guru* or spiritual guide. The offerings of rice, fruits, sweetmeats and milk, made to the god, he carries home after the close of the service. A conch is blown, a bell is rung, and a gong beat at the time of the Poojah, when the religiously disposed portion of the inmates, male and female, in a quasi-penitent attitude, make their obeisance to the god and receive in return the hollow benediction of the priest. The daily repetition of the service quickens the heartbeats of the devotees and serves to remind them, however faintly, of their religious duties. Such a worship is popularly regarded in the light of an act of great merit paving the way to everlasting bliss. A suitable endowment in, landed property is sometimes set apart for the permanent support of the idol, which is called the *debatra* land or inalienable property, according to the Hindu Shastras. Some families

the governess. The latter struck with amazement, quietly asked her pupil if she had hurt her eyes because she held fast her right hand on that part of her face. Other ladies of the family stepped forward and explained to the governess the real cause of the awkward position the girl was placed in. It was nothing more nor less than the unexpected visit of the female cook to the family of the bride. From feelings of false delicacy in presence of her husband's cook, she hung down her face and dropped down her veil. The governess learning the true cause politely desired the female cook to retire that she might be enabled to give her lessons without any interruption.

that have been reduced to a state of poverty through the reverses of fortune now live on the usufruct of the *debatra* land, which serves as a sheet-anchor in stormy weather.

Besides the daily Poojah of the household deity there are some other extraordinary religious celebrations, such as Doorga, Kali, Lakshmi, Jagaddhatri, Saraswati, Kartik, Janmáshtami, Dole, Rásh, Jhoolun, Jatras, etc., (the latter four being all Poojahs of Krishna) which excite the religious fervor of the Vaishnavas, as contra-distinguished from the Saktas, the followers of Kali or Doorga the female principle.

The internal daily details of a Hindu household next demand our attention. In the morning when the breakfast is ready the little children are served first as they have to go to their schools, and then the adult male members, chiefly brothers, nephews, etc., who have to attend their offices. They all squat down *vis-a-vis* on small bits of carpet on the floor, while the mother sits near them, not to eat but to see that they are all properly served; she closely watches that each and every one of them is duly satisfied; she would never feel happy should any of them find fault with a particular dish as being unsavoury, she snubs the cook and taxes herself for her own want of supervision in the kitchen, because the idea of having failed to do her duty in this respect is an agony to her mind.

As a mother, she avails herself of this opportunity to plunge into conversation, and consult her sons about the conduct of all domestic affairs, which necessarily expand as there are adjuncts to the original stock. For example, she takes their advice as to the amount of expenditure to be incurred at the forthcoming wedding of *Sharat Shashee*, the youngest daughter, in the month of Falgun, or February. This is an occasion, when the hearts of both the sons and the mother overflow with the milk of human kindness, yet there is a desire to avoid extravagance as far as possible.

A prudent mother wisely regulates her expenses according to the means and earnings of her sons, and she seldom or never comes to grief. The idea of an extravagant Hindoo mother is a solecism that has no existence in the actual realities of life. She is a model of economy, devotion, chastity, patience, self-denial, and a martyr to domestic affection. She may be wanting in mental accomplishment, which is not her own fault, but the very large share of strong common-sense she is naturally endowed with, sufficiently makes up for every deficiency in all the ordinary concerns of life. Accustomed to look upon her sons as the pride of her existence, she seeks every legitimate means to promote their happiness. If her daughters-in-law turn out querulous, and fall out one with another, which is not unfrequently the case, she reconciles them by the panacea of gentle remonstrance. But unhappily, such is the degeneracy of the present age that the influence of wholesome admonition being shamefully ignored is often lost in the cataclysm of discord, and the inevitable consequence is, that vicious selfishness disturbs Heaven's blessed peace, and "love cools, friendships fall off, brothers divide."

After the sons have gone to their respective offices, the mother changing her clothes retires into the *thakurghar* (the place of worship) and goes through her morning service, at the close of which she prostrates herself, invokes the blessing of her guardian deity, and then again changing her clothes, takes her breakfast and enjoys a short siesta, while chewing a mouthful of betel sometimes mixed with tobaco leaf, in order to strengthen her teeth.

In any sketch of a Hindu family it is necessary that something should be said about the domestic servants attached to a Hindu household. The cook, whose employment involves some very important considerations, may be either a male or a female. In most families, a preference is generally shewn for a female cook* for reasons which are obvious. The kitchen, being as a rule, placed in the inner division of the house, the females have an opportunity to assist her in various ways, so as to facilitate and expedite her work, which certainly is not always of the most pleasant nature. The dietary of a Hindu family, as may be easily anticipated, is of the simplest description, consisting for the most part of vegetables and fishes, with a little milk and ghee, but no eggs or meat of any kind. Not like the prepared dishes of the French and Moguls, highly flavored and richly spiced, the daily preparations are very simple; no onion, garlic, or strong aromatic spices are used. They are easy of digestion and palatable to taste, being altogether free from offensive and fœtid smell. The simple turmeric, pepper, cummin, coriander and mustard seeds, etc., generally impart a fine flavor to the preparations, which the frugal and abstemious Hindus eat with great zest. I have known the wives of several rich Baboos, take a delight in preparing with their own hands the evening meal of their husband and sons. This is entirely a labor of love, which they go through with the greatest cheerfulness. It is necessary to mention here that without fishes, which are very abundant, a nice little Hindoo breakfast or dinner in Bengal is an impossibility. The art of cooking should not be a mystery to all save the initiated few, it should be the study of every good and thrifty woman who is willing to sacrifice needless elegance and pomp to comfort and economy.

This gastronomical digression will serve to indicate the taste of the Hindu in Bengal, and the very simple style of their living. Even in the selection of articles of food a nice distinction is observed; fishes are dressed in a part of

* Whether descended from a Brahmin or Kayasth family, she goes by the general name of *Bamun Didi* (sister) so named that the members of other families might unsuspectingly eat out of her hands. She is also called *Maye* (woman). The entertaining of a middle aged female (generally a widow) is considered safe and irreproachable.

the kitchen quite distinct from where the vegetable dishes are prepared, because a widow is strictly forbidden to use anything which comes in contact with fishes. Moreover, a widow would not accept a dish unless it is prepared by a real Brahmin cook, male or female. Should a male member of the family be ever disposed to eat goat flesh (he being forbidden to use any other kind of meat, save mutton, when sacrificed) a *Sakta* cook undertakes to prepare it for him. When finished, she changes her clothes and purifies her body by sprinkling over it a few drops of Ganges water. Excepting little unmarried girls, whose parents are *Saktas* (worshippers of female deities) no other Hindu female is permitted to use meat even by sufferance. In other rigidly orthodox families a similar concession is withheld.

The wage of a female cook, who in nine cases out of ten is a widow, is about six to seven Rupees a month, with a few annas extra for *Ekadashi*—the day of close fast for all widows—and cocoanut oil for her hair,* six pieces of grey shirtings each ten cubits long, and three bathing napkins a year. She also gets an extra piece of cloth at the Doorga Poojah festival, when the most wretched pauper, somehow or other, puts on new clothes. Some of the widow cooks have certainly seen better days, but the vicissitudes of fortune have made them hopelessly destitute. As a rule, they bear the load of misfortune with the greatest patience. They chiefly come from the villages, and it speaks much in favor of the purity of their character that they ungrudgingly submit to the menial offices of a drudge, instead of being seduced into the forbidden paths of life. Of course there are a few black sheep in the flock, but happily their number is very limited. A male

---

* In order to preserve the hair and keep it clean, all Hindu females in Bengal use cocoanut oil for the head ; they however rub their bodies with mustard oil before bathing. Young ladies occasionally use pomatum, bear's grease, soap, etc., which, in a religious sense, is desecration.

cook is always a Brahman. It is almost superfluous to add that the employment in a family or the admittance of any man-servant into the inner apartment of a Hindoo household, which is emphatically the great centre, as well of domestic happiness as of religious sanctity, is open to many objections.

The second domestic servant that demands a notice at our hands is the *Jhee*, or maid-servant of the family. Her duties are alike onerous and troublesome. Like the potter's wheel she incessantly turns backwards and forwards and knows no rest till about ten o'clock at night. She rises early in the morning, sweeps and washes all the rooms and verandahs inside the house, cleans all the brass utensils of the family, makes fire in the stove, pounds the kitchen spices prepares fishes for cooking purposes, and attends to other duties of a household nature. Some maid-servants are almost exclusively employed in taking care of children. Their duties are not so hard as those of the family *Jhee* indicated above. These females are often drawn from the dregs of society, and their conduct, or rather misconduct, sometimes leads to the most unhappy results. Their wage is about two Rupees a month, exclusive of food and clothes. They occasionally also make something by carrying presents to relatives and friends.

I next come to the male servants: there are more than a half-dozen of them in a respectable family, and their services are in the main confined to the outer apartment of the household. They sweep and clean all the rooms, spread white cloth bedding on the floor, change the water of the *hookah* (the first essential both at an ordinary and special reception) fill the *chillum* with tobacco, *kochay*, or trim the fine black bordered Simla *Dhuti* and *Kalmay Urani* (Baboo's native dressing attire) put in order the lamps, and go to Bazar to make purchases. Their pay ranges from three to four Rupees a month, exclusive of food and clothes.

A rich Hindoo, however, has a large establishment of servants in addition to those mentioned above. There are durwans (door-keepers) ; syces (grooms) ; coachmen, gardeners, sircar, cashier, accountant, etc., each of whom discharges his functions in his own sphere, but they seldom or never come in contact with the female inmates of the household. The cashier is the most important and responsible person, and his income is larger than that of any other servant, because he gets his commission from all tradespeople dealing with the family. All of them get presents of clothes at the great national festival the Doorga Pujah.

The *khansamah* of a Baboo is his most favorite servant. From the nature of his office he comes into closest contact with his master, he rubs his body with oil before bathing and sometimes shampooes him,—a practice which gradually induces idle, effeminate habits, and eventually greatly incapacitates a man for the manifold duties of an active life. Indeed, to study the life of a "big native swell" is to study the character of a consummate Oriental epicure, immersed in a ceaseless round of pleasures, and hedged in by a body of unconscionable fellows, distinguished only for their flattery and servility

Except in isolated instances, the general treatment of domestic servants by their masters, is not reprehensible.

Except such as possess a thorough insight into the peculiar mysteries of the inner life of the Hindoo society, very few are aware that a wife—perhaps the mother of three or four children—is forbidden to open her lips or lift her veil in order to speak to her husband in presence of her mother-in-law, or any other adult male or female member of the family. She may converse with the children without fear of being exposed to the charge of impropriety ; this is the systole and diastole of her liberty, but she is imperatively commanded to hold her tongue and drop down her veil whenever she happens to see an elderly member in her way. A phrase used in common parlance (*Bhasur Bhadrabau*) denotes the utmost privacy, as that which the *wife* of a younger brother should observe towards the elder *brother* of her husband. It is an unpardonable sin, as it were, in the former, even to come in contact with the very shadow of the latter. The rules of conventionalism have reared an adamantine partition wall between the two. We have all learnt in our school-days that modesty is a quality which highly adorns a woman, but the peculiar domestic economy of the natives, carries this golden rule to the utmost stretch of restriction, verging on sacred, religious prohibition.

The general state of Hindoo female society, as at present constituted, exhibits an improved moral tone, presenting an edifying contrast to the gross proclivities of former times as far as popular amusements are concerned. The popular amusements of the Hindoos, like those of many European nations, have rarely been characterised by essentially moral principles. But the loose and immoral amusements of the former time do not now so much interest our educated females. The popular Native *Jatras* (representations) do not now breathe those low, obscene expressions, which was the wont only some thirty years back, yet they are not, withal, absolutely pure or elevated. It is true that some of them are touching and pathetic in their themes, not jarring to a moral sense but admirably adapted to the taste of a people having a supreme respect for their idolatrous and mythological systems, from which most of these *Jatras* are derived. The marvellous and the supernatural always exact an instinctive regard from the ignorant and the credulous multitude, destitute of the superior blessings of enlightenment. The *Panchaly* (represented by female actresses only) which is given for the amusement of the females, especially at the time of the second marriage, is sometimes much too obscene and immoral to be tolerated in a zenana having any pretension to gentility. On such an occasion, despite a strict conventional restriction, a depraved taste clearly manifests itself. Much has yet to be done to develope among the females a taste for purer amusements, and such as are better adapted to a healthy state of society.

In Hindoo females there is a prominent trait which deserves to be commended. Moses, Mohammed, and Manu, observes Benjamin Disraeli, say cleanliness is religion. Cleanliness certainly promotes health of body and delicacy of mind. When that excellent prelate, Heber, travelled in a boat on the sacred stream of the Ganges, seeing large crowds of Hindu females engaged in washing their bodies and clothes on both sides of the river, at the rising and setting of the sun, he most emphatically remarked that cleanliness is the supreme virtue of Hindoo women. In the Upper Provinces, at all seasons of the year, hundreds of women could be daily seen with baskets of flowers in their hands slowly walking in the direction of the river, and chanting songs in a chorus in praise of the "unapproachable sanctuary of Mahadev, the great glacier world of the Himàlayà, with its wondrous pinnacles, rising 24,000 feet above the level of the sea, and descending into the amethyst-hued ice cavern, whence issues, in its turbulent and noisy infancy, the sacred river of India." They display a purity, a sincerity, a constant and passionate devotion to their faith, which present a striking contrast to the conduct of men steeped in the quagmire of profligacy.

Our ladies bathe their bodies and change their clothes twice in a day, in the morning and in the afternoon, neglecting which they are not permitted to take in hand any domestic work.

In the large Hindoo households, the lot of the wife who is childless is truly deplorable. While her sisters are rejoicing in the juvenile fun and frolics of their respective children, sporting with all the elasticity of a light, free, and buoyant heart, she sits sulkily aloof, and inwardly repines at the unkind ordinance of *Bidhátá* and earnestly invokes *Ma Shasthi* (the patron deity of all children) to grant her the inestimable boon of offspring, without which this butterfly life is unsanctified, unprofitable and hollow.

The barrenness of a Hindoo female is denounced as a sin, for the atonement of which certain religious rites are performed, and incessant prayers offered to all the terrestrial and celestial gods; but all her superstitious practices proving in vain, only tend to intensify her misery.

In the beginning of this sketch I set out by stating that the peculiar constitution of Hindoo society bears an affinity to the old patriarchal system. This is true to a very great extent. The system has its advantages and disadvantages, which are, in a great measure, inseparable from the outgrowth of the social organism. If properly weighed in the scale, the latter will most assuredly counterbalance the former, so much so, that in the great majority of cases, discord and disquietude is the inevitable result of joint fraternisation. Leadership is certainly organisation; it formed the nucleus of the patriarchal system. But it is simply absurd to expect that there should always be a happy marriage of minds in all cases, between so many men and women living together, endowed with different degrees of culture and influenced by adverse interests and sentiments. In the nature of things, it is impossible that all the members of a large family, having separate and specific objects of their own, should coalesce and cordially co-operate to promote the general welfare of a family, under a common leader or head. The millennium is not yet come. Seven brothers living together with their wives and children under one and the same paternal roof, cannot reasonably be expected to abide in a state of perfect harmony so long as selfishness and incongruous tastes and interests are continually at work to sap the very foundation of friendliness and good fellowship. Union is strength, but harmonious union under the peculiar regime indicated above, is already a remarkable exception in the present state of Hindoo society. If minutely probed, it will be found that women are at the bottom of that mischievous discord, which eats into the very vitals of domestic felicity. Segregation, therefore, is the only means that promises to afford a relief from this social incubus; and to segregation many families' have now resorted, much after the fashion of the dominant race, with a view to the uninterrupted enjoyment of domestic happiness.

Having briefly indicated in the preceding lines the chief family constituents of a Hindoo household in their several relations and characteristics, it is scarcely necessary for me to add, that whenever this interesting group, consisting of sweet children, loving husbands and wives, and affectionate parents and brothers, is animated by the vital, indestructible principles of virtue, practically recognising the obligations of duty, the divinity of conscience, and the moral connection of the present and future life, it will be found to diffuse all the blessings of peace, joy and moral order around the social and domestic hearth.

II.
THE BIRTH OF A HINDOO.

THE birth of a Hindoo into the household of which he is to form an essential constituent is attended with circumstances which partake, more or less, of the religion he inherits. It has been said that by tradition and instinct as well as by early habits, he is a religious character. He is born religiously, lives religiously, eats religiously, walks religiously, writes religiously, sleeps religiously and dies religiously. His everyday life is an endless succession of rites and ceremonies which he observes with the utmost of scrupulousness sanctioned by divine veneration. From his very birth his mind is imbued with superstitious ideas, which subsequent mental culture can hardly ever eradicate, so strong being the influence of his early impressions.

It is now generally known that Hindoo girls are betrothed even in their tenderest years, and that the solemnisation of the marriage takes place whenever they attain to the age of puberty. Thus it is not uncommon for a young wife to be delivered of her first child in her thirteenth year, although the glory of motherhood is more frequently not realised until the fourteenth or fifteenth year. When the period of delivery arrives, and to her it is an awful period, which can be more easily conceived than described, the girl writhing under agony is taken into a room called Sootikaghur or Antoorghur, where no male members of the family are admitted. She is made to wear a red-bordered robe and two images of the goddess *Shashthi* made of cow-dung are placed near the threshold of the room for her daily worship with rice and *durva* grass, for one month—the period of her confinement. If in her tender age, the labor be a protracted one, she often suffers greatly from the want of a skilful surgeon or even a proper midwife. Before the founding of that noble Institution, the Calcutta Medical College, proper midwives were not procurable, because they had had no systematic training ; their profession was chiefly confined to the Dome and Bagthee caste, yet some of them were known to have acquired a tolerable fortune. Their fee varied from 5 to 50 Rupees, besides clothes and other gifts; the poor, certainly, giving less. For some years past, a strong belief has sprung up among some women that delivery in the name of god Hari Krishna is very safe. They that follow this religious regime, are believed, in the majority of cases, to have passed through the struggle of childbirth quite scathless. They use no *jhall* or *thap*,* bathe in cold water immediately after delivery, take the ordinary food of *dhall vath*, curry, fish and tamarind, after offering them to the god Hari, and on the 30th day make a Poojah (worship) consecrating in honor of the god a quantity of sweetmeats (*sundesh and batasha*) and finally distribute them among children and others. This distribution is called Hariloot. This strong faith in the god seems to enable them to pass the period of confinement without danger. If the offspring of such women become strong, their strength is attributed to the mercy of the said god.†

A woman that follows the old prescribed practice has to take *jhall* and *thap* and go through a strict course of dietetics, abstaining altogether from the use of cold water or any cooling beverage. She has to undergo the action of heat for at least five hours a day. The body and head of the newborn babe is rubbed with warm mustard oil—an application which is considered the best preservative of health in children. Exposure of the mother in any shape, is most strictly prohi-

---

* *Jhall* is a preparation of certain drugs to act as an antidote against cold, puerperal fever and other diseases incident to child birth. It often proves efficacious. *Thap* is the application of heat to the body.

† For observances during the period of pregnancy, see Note A in appendix.

bited, and the use of certain indigenous drugs and warm applications is made as an antidote against all diseases of a puerperal character.

While undergoing the throes of nature, the exhausted spirit of the expectant mother is buoyed up by the fond hope of having a *male* child, which, in the estimation of a Hindoo female, is worth a world of suffering.

In the event of the offspring turning out a female, her friends try to encourage her for the moment by their assurance that the child born is a male, and a lovely and sweet child, ushered into the world under the peculiar auspices of the goddess Shasthi. Such assurances serve very much to keep up her spirit for the time being, but when she is brought to her senses and does not hear the sound of a conch* her delusion is removed, sorrow and disappointment take the place of joy and excitement, her buoyant spirit collapses and a strong reaction sets in. Thus in a moment, a grace is converted into a gorgon, a beauty into a monstrosity, an angel into a fiend. She curses the day, she curses her fate. But "such is the make and mechanism of human nature" that she soon resigns herself to the wise dispensations of an overruling Providence. She gradually feels a strong affection for the female child and rears it with all the care and tenderness of a mother; she caresses and fondles it as if it were a boy, and her affection grows warmer as the child grows. This is natural and inevitable. At the birth of a male child, the occurrence is immediately announced by *sanka dhani* (sound of a conch); musicians without being sent for, come and play the *tom tom;* the family barber bears the happy tidings to all the nearest relatives, and he is rewarded with presents of money and cloths. Oil, sweetmeats, fishes, curdled milk, and other things, are presented to the relatives and neighbours,

* According to custom, a conch or large shell is sounded at the birth of a male child. Its silence is the sign of sorrow.

who, in return, offer their congratulations. A rich Hindoo, though he studies practical domestic economy very carefully, is, however, apt to loosen his purse string at the birth of a son and heir. The mother forgetting her trouble and agony implores *Bidhátá** for the longevity of the child. She cheerfully suckles it and her heart swells with joy every time she looks at its face.

On the second day after delivery, she gets a little sago and *cheeray vájáh* (a sort of parched rice). On the third day the same diet, with the addition of a single grain of boiled rice, and a little fried potatoe or *pull bull*, that she may use those things afterwards with safety. On the fifth day, if everything is right, the room is washed and she is allowed to come out of it for a short time; a little boiled rice and *moong dhall* is her diet that day.

On the sixth day, the image of the goddess *Shasthi* is worshipped in front of the room where the child was born, because she is the protectress of all children. The Poojah is called the *Seytayra* Poojah (worship). Offerings of rice, plantain, sweetmeat, clothes, milk, &c., are presented to the goddess by the officiating priest, and the following articles are kept in her room for the *Bidhátá Pooroosh* (god of fate) in order that he may note down unseen on the forehead of the child its future destiny, *viz.*, a palm leaf, a Bengalee pen with ink, a serpent's skin, a brick from the temple of the god Shiva, and two kinds of fruits, *atmora* and *veyla*, a little wool, gold and silver. On the eighth day is held the ceremony of *Autcowroy*, or the distribution of eight kinds of parched peas, rice, sweetmeats, with cowries and pice, amongst the children of the house and neighbourhood. On the evening of that day, the children assemble and with a *Koolo* (winnowing fan) going up three times to the door of the room beat it (the koolo) with small sticks, asking at the same in a chorus "as to how

* Bidhátá is the god of fate.

the child is doing," and shouting, "let it rest in peace on the lap of its mother." These juvenile ceremonies, if ceremonies they can be called, give infinite delight to the children, who are sometimes prompted by the adult members of the family to indulge in jocularity by way of abusing the father, not of course to irritate but to amuse him. At the birth of a female child, in common with the depreciation in which it is held, this ceremony is observed on a very poor scale. On the thirty-first day after the birth, the ceremony of *Shasthi* Poojah is again performed. Hence a woman who has had as many as twelve or fifteen or more children, is called the *Shasthi Booree*, or "the old woman of Shasthi." Before a twig of a *Bátá* tree, the priest, while repeating the usual incantation, presents offerings of rice, fruits, sweetmeats, cloths, parched peas and rice, oil, turmeric, betel, betel-nuts, two eggs of a duck, and twenty-one small wicker baskets filled with *khoyee* (parched rice) plantain and *bátásá*, which are all given to a number of women whose husbands are alive. It is on this occasion that the priest is also required to perform the worship of the goddess *Soobachinee*,* said to be one of the forms of the goddess Doorga.

When the father first goes to see the child, he puts some gold coin into its hand and pours his benediction on its head. Other relatives who may be present at the time do the same.

All respectable Hindoos keep an exact record of the birth of a child, especially a male child. Every family has its *Dowyboghee* or astrologer who prepares a horoscope in which he notes down the day, the hour and the minute of the birth of the child, opens the roll of its fate and describes what shall happen to it during the period of its existence. These horoscopes are so much relied on, that if it is stated therein that the stellar mansion under which the child was born was not good, and that it shall be exposed to serious dangers,

* For the popular story of the goddess Soobachinee see Note B.

either from sickness or accident, at such a period of its life, every possible care is taken through *Grohojag* and *Sustyan* (religious atonement) to propitiate the god of fate, and ward off the apprehended danger before it comes to pass. These papers are carefully preserved by the parents, who occasionally refer to them when anything, good or evil, happens to the child. A Hindoo astrologer is a man of high pretensions; he dives into the womb of futurity and foretells what shall happen to a man in this life, without thinking for a moment, that our Creator has not vouchsafed to us the powers of divination. In a court of justice these papers are of great value in verifying the exact age of a person, and at the time of marriage, or rather before it, they are carefully consulted as to the nature of the stellar mansion under which both the boy and girl were born, and the peculiar circumstances by which they were surrounded. Many a match is broken off because the twelve signs in the zodiac do not coincide; for instance, if the boy be of the *Lion rass* (sign) and the girl of the *Lamb rass*, the one, it is said, will destroy the other; so these papers are of very great importance when a matrimonial alliance is in course of being negotiated.

When a male child is six months old, the parents make preparations for the celebration of the *Unnoprássun*, or christening, when not only a name is given to the child, but it gets boiled rice for the first time. On this occasion, the father is required to perform a *Bidhi Shrád* so called from the increase and preservation of the members of the family. Some who live near Calcutta celebrate the rite by going to Kallee Ghaut, and procuring a little boiled rice through one of the priests of the sacred fane at a cost of eight or ten Rupees. When the rice is brought home a few grains are put into the mouth of the child by a male member of the family. The ceremony being thus performed the child from that day is allowed to take prepared food if necessary. Such families as do not choose to go to Kallee Ghaut observe the ceremony at home, and spend from 200 to 300 Rupees in feeding the Brahmans, friends and relatives, who, in return, offer their benediction and give from one to ten Rupees each to the child, which being shaved, clad in a silk garment, and adorned with gold ornaments, is brought out for the purpose after the entertainment. It is on such occasions that splendid dowries are settled on some children in grants of land or of Government securities, and I have known instances in which a dowry amounted to a lakh of Rupees. Of late years, the practice of making gifts to the child being held in the obnoxious light of a tax, the good taste of some has led them to confine the rite within the circumscribed limit of their own family. Superstition has its influence in making the choice of the name given to the child. The Hindoos are generally named after their gods and goddesses, under a belief that the repetition of such names in the daily intercourse of life will not only absolve them from sins, but give them present happiness and hope of blessedness in a state of endless duration. Some parents purposely give an unpleasant name to a child, that may be born after repeated bereavements, believing thereby the curses of the wicked shall fall innocuous on its head. Such names are Nafar, Goburdhone, Ghooie, Tincurry, Panchcurry, Dookhi, &c. In the case of females, she who has many daughters, and does not wish for more, gives them such names as *Khaynto* (cessation,) *Arnά* (no more,) *Ghyrnά* (despised,) *Chee chee* (expression of contempt.)*

* Apart from the horrid practice of female infanticide, now put a stop to by a humane Government, many instances might be given of the extreme detestation in which the birth of a girl is held even by her mother. Among others I may cite the following: A woman who was the mother of four daughters and of no son, at the time of her fifth delivery laid apart one thousand Rupees for distribution among the poor in the event of her getting a son, when, lo! she gave birth to a female child *again*, and what did she do? she at once flung aside the money, mournfully declaring at the same time, that "she has already four firebrands incessantly burning in her bosom and this is the *fifth*, which is enough to burn her to death."

Except under extraordinary circumstances, a Hindoo mother * seldom engages a wet nurse; she continues to suckle her child till it is three or four years old, and attends at the same time to her numerous household duties, which are by no means light or easy. Indolent loveliness, reclining on a sofa, is not a truthful picture of her life; it may be she has to cook for her husband, because he is such an orthodox Hindoo that he will on no account accept prepared food (such as rice, dhall, vegetables, curry, &c.) from any other hand. In such families, the woman has to rise very early, perform her daily ablutions and attend to the duties of the kitchen, and before nine the breakfast must be ready, as the husband has probably to attend his office at ten. It is not an uncommon sight to see a woman cooking, suckling her child, and scolding her maid servant at one and the same time. A Hindoo woman is not only laborious, but patient and submissive to a degree; let the amount of privation be ever so great, she is seldom known to murmur or complain. All her happiness is centred in the proper discharge of her domestic and social duties. So simple and unambitious is a Hindoo female, that she generally considers herself amply rewarded if the food prepared by her hands is appreciated by those for whom it is intended. It is a lamentable fact that, expert as she doubtless is in the art of cooking, she is totally incapable of nourishing the minds of her children with any solid intellectual food worthy of the name. As already indicated, she communicates to her child what she can out of her own store of simple ideas and superstitious beliefs, but her best gift is the care and tenderness which she lavishes upon it, and the wakening of its young soul to return the sense of her own love.

* In cases where a woman is prolific enough to give birth to a child every year she is placed under the necessity of weaning her first-born, and giving it cow milk, a mode of sustenance not at all conducive to its health.

III.

THE HINDOO SCHOOL BOY.

FROM the time when the young Hindoo passes from the infant stage of "mewling and puking in the nurse's arms," till he goes to school, he is generally a bright-eyed, active, playful boy, full of romping spirits and a favourite of all around him. His diet is light, and his health generally good. He usually runs about for three or four years *in puris naturalibus*, and among the lower classes a string is tied round his loins with a metal charm attached to frighten away the evil spirits. When he attains the age of five, the period fixed by his parents for the beginning of his education, he is sent to a *Pátsálá* (vernacular infant school) not, however, without making a Poojah to *Saraswattee*, the goddess of learning. On the day appointed, and it must be a lucky day, according to the Hindoo almanac, the child bathes and puts on a new *Dhooty* (garment) and is taken to the place of worship, where the officiating priest has previously made all the necessary arrangements. Rice, fruits, and sweetmeats, are then offered to the goddess, who is religiously invoked to pour her benediction on the head of the child. After this, the priest takes away all the things offered to the goddess, with his usual gift of one or two rupees, and the child is taken by his parents to the *Pátsálá* and formally introduced to the *Gooroomaháshoy*, or master of the school. Curious as little children naturally are, all present gaze on the new comer as if he were a being of a strange species. But time soon wears off the gloss of novelty and everything assumes its normal aspect. The old boys soon become familiar with the new one, and a sort of intimacy almost unconsciously springs up amongst them. In this country a boy learns the letters of the alphabet, not by pronouncing them, but by writing them on the ground with a small piece of *kharee*, or soft stone, and copying them over and over again until he thoroughly masters them. Five letters are set him at a time. After this he is taught to write on palm leaves with a wooden pen and ink, then on slate and green plantain leaves, and, finally, on paper. At every stage of his progress he is expected to make some present to his master in the shape of food, clothes and money. A village school begins early in the morning, and continues till eleven, after which the boys are allowed to go home for their breakfast; they return at two, and remain in the school till evening, when all the boys are made to stand up in a systematic order, and one of the most advanced amongst them enumerates aloud the multiplication and numeration tables, and all are taught to repeat and commit to memory what they hear. By the daily repetition of these tables, their power of memory is practically improved. With a view to encourage the early attendance of the boys, a *Gooroomahashoy* resorts to the queer method of introducing the *hathchory* system into his *Pátsálá*, which requires that all the boys are to have stripes of the cane in arithmetical progression, on the hand, in the order of their attendance, that is, the first comer to have one stripe, the second two, and so on, in consecutive order. The last boy is sometimes made to stand on one leg for an hour or so to the infinite amusement of the early comers. The system certainly has a good effect in ensuring early attendance.

The course of instruction in such schools embraces reading in the vernacular, a little of arithmetic and writing, and such as become capable of keeping accounts pass for the clever boys. Stupid and wicked pupils are generally beaten with a cane, but their names are never struck off the register, as is the case in English schools. Sometimes a truant is compelled to stand on one leg holding up a brick in his right hand, or to have his arms stretched out till he is completely exhausted. Another mode of punishment consists in applying the leaves of *Bichooty* (a stinging plant) to the back of a naughty boy, who naturally smarts under the torturing. The infliction of such cruel punishments sometimes leads the boys to make a combination against the master for the purpose of retaliation, which generally results in bringing him to his senses. Hindoo boys are extremely sensitive, and are very apt to resent any affront to which they are cruelly subjected by their master.* The rate of fee in a village school is from one to three-pence a head per month, but the master has his perquisites by way of victuals and pice. There is a common saying among the Hindoos that in twelve months there are thirteen *parbuns*, or school festivals, implying thereby, that they are encountered by a continuous round of *parbuns*. On every such occasion the boys are expected to bring presents for the master, and any unfortunate boy who fails to bring such is denied the usual indulgence of a holiday. Little boys are seldom fond of reading, they would gladly sacrifice anything to purchase a holiday. It is not an uncommon thing to find a boy steal pice from his mother's box in order to satisfy the demands of his master at the festival. The principle on which a village school is conducted is essentially defective in this respect. Instead of teaching the rules of good conduct and enforcing the first principles of morality, it often sadly defeats the primary object of a good education, namely, the formation of a sound, moral and virtuous

---

* *Apropos*, I may mention here the following incident. A few years back a well-known master of the Hindoo school being placed in a very awkward position, had to call in the aid of the Police to get himself out of the difficulty. Sailors and Kaffries—always a set of desperate characters—were retained by the boys for the purpose of insulting him on the high road, but the timely interference of the Police put a stop to the contemplated brutal assault. This had the effect of inducing the master to behave in future with greater forbearance, if not with more sober judgment. I forbear giving the name of the indiscreet, but well-intentioned master, whose connection with the school had contributed very largely to its efficiency and usefulness.

character. It is a disgrace to hear a schoolmaster, whose conduct should be the grand focus of moral excellence, use the most vulgar epithets towards his pupils for little faults the effects of which are seldom obliterated from their minds, even in the more advanced period of their life. However, such days of obnoxious pedagogism are almost gone by, never to come back again, now that the system of primary education has been extended to almost every village in India, under the auspices of our liberal Government. Whilst on this subject I may as well state here that some forty years ago our Government had appointed the late Rev. William Adam to be the Commissioner of Education in Bengal. That highly talented and generous philanthrophist, after a minute and searching investigation, submitted in his report to Government a scheme of education very similar to what is now introduced throughout Bengal. The scheme was then ignored on account of its vast expense, and the Commissioner was so disheartened at the apathy of Government towards the education of the masses, that a few days before his departure from Calcutta he took a farewell leave of some of his most distinguished native friends, and his parting words were to the following effect: "Your Government is not disposed to encourage those who are its real friends." This reproach has, however, been subsequently removed by the adoption of a primary system of education. The spirit of the times and the onward progress of enlightened sentiments have gradually inaugurated a comprehensive scheme, which, although still limited in its range, embraces the moral and intellectual improvement of the people in general.

In Calcutta, when a boy is six years old, his parents are anxious to have him admitted into one of the public schools, where he has an opportunity to learn both the Vernacular and the English languages. He may be said from that day to enter on the first stage of his intellectual disintegration. The books that are put into his hands gradually open his eyes and expand his intellect; he learns to discern what is right and what is wrong; he reasons within himself and finds that what he had learnt at home was not true, and is led by degrees to renounce his old ideas. Every day brings before his mind's eye the grand truths of Western knowledge, and he feels an irresistible desire, not only to test their accuracy but to advance farther in his scholastic career. He is too young however, to weigh well everything that comes in his way, but as he advances he finds the light of truth illumine his mind. His parents, if orthodox Hindoos, necessarily feel alarmed at his new-fledged ideas and try to counteract their influence by the stereotyped arguments, of the wisdom of our forefathers, but however inimically disposed, they dare not stop his progress, because they see, in almost every instance, that English education is the surest passport to honor and distinction. In this manner he continues to move through the various classes of the middle schools till he is advanced to one of the higher educational institutions connected with the University, and attains his sixteenth or seventeenth year, which is popularly regarded as his marriageable age.

IV.

VOWS OF HINDOO GIRLS.

WHEN a girl is five years of age, she is initiated by an elderly woman in the preparatory rites of *Bratas*, or vows, the primary object of which is to secure her a good husband, and render her religious and happy throughout life. When the boy is sent to the Pátsálá, the girl is commonly forbidden to read or write, but has to begin her course of Bratas. The germs of superstition being thus early implanted in her mind, she is more or less influenced by it ever after. Formed by nature to be docile, pliant and susceptible, she readily takes to the initial course of religious exercises.

The first rite with which she has to commence is called the "Shiva Poojah," after the example of the goddess Doorga, who performed this ceremonial that she might obtain a good husband; and Shiva is regarded as a model husband. On the 30th day of Choytro, being the last day of the Bengallee year, she is required to make two little earthen images of the above goddess, and placing them on the coat of a bale-fruit (wood apple) with leaves, she begins to perform her worship; but before doing so, she is enjoined to wash herself and change her clothes, a requisition which enforces, thus early, cleanliness and purity in habits and manners, if not exactly in thought and feeling. Her mind being filled with germinal susceptibilities, she imbibes almost instinctively an increasing predilection for the performance of religious ceremonies. Sprinkling a few drops of holy water on the heads of the images, she repeats the following words: "All homage to Shiva, all homage to Shiva, all homage to *Hara*, (another name of Shiva); all homage to Bujjara," meaning two small earthen balls, like peas, which are stuck on the body of the images. She is then to be absorbed in meditation about the form and attributes of the goddess, and afterwards says her prayers three times in connection with Doorga's various names, which I need not recapitulate here. Offerings of flowers and bale leaves are then presented to the goddess with an incantation. Being pleased, Mahádev (Shiva) is supposed to ask from heaven what Brata or religious ceremony is Gouri (Doorga) performing? Gouri replies, she is worshipping Shiva, that she may get him for her husband, because, as said before, Shiva is a model husband.

Then comes the Brata of Hari or Krishna. The two feet of the god being painted in white sandal paste on a brass plate, the girl worships him with flowers and sandal paste. The god seeing this, is supposed to ask what girl worships his feet, and what boon she wants? She replies: May the prince of the kingdom be her husband, may she be beautiful and virtuous, and be the mother of seven wise and virtuous sons and two handsome daughters. She asks that her daughters-in-law may be industrious and obedient, that her sons-in-law may shine in the world by their good qualities, that her granary and farm-yard may be always full, the former with corn of all sorts, and the latter with milch cows, that when she dies all those who are near and dear to her may enjoy long life and prosperity, and that she may eventually, through the blessing of Hari, die on the banks of the sacred Ganges, and thereby pave the way for her entrance into heaven.

It is worthy of remark here that even young Hindoo girls, in the exercise of their immature discretion, make distinction between the gods in the choice of their husbands. In the first Brata, that of Shiva, a tender girl of five years of age is taught, almost unconsciously as it were, to prefer him to Krishna for her husband, because the latter, according to the Hindoo Shasters, is reputed to have borne a questionable character. I once asked a girl why she would not have Krishna for her husband. She promptly answered that that god disported with thousands of Gopeenees (milk-maids) and was therefore not a *good* god, while Shiva was devotedly attached to his one wife, Doorga. The explanation was full of significance from a moral and religious point of view.

The third Brata refers to the worship of ten images. This requires that the girl should paint on the floor ten images of deified men, as well as of gods, with *alapana* or rice paste. Offering them flowers and sandal paste, she asks that she may have a father-in-law like Dasarath, the father of Ram Chunder; a mother-in-law like Kousala, the mother of Ram Chunder; a husband like Ram Chunder; a *dayur* or husband's brother, like Luchmon, Ram's younger brother; a mother like Shasthi, whose children are all alive; like Koontee whose three sons were renowned for their love of justice, piety, courage and heroism; like Ganges, whose water allays the thirst of all; like the mother earth, whose patience is beyond all comparison. And, to crown the whole, she prays that she may, like Doorga, be blessed with an affectionate and devoted husband like Dropadi (the wife of the five Pandooas), be justly remarkable for her industry, devotedness and skill in the culinary art, and be like Sita (the wife of Ram Chunder) whose chastity and attachment to her husband are worthy of all praise. The above three Bratas take place in the Bengalee month of Bysack, (April) which is popularly regarded as a good month for the performance of meritorious works. The prayer contained in the above expresses the culminating female wish in entire accord with the injunctions of the holy shaster, but how often are the amiable qualities ennumerated above set at naught in the actual conflicts of life, in which the predominance of evil desires swallows up every generous impulse!

The next Brata is called the *Sajooty* Brata. It is solely

intended to counteract the thousand evils of polygamy—an unhealthy, unnatural institution, which ought to be expunged from the midst of every civilized community. Though God "has stamped no original characters on our minds wherein we may read his being," still we can clearly discern in His superior arrangements for the happiness of His creatures, that this abnormal practice is directly opposed to His dispensations, so much so that any one countenancing it, is guilty of a crime, for which, if he is not amenable to an earthly tribunal, he is assuredly accountable to a superior and superintending Being, the infringement of whose law is sure to be attended with misery. To get rid of the consequences of this monstrous evil, a girl of five years of age is taught to offer her invocation to God, and in the outburst of her juvenile feeling is almost involuntarily led to indulge in all manner of curses and imprecations against the possible rival of her bed. Nor can we find fault with her conduct, because "an overmastering and brooding sense" of some great future calamity thus early haunts her mind.

In performing the *Sajooty Brata*, the girl paints on the floor with rice paste a variety of things, such as the bough of a flower tree, a Palkee containing a man and a woman, with the sun and moon over it, the Ganges and the Jumna with boats on them, the temple of Mahadeo with Mahadeo in it, various ornaments of gold and precious stones, houses, markets, garden, granary, farm-yard and a number of other things, all intended to represent worldly prosperity. After painting the above, she invokes Mahadeo and prays for his blessing. An elderly lady more experienced in domestic matters then begins to dictate, and the girl repeats a volley of abuses and curses against her *Sateen* or rival wife in the possible future.

> "There, stripped, fair rhetoric languished on the ground,
> And shameful Billingsgate her robes adorn."

The following are a few of the specimens; I wish I could have transcribed them in metre.:—

"*Barrey, Barrey, Barrey* (a cooking utensil)
May *Sateen* become a slave!
Khangra, Khangra, Khangra, (broomstick)
May *Sateen* be exposed to infamy!
Hatha, Hatha, Hatha, (a cooking utensil)
May she devour her *Sateen's* head!
Geelay, Geelay, Geelay (a fruit)
May *Sateen* have spleen!
Pakee, Pakee, Pakee (bird)
May *Sateen* die and may she see her from the top of her house!
Moyna, Moyna, Moyna (bird)
May she never be cursed with a *Sateen*!

May she cut an *Usath* tree, erect a house there, cause her *Sateen* to die and paint her feet with her *Sateen's* blood!

I might swell the list of these curses, but I fear they would prove grating to the ears of civilized readers.

The performance of the *Sajooty Brata* springs out of a desire to see a *Sateen* or rival wife become the victim of all manner of evils, extending even to the loss of life itself, simply because a plurality of wives is the source of perpetual disquietude and misery. By nature, a woman is so constituted that she can never bear the sight of a rival wife. In civilized countries, the evil is partially remediable by a legal separation, but in Hindoostan the legislature makes no provision whatever for its suppression. A feeling of burning jealousy becomes rampant wherever there is a case of polygamy to poison the perennial source of domestic felicity. So acutely sensitive is a Hindoo lady in this respect that she would rather suffer the miseries of widowhood than be cursed with the presence of a *Sateen*, whose very name almost spontaneously awakens in her mind the bitterest and the most envenomed feelings. She can make up her mind to give away a share of her most valuable worldly enjoyments, but she can never give a share of her husband's *affection* to any one on earth. To enjoy the exclusive monopoly of a husband's love is the life-long prayer of a Hindoo female. She expresses it in the incipient stage of her girlhood; and practically carries it with her until the last spark of life becomes extinct. This certainly indicates the prompting of a very strong *natural* feeling.

V.

MARRIAGE CEREMONIES.

THE Hindoos have a strong belief that to solemnise the marriage of their children at an early age, is a meritorious act as discharging one of the primary obligations of life. They are, therefore, very anxious to have their sons and daughters formally married during their own life-time. Sometimes children are pledged to each other even in infancy, by the mutual agreement of the parents; and in most cases the girl is married when a mere child of from eight to ten years, all unconscious as yet of the real meaning and obligations of the relation, although her girlish fancies have been continually directed to it. Matches in the case of good families are commonly brought about in the following way.

When an unmarried boy attains his seventeenth or eighteenth year, numbers of professional men called *Ghatucks* or match-makers come to the parents with overtures of marriage. These men are destitute of principle, they know how to pander to the frailties of human nature; most of them being gross flatterers, endeavour to impose on the parents in the most barefaced manner. As they live on their wits, their descriptive powers and insinuating manners are almost matchless. When the qualities of a girl are to be commended, they, indulging in a strain of exaggeration, unblushingly declare, "she is beautiful as a full moon, the symmetry of her person is exact, her teeth are like the seeds of a pomegranate, her voice isr emarkably sweet like that of the cuckoo, her gait is graceful, she speaks like the goddess *Luckee*, and will bring fortune to any family she may be connected with." The Hindoos have a notion that the good fortune of a husband depends on that of the wife, hence a woman is considered as an emblem of *Luckee*, the goddess of fortune. This is the highest commendation she can possess.*

If the qualities of a youth are to be appraised, they describe him thus: he is as beautiful as *Kartick* (the god of beauty), his deportment is that of a nobleman, he is free from all vices, he studies day and night, in short, he is a precious gem and an ornament of the neighbourhood. The Hindoos know very well that the *Ghatucks* as a body are great impostors, and do not believe half that these people say. From the day a matrimonial alliance is proposed, the parents on both sides begin to make all sorts of preliminary enquiries as to the unblemished nature of the caste, respectability and position in society of the parties concerned. When fully satisfied on these points, they give their verbal consent to the proposed union, but not before the father of the boy has demanded of the father of the girl a certain number of gold and silver ornaments, as well as of *Barabharun*, *i.e.*, silver and brass utensils, couch, &c. exclusive of (with but few exceptions) a certain amount of money in lieu of *Foolshajay*.† Before proceeding further, I should observe that of late years a great change has taken place in the profession of the *Ghatucks*. The question of marriage, though not absolutely, yet chiefly, is a question the solution of which rests with the females. Their voice in such matters has a preponderating influence. Availing themselves of this powerful agency a new class of female *Ghatucks* or rather *Ghatkees* have sprung up among the people. Hence the occupation of the male

* I may be permitted here to observe *en passant* that a civilized nation in describing the beauty of a woman, is sometimes apt to adopt the flowery language of Hafiz. At a Ministerial banquet sometime ago, the Lord Mayor of London was reported to have said about the Princess of Wales; "she is perfection, she sparkles like a gem of fifty facets, she is light when she smiles and she is beauty whenever you see her."

† Presents of sweetmeats, fruits, clothes, flowers and sundry other articles on a pretty grand scale from the bride to the bridegroom, which will be described more in detail afterwards.

Ghatucks is nearly gone, except in rare cases where nice points of caste distinction are to be decided. The great influences of *Shibi Ghatkee* and *Badnee's* mother—two very popular female *Ghatkees*,—is well known to the respectable Hindoo community of Calcutta. These two women have made a decent fortune by plying this trade. Though certainly not gifted with the imaginative powers of a poetic bard of Rajpootana, * their suasive influence is very telling. They have the rare faculty of making and unmaking matches. From the superior advantage which their sex affords them, they have a free access to the inner apartments of a house (even if it were that of a millionaire)—a privilege their male rivals can never expect to enjoy. When balked by the subtlety of a competitor in trade, by their bathos they contrive to break a match. Their representations regarding a proposed union seldom fail to exercise a great influence on the minds of the Zenana females. Relying on the accuracy of their description, which sometimes turns out exaggerated, if not false, the mother and other ladies are often led to give their consent to a proposed union. The husband, swayed by the counsel and importunity of his wife, is forced to acquiesce in her choice. He cannot do otherwise because, as our friend, Baboo Keshub Chunder Sen, has very facetiously observed, "man is a noun in the objective case governed by the active verb woman." †

* A Rajpoot prince was said to have given a lakh of Rupees to a bard in order to purchase his rhythmic plaudits in a respectable assemblage of his countrymen.

† If we consult properly the pages of the history of this country from the earliest period, we shall find abundant proofs of the very great influence of women on Hindoo society in general. I cannot do better than give the following quotation from Tod's Annals of Rajasthan. "What led to the wars of Rama? The rape of Sita. What rendered deadly the feuds of the Yadus? The insult of Dropadi. What made prince Nala an exile from Nirwar? His love for Damayanti. What made Raja Bharti abandon the throne of Avanti? The loss of Pingala. What subjected the Hindu to the dominion of the Islamite? The rape of the princess of Canouj. In fine, the cause which overturned kingdoms, commuted the sceptre to the pilgrim's staff and formed the ground-work of all their grand epics, is woman."

When a *Ghatkee* comes up with the proposal of a matrimonial alliance with an educated youth, the first question generally asked her is, "Has he passed his examinations?" If so, how many *passes* has he got? meaning thereby how many examinations of the University has he passed through? "Has he yet any Jalpany or scholarship?" These are difficult questions which must be satisfactorily answered before a negotiation can be effected. That a University degree has raised the marriageable value of a boy, there can be no doubt. If he have successfully passed some of these examinations and got a scholarship, his parents, naturally priding themselves on their valuable acquisition, demand a preposterously long catalogue of gold ornaments, which, it is not often in the power of a family in middling circumstances easily to bestow. The parents of the girl, on the other hand, seeing the long list, demur at first to give their consent, but their demurring is of no avail; marry their daughter, they must. The present ruinous scale of nuptial expenses must be submitted to at any sacrifice, and after deep cogitation they send a revised schedule, (as if marriage were a mere matter of traffic) taking off from it some costly items, which would press heavily on the purse. In this manner the *Ghatkee* continually goes backwards and forwards for some time, proposing concessions on both sides and holding out delusive hopes of future advantages in the event of the carrying out of the marriage. There is a trite saying among the Hindoos, that "a matrimonial alliance could not be completed without uttering a lakh of words."

The parents of the girl on whose head falls the greatest burden, are eventually made to succumb from a consideration of their having secured a desirable match, namely, a *passed* student. If not placed in affluent circumstances, as is generally the case, they are obliged to raise the requisite sum of money by loan, which sows, in many instances, the seeds of much future embarrassment. At a very moderate calculation, a tolerably respectable marriage now-a-days costs between two and three thousand Rupees (about £200),—sometimes more. There is another native adage which says, "we want twine for thatching and money for wedding." A respectable Hindoo gentleman who has four or five daughters to give in marriage and whose income is not large, is often reduced to the greatest difficulty and embarrassment by reason of the extravagantly enormous expenses of a marriage. The rich do not care much what they are required to spend. All that they look for is a desirable match. It is the middle and poorer classes, who form by far the largest aggregate of population in every country, that suffer most severely from the present enhanced scale of matrimonial charges. The late Rajah Rajkissen, Baboos Ramdoolal Dey,* Nemy Churn Mullick and other Hindoo millionaires, spent extraordinary sums of money on the marriage of their sons. The amount in each instance far exceeded a lakh of Rupees. The annals of Rájasthan furnish numerous instances of lavish expenditure, varying from five to ten lakhs of Rupees and upwards, on the solemnization of nuptials. There was a spirit of rivalry which animated the princes to surpass each other in magnificence and splendour on such occasions, regardless alike of the state of their exchequer, and the demoralizing effects of such conduct. Marriages in such a magnificent style are seldom to be seen in Calcutta now-a-days, not because of the distaste of the people for such frivolities, but because of the lamentable decline and impoverishment of the former magnates of the land. It is painful to contemplate that the present scale of expenditure among the middle classes has been in an inverse ratio to their

* Besides the marriage expenses, this man gave to his five sons-in-law fifty thousand Rupees each, as well as a house worth ten thousand Rupees more.

income. The exertions made sometime ago by Moonshee Peary Lall for the reduction of marriage expenses would have doubtless conferred a lasting boon on the Hindoo community in general, if the object had been crowned with success, but as the Legislature has no control over such matters, relating as they do to purely private affairs, the noble scheme resulted in failure. It is quite optional with parties to go to heavy expenses on such occasions; no act of Government without the voice of the people could restrain them in this respect. Any social reform to be permanent and effectual must be carried out by the universal suffrages of the people.

When the preliminaries of a marriage are settled, a person, on each side, is deputed by turns to see the boy and the girl. It is customary to see the girl first. When the friends of the bridegroom, therefore, come for the purpose, they sit down in the outer apartment of the house, whilst the bride is engaged in her toilet duty. After fifteen or twenty minutes, she, glittering in jewels and accompanied by a maid servant as well as by the *Ghatkee*, makes her appearance. The first thing she does in entering the room is to make a *pranám* or bow to all present, and then she is asked to squat down on the clean white sheet spread on the floor. A solemn pause ensues for a minute or so, when one of the company, more officious than the rest, breaks the silence by putting to her a few questions. She naturally feels herself somewhat out of her element in the midst of so many strangers, and unconsciously shows a sort of embarrassment even of self conflict almost distressing to witness. This internal agitation of feeling, arising partly from modesty and partly from anxiety, causes her even to stammer. Her engrossing thought for the time being is, according to the early vow she has made, that she may have a *good* husband with lots of jewels. "What is your name, mother?" is the first question. She may diffidently reply in a half suppressed tone "*Gri Balla.*"

"Who is that sitting before you?"—perhaps pointing to the girl's father. She says, "My father." "Can you read and write?" If she say, "yes," she is asked to read a little out of her book.

The *Ghatkee* here plays the part of a panegyrist by admiring the amiable qualities of the girl, who, she adds, is the very type of *Luckee* (the goddess of prosperity.) While this examination is going on in the outer apartment, the anxious mother, whose heart beats with throbbing sensations while watching the scene from behind a half closed window, does not feel herself at ease, until she hears that her daughter has acquitted herself creditably. Before the girl leaves the room, the father or brother of the boy puts a gold mohur into her hand as a tangible proof of approval and bids her retire. It is needless to say, that she feels herself relieved, quite glad and free, when she again sees the faces of her mother and sisters, whose joy returns with her return.

This interview is called *pucca dheykha* or the confirmatory visit. All the Brahmins, *Ghatucks* and *Ghatkees*, and other Koolins who may be present on the occasion receive two or four Rupees each. The servants of the house are not forgotten, they too receive each a Rupee. If this interview take place in the morning, the parties return home without breakfast, it being customary with them not to eat anything before bathing and performing their daily worship. If in the evening, they are treated to a good dinner consisting of the best fruits of the season, sweet and sour milk and sweetmeats of various kinds. It is on such ceremonious occasions, that the Hindoos make a display of their wealth by serving the dinner to their new friends with silver salvers, plates, glasses and *paundan*, (betel box). Almost every respectable gentleman keeps a good assortment of these silver articles. They are, however, reserved for special purposes, and used only on special occasions. As a rule, the people are not fond of investing their money, like Europeans, in plated-ware, because it is, comparatively speaking, of little exchangeable value in times of need and distress.

It is now the turn of the boy to be examined in a similar way as to his scholastic acquirements. When the father and the relatives of the girl pay a return visit, they generally bring with them a graduate of the University. Should the boy be one who has successfully passed the Matriculation standard, he is not subjected to so strict an examination as one who does not enjoy the same dignity. In both cases, however, they must undergo some examination in English literature, composition, grammar, history, &c. It is a noteworthy fact that a boy however intelligent and expert in other respects, betrays a lamentable deficiency, arising from diffidence, when required to undergo an examination in the presence of his father-in-law and a University graduate. The thought of failure acts as a heavy incubus on his mind. He finds himself bewildered in a maze of confusion. If he do not actually stammer, he talks at least very slowly and diffidently, and if called upon to write, his hand shakes, and in fact he becomes extremely nervous. After this trial is over, the boy retires with mingled feelings of misgiving and complacence. He receives, however, in his turn a gold mohur. The gentlemen who had come to see him are then asked to a dinner in the way described above. The same display of silver-ware is made on the occasion, and nearly the same amount of presents of money made to the Brahmins, Koolins and others.

When both parties are satisfied as to the desirableness of the union, a good day is fixed for drawing a *pattra* or written agreement in which, say, a Koolin of superior caste, engages in writing to give his son in marriage with the daughter of either a second Koolin, or, as is often the case of a Mowleek, an inferior in caste. This *Pattra* is written by a Brahmin on Bengallee paper with Bengallee pen and ink (as if English writing materials would desecrate such a sacred contract) and must consist of an odd number of lines, such as seven or nine lines. An invocation of the Butterfly must head the *Pattra*, the purport of which will run as follows: "I, Ram Chunder Bose, do engage to give my second son, Gopeenauth Bose, in marriage with Nobinmoney Dossee, the eldest daughter of Issen Chunder Dutt, who is also bound by his contract; the marriage to be solemnized on a day to be named hereafter." Here the signatures of both the fathers as well as of the witnesses follow. When finished, it is rolled up in red thread. The *Koolin* gentleman hands it to the *Mowleek* gentleman, when the latter embraces the former, and gives him at the same time *Koola marjádá* and *Pattra Darshanee*, as a mark of respect for his superior caste,—or about fifty Rupees. The articles required for the matrimonial contract are paddy, doov grass, turmeric, betel leaf, betel-nuts, sandal paste, cowries (small shells) and *alta* * all which are considered as conducive to the future welfare of the boy † and girl. When the contract is religiously ratified, a couple of conchs—one for the bridegroom and another for the bride—are sounded by the females, announcing the happy conclusion of this important preliminary, at which all hearts are ex-

* A thin stuff like paper with which Hindoo females redden their feet. A widow is not allowed to use it. In the absence of shoes, which they are forbidden to wear, this red color heightens the beauty of their tiny feet. It is applied once a week.

† In the selection of a bridegroom, outward appearances are not always to be trusted. The late Baboo Aushotosh Dey, a millionaire, had a very beautiful granddaughter to give in marriage. As was to be expected, *Ghatacks* and *Ghatkees* had been rummaging the whole town and its suburbs for a suitable match, one who would possess all the recommendations of a good education, a respectable family, and a fair, prepossessing appearance—qualities which are rarely combined in one. Among others, the name of the late Honorable Baboo Dwarkey Nauth Mitter (afterwards a Judge of the Calcutta High Court,) was mentioned. He was then a bachelor, and his reputation as a scholar spread far and wide. Some how or other he was brought into the house of Baboo Aushotosh Dey for the purpose of giving the ladies an opportunity of seeing him. His scholastic attainments were pronounced to be of very superior order, but not being blessed with a prepossessing appearance, he was rejected.

hilarated. Arrangements are now being made for the dinner of all who may be present at the time. Sometimes fifty to sixty persons are fed. Every care is taken to provide a good dinner for the delectation of the guests and a *Pattra* on this scale costs from 300 to 400 Rupees. The Brahmins, Koolins, and others, receive, as usual, presents of money and return home replenished in body as well as in purse.

It is worthy of remark that though the distinction of caste still exerts its influence on all the important concerns of our social and domestic life, it is nevertheless fast losing its prestige in the estimation of the enlightened Hindoos. In former days a Koolin occupied a prominent position in society, be his character what it might, but now-a-days the rapid spread of English education, and the manifold advantages derivable from it, has practically impaired his influence and lowered his dignity. A *Koolin* who happens to be the father of a girl married to a *Mowleek*, is, in the present day, degraded into the rank of his traditional inferior, simply because he is the father of the girl; he must even be prepared to submit to all sorts of humiliation and continue to serve the *Mowleek* father of the boy as long as the connection lasts. At every popular festival for at least one year he must, according to his rank, make suitable presents to his son-in-law, failing which a latent feeling of discontent arises which eventually ripens into bitter misunderstanding.

But to return to the marriage contract. After the entertainment, both parties consult the almanac and fix a day for the ceremony, called *Gátray haridrá* or the anointment of the boy with turmeric. On that day the bridegroom, after bathing and putting on a red bordered cloth,* is made to stand on

* In Hindoo marriages and other ceremonies of a similar nature *red* color is indispensably necessary for all kinds of wearing apparel, even the invitation cards must be on *red* paper. Red color is the sign of joy and gaiety as opposed to black, which is held to be ominous.

a grindstone surrounded by four plantain trees, while five women (one must be of Brahmin caste) whose husbands are alive, go round him five or seven times, anoint his body with turmeric, and touch his forehead at one and the same time with holy water, betel, betel-nuts, a *Sree* made of rice paste in the shape of a sugarloaf, and twenty other little articles consisting of several kinds of peas, rice, paddy, gold, silver, &c. From this day, the boy carries about a pair of silver nut-crackers, and the girl a pair of *kajulnatha*,* which must remain with them till the solemnization of the nuptials, for the purpose of repelling evil spirits. A little of the turmeric paste with which the body of the bridegroom was anointed is sent by the family barber to the bride in a silver cup, her body is also anointed with it. A number of other gifts follow, namely, a large brass vessel of oil, various kinds of perfumery, three pieces of cloth (one must be a richly embroided Benares *saree*, one Dacca, and the other red bordered), a small carpet, a silk musnud with pillows, two mats, some gold trinkets for the head, a few baskets of sweetmeats, some large fishes, sweet and sour milk, and a few garlands of flowers, &c., all which cost from two to three hundred Rupees, or sometimes more. A rich man sometimes gives a pair of diamond combs and flowers for the hair, of the value of two thousand Rupees and upwards. From this, an idea may be formed as to the lavish expenditure of the Hindoos on marriages, even in these hard times. A *few* can afford it, but the *many* are put to their wits'-end in meeting the demands thus made upon them.

Two or three days after the ceremony of anointment, the Bengali almanac is again consulted, and a lucky day is appointed for the celebration of *Ahibarrabhàt*, so called from its being a feast given just before the wedding. On this

* A collirium case which contains the black dye with which native females daub their own and their childrens' eyelids.

occasion the father of the bridegroom gives a grand entertainment to the male relatives of the family. As a counterpart to the same the father of the bride gives a similar entertainment to the female relatives of his own family, with this difference only, that in the case of the former no Palkees are required, whereas in the case of the latter these covered conveyances have to be engaged for bringing in the females. In either case the number of guests generally varies from two to three hundred, and as the present style of living among the Hindoos in the metropolis has become more expensive than that which prevailed in the good old days, partly from a vain desire to make an ambitious display of wealth, and partly from the unprecedentedly rapid increase of the population, which has, as a necessary sequence, considerably raised the prices of all kind of provisions, an entertainment of this nature costs from four to five hundred Rupees on each side. The very best kinds of *loochees*, *kocharees*, vegetable curries, fruits, sweetmeats* and other delicacies of the season are to be provided for this special occasion.

English friends are often invited to the marriages of rich families in Calcutta and regaled with all sorts of delicacies from the Great Eastern Hotel. "The family mansion

* The Bengalis have become so much anglicised of late that they have not hesitated to give an English name to their sweetmeats. When the late Lord Canning was the Governor General of India, it was said his Baboo made a present of some native sweetmeats to Lady Canning, who was kindly pleased to accept it. Hence the sweetmeat is called "Lady Canning," and to this day no grand feast among the Bengalis is considered as complete unless the "Lady Canning" sort is offered to the guests. The man that first made it is said to have gained much money by its sale. It is not the savoury taste of the thing that makes it so popular, but the name of the illustrious Lady. While treating the subject of Hindoo entertainment, it would not be out of place to make a few observations on a branch of it, for the information of European readers. At all public entertainments of the kind I am referring to, respectable Hindoos strictly confine themselves to *vegetable curries*. Though those of the *Sakto* denomination (the followers of Kali and Doorga) have no religious scruples to use goat-meat (male) and onion in the shape of curry among select friends at home, they dare not expose themselves by offering it to strangers. Hence, in large assemblies, they strictly confine themselves to vegetable curries of different kinds. The principle is good, were it honestly observed; because meat, if not necessarily, yet generally, is the concomitant of *drink*. *Privately*, however, both meat and drink are largely used. Respectable females are entirely free as yet from these carnal indulgences.

is splendidly furnished and brilliantly illuminated. There is literally a profusion of pictures and chandeliers. All the furniture and surroundings are indicative more of an English than of a Native house. Dancing girls are hired to impart *eclât* to the scene. A *nabat* covered with tinsel is put up in front of the house, where native musicians play at intervals, much to the satisfaction of the mother of the bridegroom and the boys of the neighbourhood, and a temporary scaffolding made of bamboos and ornamental paper is erected on the highway in the form of a crescent bearing on it the inscription, "God save the bridegroom." Male and female servants receiving presents of gold and silver bangles move about the house gaily dressed in red uniform, or clothes. As tangible memorials of the happy union, presents of large brass pots, with oil, plates with sweetmeats, fruits, and clothes, &c., are largely distributed among the Brahmins and numerous friends and relatives of the family. This present is called *Samajeek*. With the exception of Brahmins, who are content with offering hollow benedictions, in which the sacerdotal class, as a rule, is so very liberal, everyone else who receives them makes in return presents of clothes and sweetmeats, the nearest relatives making the most costly ones. In times of great *loganshá*, *i.e.*, when numerous marriages take place, the demand for clothes and sweetmeats is really enormous. Dealers in those things make a harvest of profit and "the town becomes a jubilee of feasts."

During the night preceding the marriage, the women of both the families scarcely sleep, being busily engaged in making all sorts of preparations for the next day. Very early in the morning, five *Ayows*, or females whose husbands are alive, take with them a light, a knife, a *Sree*, a *Brundálá*, containing sundry little articles, described before, a small brass pot, some sweetmeats, *choora* and *moorkee*, oil, betel, betel-nuts and turmeric, and go to the nearest tank, sounding a conch, and touching the water with the knife, fill the brass pot with water. The above articles being presented as an offering to the brass pot, the females receive a portion of the eatables and return home sounding the conch, which is a necessary accompaniment of all religious ceremonies.

What I am now about to describe may be called the *first* marriage, because it is invariably followed by a second ceremonial when the union is really consummated. But it properly forms the binding ceremony, as constituting the marriage relative between the two youthful parties, with all its legal and social rights, even if they should not be spared to live together as husband and wife.

The emptiness and superficiality of the relation, especially on the side of the childish bride, will be but too apparent, and is but too often realised in this uncertain life, in the prolonged misery of a virgin widowhood. On the day of the marriage both the bridegroom and the bride are forbidden to eat anything except a little milk and a few fruits. The father of the bride also fasts, as well as the officiating priests of the two families.

About twelve o'clock in the day, the Mowleek family sends presents of clothes, sweetmeats, fishes, sour and sweet milk and some money, say about twenty-five rupees, to the house of the Koolin family, as a mark of honor to the latter, to which, from his superior caste he is fairly entitled. This present is called *Adhibassy*. Both the fathers are also required during the day to perform the ceremony of *Nannimook* or *Bidhishrad*,—a ceremony, the meaning of which, as said before, is to make offerings to the manes of ancestors, and to wish for the increase and preservation of progeny.

After the performance of the above ceremonies, both the bridegroom and the bride putting on new red bordered *dhooty* and *saree* respectively at their several houses, are made to bathe ; and five women whose husbands are alive touch their foreheads with sundry little things, as mentioned before. They have afterwards to go through a few minor rites which are purely the inventions of the females, not being at all enjoined in the *Shásters*. It is obvious that the primary object of all these female rites is to promote conjugal felicity. Strange as it may appear, it is nevertheless a fact that the mother of the bridegroom eats *seven* times (of course but little at a time) that day through a fear lest the bride, when she comes, will give her but scanty meals,* while the mother of the bride does not eat anything until the marriage ceremony is over, being impressed with a notion that the more she fasts the more she will get to eat afterwards.

The females on the side of the bride, with the help of a matron, exercise their utmost ingenuity, and literally rack their brains, in devising all manner of contrivances partaking of the character of charms to win the devoted attachment of the bridegroom towards the lovely little bride. They resort to numerous petty tricks for the purpose which are too absurd and childish to be dwelt upon. Credulous as they naturally are, and simple as they are known to be in their habits, not to speak of the normal weakness of their intellect, they fondly imagine that their *thook thak* or trick is sure to triumph and produce the desired effect. To give an instance or two. They write down in red ink on the back of the *Peray*, or wooden seat on which the bride is to sit, the names of twenty-one uxorious husbands, and go round the bride seven times. They also write the name of the goddess, Doorga, on the silk *saree* or garment which the bride is to wear at the time of the marriage ceremony, because Shiva, her husband,

* The cause of the fear is as follows: When Kartick (the god of beauty and the son of the goddess Doorga) went out to marry, he had forgotten to take with him the usual pair of nut-crackers. When he remembered this on the way, he immediately returned home, and to his great surprise, saw his mother eating with her ten hands, she being a ten handed goddess. On asking the reason, he was told that it was lest, when he should bring his wife, she would not give her the proper quantity of food. Under what strange hallucinations, even the gods and goddesses of the Hindoos laboured!

was excessively fond of her. They place before her the *Chundi Pooty*, a sacred book treating of Doorga and Shiva, while her mouth is filled with two betel-nuts to be afterwards chewed with betel by the bridegroom unawares. Meantime active preparations are made on both sides for the auspicious solemnization of the nuptials. At the house of the bridegroom, arrangements are being made for illumination and fireworks, and the grand *Nacarras* announce the approaching departure of the procession. Fac-similes of mountains and peacocks are made of colored paper spacious enough to accommodate a dozen persons; hundreds of *Khás gaylap* and silver staves are seen on the roadside; groups of songsters and musicians are posted here and there to give a passing specimen of the vulgar songs of the populace; a *Sookasun* or bridegroom's seat elegantly fitted up is brought out with two boys gaily dressed to fan the bridegroom with *chamurs*;* hundreds of blue and red lights are distributed among the swarthy coolies, who are to use them on the road when the procession moves. The bridegroom, being washed, is helped to put on a suit of superbly embroidered Benares *kinkob* dress, with a pearl necklace of great value, besides bangles and armlets set in precious stones and garlands of flowers. Durwans and guards of honor are paraded in front of the house; and in short, nothing is left to impart an imposing appearance to the scene. As has been already observed, there is a growing desire among the Hindoos to imitate English manners and fashions. A marriage procession is considered quite incomplete unless bands of English musicians are retained, and a cavalcade of troopers like a burlesque of the Governor-General's Body Guard is seen to move forward to clear the way. A Cook's carriage with a postillion is not unfrequently observed to supersede the old *Sooksun*, or gilt Palkee.

* The *chamurs* are fans made of the tails of Thibet cows.

Before the bridegroom leaves his house he says his prayer to the goddess Doorga, and makes his preparatory *jattrá* (departure). At this time his mother asks him, "*Baba* where are you going?" He answers, "To bring in your *Dassee* or maid-servant." Before leaving he receives from her a few instructions as to how he should conduct himself at the house of his father-in-law. He is to gaze on the stars in heaven, keep his feet half on the ground and half on the wooden seat when engaged in performing a ceremony, and not to use any other betel but his own. The object of these instructions is to thwart the intention of his mother-in-law that he may become a uxorious husband, a wish in which his mother does not share at all, because it is calculated to diminish his regard for her. In the majority of cases the wish of the mother-in-law prevails over that of the mother, as is quite natural.

He has next to perform the rite of *Kanakángoolee*, surrounded by all the women of the family. A small brass plate containing rice, a small wooden pot of vermilion, and one Rupee, are thrown right over his head by his father into the *Saree*, or robe of his mother, who stands behind him for the purpose of receiving the same. This is a signal for him to come out, and if all arrangements are complete, take his seat on the bridal *Sookasun*, or carriage. The procession moves forward amid the increasing darkness. One or two European constables march ahead. The usual cortége of stalwart durwans follow. The torches and flambeaus are lighted. The *Khasgalabullahs* are ranged on both sides of the road; in the midst are placed bands of native and English musicians. Parties of songsters in female dress begin to sing and dance on the *Moworpunkhee*, borne on the shoulders of coolies. The flaring torches are waved around the procession. Blue and red lights are flashed at intervals. Noise, confusion, and bustle ensue. Men, women and children all flock to see the támáshá. Mischievous boys try to rob the lights. And to lend, as it were, an enchantment to the scene, gay Baboos in open carriages, in their gala dresses bring up the rear. It is on such occasions that modest beauties and newly-married brides (*bahus*) come out from the Zenana, and, unveiling their faces, rise on the tops of their houses on both sides of the road, in order to feast their eyes on all the pompous accompaniments of a marriage exhibition. As soon as the procession arrives near the house of the bride, the people of the neighbourhood assemble in groups to have a sight of the lord of the day, and four or five gentlemen of the party of the bride advance to welcome the bridegroom and his party of friends, who enter, receiving the stares of the idle and the salutations of the polite. The barber of the family brings out a light in a *sará* (earthen vessel) and places it on the side of the road. Decency forbids me to mention certain of its constituents.

As the initiatory rite of the auspicious event, the females blow the conch-shell in the inner apartment, and some more impatient than the rest peep through the latticed corridor or window, while the bridegroom is slowly conducted to his appropriate seat made up of red satin with embroidered fringes, having three pillows of the same stuff on three sides. An awning is suspended over the spacious compound, and it is splendidly illuminated with gas lights. Polite and complimentary expressions of good wishes and of refined native etiquette are exchanged on both sides, comparing favorably with the rude manners of past times. "Come in, come in, gentlemen, and sit down, please," is the general cry. "Bring tobacco, bring tobacco, for both Brahmin's and Soodras," is the next welcome expression. Boys, especially the brother-in-law of the bridegroom, now bring him a couple of betel-nuts, to be cut with the pair of nut crackers he holds in his hand. He objects and hesitates at first, but no excuse is admitted, no plea heard, he must cut them in the best way he can.* When all the guests are properly seated, numbers of school boys sit face to face and begin to wrangle, much to the amusement of the assemblage. As English education is now all the "go" among the people, questions in spelling, grammar, geography and history, are put to each other. The following may be taken as a specimen: Aushotosh asks Bholanauth, "In what school do you read?" Bholanauth answers, "In the Hare School." A. continues, "What books do you read"? B. enumerates them.

A. asks, "What is your pedagogue's name?" B., a little confounded, remains quiet, meditating within himself what could a *pedagogue* mean. A. drawing nearer, asks him to spell the word, housewife? B. answers, "h-u-z-z-i-f." A. laughs heartily in which he is joined by other boys. Continuing the chain of interogations, he asks B. to parse the sentence: "To be good is to be happy." B. hanging down his head, attempts, but fails. "Where is Dundee, and what is it famous for?" B. answers, "Dundee is in Germany." (laughter): A. pressing his adversary, continues, "What was the cause of the Trojan war?" B. answers hesitatingly, "The golden fleece!" Thus discomfited, B. takes refuge in ignoble silence, while A., in a triumphant mood, moves prominently forward amidst the plaudits of the assembled multitude. "Long live Aushotosh," is the universal blessing.

Here two or three professional genealogists, having tunics on their bodies and turbans on their heads, stand up, and in measured rhyme recite the genealogical table of the two families now affianced, blazoning forth the meritorious

* Every commonplace minutiæ in the domestic economy of a Hindoo family is fraught with meaning: the nuts are kept all-day in the bride's mouth and are saturated with her saliva. When cut by the hand of the bridegroom they are supposed to possess a peculiar virtue. Somehow or other, the bridegroom must be made to use them with the betel, in spite of the warning of his mother, forbidding him to use them on any account. When used, his love for his wife is supposed to be intensified, which is prejudicial to the interests of his mother.

deeds of each succeeding generation. They keep a regular register of all the aristocratic Hindoo families, especially of the Koolin class, and at respectable marriages they are richly rewarded. It is quite amusing to hear how seriously they rehearse the virtuous acts of the ancestors, carefully refraining from making any allusion to disreputable acts of any kind. Though not like Chundá, the inimitable bard and pole-star of Rajasthan, as Colonel Tod says, their services are duly appreciated by all orthodox Hindoos, who exult in the glowing recital of ancestral deeds. Their language is so guarded and flattering that it can offend nobody, except such as do not reward them. Having the genealogical table in their possession they can easily turn the good into bad, and *vice versa*, to serve their own selfish ends. An upstart, or one who has a family stain, pays them liberally to have his name inserted in the genealogical register, and to be mentioned in laudatory terms.

In the *Thakoor dhallan*, or chamber of worship, all preparations for the solemnization of nuptials are now made. The couch-cot, beddings, carpet, embroidered and wooden shoes—here English shoes will not do—gold watch with chain, diamond ring, pearl necklace, and one set of silver and one set of brass utensils,* are arranged in proper order, and flowers, sandal-paste, dooav grass, holy water in copper pans, and khoosh grass, are placed before the priests of both parties. The bridegroom, laying aside his embroidered robe, is dressed in a red silk cloth, and taken to the place of worship, where the bride, also attired in a silk *Saree*, veiled and trembling through fear, is slowly brought from the female penetralia on a wooden seat borne by two servants and placed on the left side of the bridegroom. The agitation of her internal feelings when brought before the altar of Hymen is

* The articles consist of Silver Ghará, Ghároo, Báthá, Thállá, Bátti, Glass, Raykáb, Dábur, Dipay and Pickdán.

greatly soothed by the wealth of gold ornaments—the *summum bonum* of her existence with which her person is adorned. The officiating priest puts into the hands of the bridegroom fourteen blades of khoosh grass in two small bundles which he winds and ties round his figures. The priest then pours a little holy Ganges water into the bridegroom's right hand, which he holds while the father-in-law repeats a *mantra* or incantation, at the close of which he lets it fall. Rice, flowers and doorva grass are next given him, which he lays near the copper pan containing the holy water. Water is presented as at first with a prayer, and sour milk, then again water. The officiating priest now directs him to put his hand into the copper pan, and placing the hand of the bride on that of the bridegroom ties them together with a garland of flowers, when the father-in-law says: "Of the family of Goutam, the great grand-daughter of Ram Churn Bose, the grand-daughter of Bulloram Bose, the daughter of Ramsoonder Bose, wearing such and such clothes and jewels, I, Dwarkeynath Bose, give to thee, Oma Churn Dutt, of the family of Bharadáz, the great grandson of Dinnonath Dutt, the grandson of Shib Churn Dutt, the son of Jodonauth Dutt." The bridegroom says, "I have received her." The father-in-law then takes off the garland of flowers with which the hands of the married pair were bound, and pouring some holy water on their heads, pronounces his benediction, A piece of silk cloth called *Lajá bustur*, is then put over the heads of the boy and girl, and they are asked to look at each other *for the first time in their lives.* While the marriage ceremony is being performed the boy is made to wear on his head a conical tinsel hat. Here the barber of the bridegroom gives to the priest a little *Khoye* (parched rice) and a little ghee, which are offered with doorva grass to the god Brahma. A very small piece of coarse cloth called *gatchard*, or knotted cloth, containing in all twenty-one myrobolans, *boyra* fruit and betel-nuts, is tied to the silk *dhobja* or scarf of the bridegroom, which is fastened again to the silk garment of the bride, thus symbolising a union never to be severed. The married couple are then taken into the inner court where the females are waiting on the tiptoe of expectation, wreathed for a moment in the rapturous embraces of one another. As soon as the boy appears, or rather before his appearance, conch-shells are again blown, and he is made to stand on a stone placed under a small awning called *chádldhtalah*, a emporary shed, surrounded on four sides by plantain trees. By way of merriment, some females greet him with *hayeumllah* mixed in treacle, some pull his ears, notably his sisters-in-law, while matrons cry out "*ulu, ulu, ulu*," sounds indicative of excessive joy. It would require the masterly pen of a Sir Walter Scott to adequately delineate the joyous feelings of the females on such an auspicious occasion.

The bridegroom is made to wear on his ten fingers ten rings made of twigs of creepers, and his hands are tied by a piece of thread as long as his body. Putting betwixt them a weaver's shuttle, the mother-in-law says, "I have bound thee by thread, bought thee with cowries, and put a shuttle betwixt thy hands, now bleat thou like a lamb, * Bapoo,"—a term of endearment. She also closes his mouth by touching his lips with a padlock, and symbolically sewing the same with twenty-one pins, that he may never scold the girl; touches his nose with a slender Bamboo pipe and breaks it afterwards, throws over his body treacle and rice, as well as the refuse of spices pounded on a grindstone, which has been

* I have known a young collegian of a rather humourous disposition bleat like a lamb at the time of marriage, to the great amusement of all the females, except his mother-in-law, who, simple as she was, took the matter in a serious light, and felt herself almost dejected on account of the great stupidity of her son-in-law (for she could not take it in any other sense), but her dejection gave place to joy when in the *Bdsurghur*—the sleeping room of the happy pair for the night—she heard him outwit all the females present. It is obvious that the meaning of this part of the female rite is to render the husband tame and docile as a lamb, especially in his treatment of his wife.

kept covered with a bag for eight days, are alive, by two females whose husbands and finally touches his lips with honey and small images made of sugar, that he may ever treat his wife like a *sweet* darling.

Afterwards the mother-in-law with several other married women, adorned with all their costly ornaments and dressed in their best attire, touch his forehead with *Sree*, *Barandàllà* a winnowing fan, plantain, betel and betel-nuts; and here the silk scarf of the boy, of which mention has been made before, is again more closely fastened to the silk garment of the girl, and kept with her for eight days, after which it is returned, accompanied by presents of sweetmeats, fishes and curdled milk. These puerile rites, purely the invention of females, are intended to act as charms for securing the love and affection of the husband for his wife. The wish is certainly a good one, but often the agencies employed fail to produce the desired effect! "Charms strike the sight, but merit wins the soul." Before the marriage ceremony is concluded, the boys of the neighbourhood make the usual demand of *Gramvaṭi* and *Barawari* Poojah. At first in a polite way they ask the father of the bridegroom for the gift. He offers twenty Rupees, but they insist on having one hundred Rupees. After some altercation in which sometimes high words and offensive language are made use of,* the matter is eventually settled on payment of thirty-two Rupees. This money is used in giving a feast to the boys of the

* In former days when education was but very scantily cultivated, unpleasant quarrels were known to have arisen between the two parties from very trivial circumstances. The friends of the bridegroom, often pluming themselves on their special prerogatives as members of the strong party readily resented even the slightest insult offered them rather incautiously by the bridal party. These altercations sometimes terminated in blows, if not in lacerated limbs. Instead of waiting till the conclusion of the ceremony, the whole of the bridegroom's party has been known to return home without dinner, to the great mortification of the other party. There is a common saying among the Bengalees that "he who is the enemy of the house should go to a marriage party." It was a common sport with the friends of the bridegroom to cut with a pair of scissors the bedding at the house of the bride. But happily such practices are of rare occurrence now-a-days.

neighbourhood, reserving a portion for the *Barawari* poojah,—a mode of worship which will be more fully treated in another place.

As an epilogue to the nuptial rite, the bridegroom continues to stand on a stone, while two men setting the bride on a wooden seat, and lifting her higher than his head, makes three circumambulations, asking the females at the same time who is taller, the bridegroom or the bride? The stereotyped response is, "the bride." This being done, the females throwing a piece of cloth over the heads of both, desire them to glance at each other with all the fond endearments of a wedded pair. As is to be expected, the coy girl, almost in a state of trepidation, casts but a transient look, and veils her face instanter; but the boy, young as he is, feels inwardly happy to view the lovely face of his future wife. This look is called *Shoovádristi* or "the auspicious sight" which is held in the light of a harbinger of future felicity.

The bridegroom returns to the *Thacoordhallan* or place of worship and performs the concluding part of the marriage ceremony, while the officiating priest, repeating the usual incantation, presents the burnt offerings (*home*) to the gods, which is the finale of the religious part of the rite.* But before the bridegroom leaves the place of worship, the officiating priests of both sides must have their *dackiná* or pecuniary reward. If the boy be of the Mowleek caste and the girl of the Koolin caste, the former must give double what the latter gives, *i. e.*, 16 Rupees and 8 Rupees. Here, as in every other in-

* An English gentleman, who, to a versatile genius, combined an intelligent knowledge of, and a familiar acquaintance with, the manners and customs of the country, once advised a Native friend of his to go to England and other great countries on the continent with a number of Hindoo females and exhibit there all the important social and domestic ceremonials of this conntry in a place of public resort. The very circumstance of Hindoo females performing those rites in the manner in which they are popularly celebrated here, would be sure to attract a very large audience. The marriage ceremonies alone would form a regular night of enchantment and amusement. The time will certainly come when the realization of such an ingenious idea would no longer be held Utopian.

stance, the superiority of caste asserts its peculiar privileges. The professional genealogists, after concluding their recitation and singing their epithalamiums, also come in for their share of the reward, but they are generally told to wait till the next day, when in common with other Ghatacks they receive their recompense. The bridegroom is then permitted to have a little breathing time, after having undergone the infliction of so many religious and domestic rites, which latter formed the special province of the females.

The head of the family now stands up before the assembly, and asks their permission to go through the ceremony of *Mala Chandan*, or the distribution of sandaled garlands. This is done to pay them the honor due to their rank. The *Dullaputty*, or the head of the order or party, almost invariably receives the first garland, and then the assembled multitudes are served. For securing this hereditary distinction to a family, large sums of money have been spent from time to time by millionaires who, by the favorable combination of circumstances, had risen from an obscure position in life to a state of great affluence. The late Rajah Rajkissen Bahadoor, Baboos Ram Doolal Dey, Kisto Ram Bose, Modun Mohun Dutt, Santi Ram Singh, Ram Rutton Roy and others, expended upwards of a lakh of Rupees, or £10,000, each for the possession of the enviable title of *Dullaputty*, or head of a party. The way by which this noble distinction was secured was to induce first-class Koolins, by sufficient pecuniary inducements, to intermarry into the families of the would-be *Dullaputty*. The generally impoverished condition of the old aristocracy of the land, and the onward march of intellect teaching the people to look to sterling merit for superiority in the scale of Society have considerably deteriorated the value of these artificial distinctions. The progress of education has opened a new era in the social institutions of the country, and an enlightened proletariat is now-a-days more esteemed than an

I

empty titled *Dullaputty*, the magnitude of whose social status is not to be estimated by the numbers of Koolins he is connected with, but by the extent and character of his services to society.

The bridegroom next dines with his friends outside, notwithstanding the importunities of the females for him to dine in their presence in the inner apartment, that they might have an opportunity to indulge in merriment at his expense. As a rule, the Brahmins dine first, and then the numerous guests and attendants, numbering sometimes one thousand. Despite the precaution of the friends of the bride to prevent unwelcome intrusion, from a natural apprehension of running short of supplies, which, on such occasions, are procured at enormous cost, many uninvited persons in the disguise of respectable looking Baboos contrive somehow or other to mingle in the crowd and behave with such propriety as to elude detection. The proportion of male intruders is larger than that of female ones, simply because the latter, however barefaced, cannot entirely divest themselves of all modesty. It would not be above the mark to put down the number of the former at twenty per cent. Such men are professional intruders ; they are entirely devoid of a sense of self respect, and lead a wretched, demoralized life. Foreigners can have no idea of the extent to which they carry on their disreputable trade, including in their ranks some of the highest Brahmins of the country. It is not an uncommon sight, on such occasion, to behold numbers of people depart after dinner with bundles of *loochees* (fine edibles) and sweetmeats in their hands, which *methránees* * threaten to touch and defile.

When full justice has been done to the feast provided for the occasion, the crowd melts away and streams out at the door, well pleased with the reception they have had. It

* Sweeper-caste females.

is much easier to satisfy men than women in this respect. The latter are naturally fastidious, and the least shortcoming is sure to be found fault with. When confusion and bustle subside, the bridegroom is slowly conducted into a room in the inner apartment which bears the euphonious name of *Básurghur*, the bedchamber of the happy pair, or rather the storehouse of jokes and banter, where are grouped together his wife, his mother-in-law, * and the whole galaxy of beauty. The very name of *Basarghur*† suggests to the female a variety of ideas at once amusing and fascinating. As I have already observed, she, nursed from her cradle in a state of perfect seclusion, and immersed in all the drudgeries of a monotonous domestic life, is glad of any opportunity to share in the unreined pleasure of joviality. The mother-in-law, throwing aside conventional restraint, introduces herself, or is introduced by other women, to her son-in-law. They pull the poor lad's ears, in spite of her earnest protestation, and if they do not know what flirtation is, they assail him

* According to the prescribed rules of the Hindoo society, a mother-in-law is not permitted to appear before her son-in-law; it is not only considered indecorous, but is associated with something else that is scandalous; hence she always keeps her distance from her son-in-law, but on this particular night, her presence in the room with other females is quite consistent with feminine propriety. In the case of a very young son-in-law, however, a departure from this rule is not reprehensible.

† In the suburbs and rural districts of Bengal, females, more particularly among the Brahmin class, are tacitly allowed to have so much liberty on this special occasion that they, putting under the bushel their instinctive modesty, entertain the bridegroom not only with epithalamiums but with other amorous songs, having reference to the diversions of Krishna with his mistress, and the numerous milkmaids. Under an erroneous impression of singing holy songs they unwittingly trumpet the profligate character of their god. These songs are generally known by the names of *sákhisungbad* and *biraha;* the former as the designation implies, consist of news as conveyed by the principal milkmaids regarding his mistress, to whom he oftentimes proved false, and the latter of disappointed love, which broadly exhibits the prominent features of his sensuous life. They feel such an interest in these low entertainments, that under the hallowed name of religion they are led to indirectly perpetrate a crime. Frail as women naturally are, the example of such a god, combined with the sanction of religion, has undoubtedly a tendency to impair the moral influence of a virtuous life. I have always regretted this from my personal observation, but to strike a death blow at the root of the evil must be the work of ages. The essential elements of the Hindoo character must be thoroughly recast.

with jokes which quite puzzle him and bewilder his senses. They burst into roars of laughter and make themselves merry at his expense; he feels himself almost helpless and unprepared to make a suitable repartee, and is at length driven into all manner of excuses, as plausible reasons for a brief respite and a short repose. He complains of headache occasioned by the lateness of the hour; as a sure remedy they give him soda, ice, eau-de-cologne, and almost bathe him in rose-water; but a soporific they can on no account allow him, because it would mar their pleasure and sink their lively spirits. Keeping up their jokes, they place the lovely bride with all her gold trappings on his knee, and unveiling her face ask him to look at it, and say whether or not he likes her; she closes her eyes, moves and jerks to have the veil dropped down, but her sisters yield not to her wish, and keeping her yet unveiled, repeat the question. Of course he makes no reply, but blushes and hangs down his head; their demand being imperative, he sees no other alternative, but to gently reply in the affirmative. They next make the girl bride, much against her inclination, lie down by his side; as often as she is dragged so often she draws back, but yielding at last to the admonition of her mother, she is constrained to lie down, because, on that night, this form is strictly enjoined in the female shaster. The innocent girl, unconscious of the absurd mirth, shrinking together, turns away, and occasionally whimpering, passes the sleepless, miserable hours. The dawn of morning is to her most welcome, although it affords her but a temporary relief. As the first glimpse of light is perceived, she flies into the bosom of her aunt, who tries to animate her drooping spirit by a word or two of solace, citing perhaps at the same time the example of Surrajiney, her elder sister, placed in a similar position three years ago. The women referred to remain in the *Basarghur*. As a matter of course aged women go to sleep faster than young sprightly girls of sweet seventeen, who are bent on making the best of the occasion by indulging in jokes and witticsms. They literally rack their brains to outwit the bridegroom by their *thátá* and *támáshá* (jokes), and their stock of it seems to be almost inexhaustible. They contrive to make him chew the same beera or betel which is *first* chewed by the bride, and if he be obstinate enough to refuse it, in obedience to the warning of his mother, which is often the case, four or five young ladies open out his lips, and thrust the chewed bettle into his mouth. What young man would be so ungallant as to resist them after all? He must either submit or bear the opprobrium of a foolish discourteous boy. Thus the whole night is passed in the banter and practical joking peculiar to the idiosyncracy of the Hindoo females. When in the morning he attempts to get away from their company, one or two ladies, notably his *salees*, or sisters-in-law hold him fast by the skirt of his silk garment demanding, the customary present of *Sarjaytollánee.* * He sends a message to his man outside, and gets thirty two or fifty Rupees, on payment of which they are satisfied and permit him to go. After a short respite he is again brought into the inner apartment, and after shaving, bathing and changing his clothes, he is made to go almost through the same course of female rites as he had to perform on the preceding night, with this difference only, that no officiating priest is required to help on the occasion. This rite is named *Bassi Bibáha* (not new marriage), all the ceremonials being conducted by the females. It would be tedious to inflict on the reader a recapitulation of the same, but suffice it to say, that in all the primary pervading principle is plainly perceptible, namely, the long life and conjugal felicity of the happy pair. It is a remarkable fact that in the opinion of the Hindoo

† The fee for the trouble of removing the bed and keeping up the night, the ladies who remained in the bed-chamber are justly entitled to it for their pains; a widow, be it observed, is not permitted to touch the bed lest her misfortune would befall the bride, but she gets, however, her portion or share of the fee.

females the wider the circle of matrimonial ceremonies, the greater the chance of securing the favor of Hymen. At the conclusion, the boy and girl are directed to say that they have passed the state of celibacy and entered on that of matrimony. "Marriage is honorable in all and the bed undefiled."

As morning advances, the bridegroom walking, and the bride in the arms of her relative, are next brought into a room—the women blowing the conch and sprinkling water,—and made to sit near each other. They then play with cowries, (shells) the girl is told to take up *a few* cowries in her left hand and put them near the boy, while on the other hand the boy is told to take up as *much* as his right hand can contain and put them before the girl, the meaning of which is, that the girl would spend sparingly and the boy give her abundantly. They then play with four very small earthen pots, called *mooglivhur*, filled with rice and peas; the girl first opens the lids of the pots and throws the contents on a *Koolo*, (winnowing fan) the boy takes it up and fills the pots, the girl slowly puts the lids on and inaudibly repeats the name of her husband for the first time,* expressing a hope that by the above process she stops his mouth and curbs his tongue, that he may never abuse her. As the first course of breakfast, fruits and sweetmeats are served to the bridegroom and the bride. He eats a little and is requested to offer a portion of the same to his wife, whose modesty forbids her to accept any in his presence, but the earnest importunities of the nearest of kin overcome her shyness, and she is at length prevailed upon to taste a little which is offered her by the hand of her husband, the females expressing a desire at the same time that she may continue to eat from the same

* It should be mentioned that a female after her marriage is not allowed to utter the name of her husband or of any of his male and female relatives save those who are younger than she. There is no harm done in taking the name of a husband, but through a sense of shame she does not repeat it.

hand to the end of her days. They then receive the benedictions of the male and female members of the family in money, dooav grass and paddy, which embody a prayer to the God for her everlasting happiness. A second course of breakfast consisting of boiled rice, dhall, fish and vegetable curries in great variety, sweetmeats, sour and sweet milk, is next brought for the bridegroom ; seeing that he eats very slowly and scantily through shame, his sisters-in-law help him with handfuls of rice and curries, &c. After he has finished eating, the residue of the victuals is given to his wife in a separate room, because it is customary that she should use the same that day, with a view to cement mutual love and affection.

Preparations are now being made for the return of the procession to the house of the bridegroom, but before it starts some pecuniary matters are to be settled. The father of the bridegroom gives fifty Rupees as *Sarjaytolldnee* for the benefit of the sisters of the bride, and the father of the bride must give the same sum, if not a larger one, as *Nanadkhaymee* for the benefit of the sisters of the bridegroom. Then the difficult problem of *Samajeek* is to be solved. In almost every case, the question is not decided without some discussion. Hindoos are above all tenacious of caste when the question is one of Rupees and pice. Crowds of *Bhâts*, *fakeers*, *nagas*, *raywos*, and mendicants shouting at times "*Jay*, *Jay*," victory, victory ; " Bar, konay bachay thakoog," " may the bridegroom and bride live long," impatiently wait in the street for their usual alms. They get a few annas each and disperse. Professional *Ghatucks*, genealogists and Brahmins also come in for their share and are not disappointed. Then comes the interesting and affecting part of the ceremonial, the *jattra*, or the approaching departure of the happy pair for the house of the bridegroom. A small brass pot filled with holy water and a small wooden pot of vermillion being placed before them, they are made to sit on the two wooden *pirays* on which they sat the previous evening at the time of marriage, and the females touch their foreheads with sour milk, *shiddi* (hemp), and the consecrated *urghi* of the goddess Doorga, * which latter is kept in a tuft on the *Khopa* or ringlet of the bride's hair for eight days. Her forehead is also rubbed with vermillion, the emblem of a female whose husband is alive. This is followed by the rite of *Kanokanjooley* already described, but this time the father of the bride throws the brass plate right over her head into the cloth of his wife, who stands for the purpose behind her daughter. A sudden and solemn pause is perceptible here, betokening the subsidence of joy and the advent of sorrow. In the midst of the company, mostly females, the father and mother of the bride, alternately clasping both the hands of the bridegroom, with tears in their eyes, commit the very responsible trust of the young wife to his charge, saying at the same time in a faltering tone, among other things, that "hitherto our daughter was placed under our care, but now through the *Bhabiturbee* or kind dispensation of Providence, she is consigned for ever to your charge, may you kindly overlook her shortcomings and frailties and prove your fidelity by constancy." At this parting expression, tears start into the eyes of all the females who are naturally more susceptible than the sterner sex. With sorrowful countenances and deep emotion they look steadfastly at the married pair and imploringly beseech the bridegroom to treat the bride with all the tenderness of an affectionate husband. The scene is exceedingly affecting, and the sweet sorrow of parting does not permit him to say *Bidaya* or farewell to the bridegroom. The mother-in-law, especially, should the bride be her only

* The *Urghi* consists of *dooav* grass, rice and *áltá* (a thin red stuff made of cotton like paper with which Hindoo females daub their feet,) previously consecrated to the goddess Doorga, and is supposed to possess a peculiar virtue in promoting felicity and relieving distress.

daughter, is overwhelmed with grief, and if she does not cry bitterly, her suppressed emotion is unmistakable; the idea even of a temporary separation is enough to break her heart, and no consolation can restore the natural serenity of her mind.* Her relatives endeavour to cheer her by reminding her of their and her own cases, and declare that all females are born to share the same fate. They scarcely enter the world before they must leave their parents and intermarry into other families. This is their destiny, and this the law of *Juggut* (the world), and they must all abide by it. Instead of repining, she ought to pray to *Debta* (god,) "that her daughter should ever continue to live at her father-in-law's, use *Sidoor* (vermillion) on her grey head, wear out her *iron bangle*, and be a *junma ayestri*," blessings which are all enjoyed by a female whose husband is alive. Such powerful arguments and undeniable examples partially restore the equanimity of her mind, and she is half persuaded to join her friends and go and see the procession from the top of the house. The same tumult and bustle which ensued at the

---

* Hindoos are so passionately fond of their children, male or female, that they can but ill brook the idea of a segregation, even under circumstances where it is unavoidable. Hence wealthy families often keep their sons-in-law under their own roof. Sometimes this is done from vanity. Such sons-in-law generally become indolent and effeminate, destitute alike of mental activity and physical energy. They eat, drink, smoke, play and sleep. Fattening on the ample resources of their father-in-law they contract demoralizing habits, which engender vice and profligacy. The late Baboos Ramdoolal Dey, Ramruttun Roy, Prannauth Chowdry, the Tagore families, the old Rajahs of Calcutta and some of the newly fledged English made Rajahs and others, countenanced this practice, and the result is, they have left with but few exceptions a number of men singularly deficient in good moral character. These men are called *Ghar Jamayes*, or home bred sons-in-law, which is a term of reproach among all persons who have a spark of independence about them. The late Baboo Dinno Bundho Mitter, the celebrated author of "*Nil Durpun*," strongly satirises such characters in a book called "*Jamay Bareek.*" While on this subject I may as well mention here that Baboo Ramdoolal Dey of Calcutta, who had risen from obscurity to great opulence, had five daughters, to each of whom he gave a marriage dowry of Rupees 50,000 in Government securities, and 10,000 Rupees for a house. Of course all his sons-in-law were first class *Koolins*, and used to live under the roof of their father-in-law. Some of their sons and grandsons are now ranked amongst the Hindoo millionaires of this great City, while most of the members of the original stock have dwindled into insignificance, strikingly illustrating the instability of fortune.

time of coming now prevail at the departure of the bridegroom in his *Sookasun*, and the bride in her closely covered crimson *Mohápáyá*, preceded by all the *tinsel trappings* and bands of English and Native musicians. The procession slowly moves forward with all the pomp and consequence of a grand, imposing exhibition, amidst the staring of the wondering populace and of the sight-seeing public. "It is on such occasions," as Macaulay observes, "that tender and delicate women, whose veils had never been lifted before the public gaze, came forth from the inner chambers in which Eastern jealousy keeps watch over their beauty." The great body of *Barjattars*—bridegroom's friends—who graced the procession with their presence the previous night, do not accompany it now on its return homewards, and notwithstanding all the vigilance of the extra guards, the mob scrambles and forcibly takes away the tinsel flower and fruit trees on the way. In an hour or two, all the objects of wonder vanish from the sight, and leave no mark behind them: "the gaze of fools, the pageant of a day."

On the arrival of the procession at its destination, the bridegroom alights from the *Sookasun* and the bride from the *Mohápáyá*, under which, by way of welcome, is thrown a *ghara*, or pot of water. Hereupon the silk *chadur* or scarf of the bridegroom, so long in the possession of the bride, being entwined between both while the conch is blowing, they are taken into the inner apartment, the former walking, the latter in the arms of one of her nearest female relatives whose husband is alive. The boy is made to stand on an *allpana piray* (white-painted wooden seat), the girl on a thálá or metal plate filled with milk and altawater, and holding in her hand a live *shole* fish. A small earthen pot of milk is put upon the fire by a female whose husband is alive, and when through heat it overflows, the veil of the girl being lifted, she is desired to witness the overflowing process and say gently three times, "may the wealth and resources of her father-in-law overflow," while her mother-in-law puts round her left hand an iron bangle,* and with the usual benediction that she may be ever blessed with her husband, rubs the middle of her forehead with a little vermillion. A small basket of paddy or unhusked rice, over which stands a small pot of vermillion, is placed on the head of the bride, which the bridegroom holds with his left hand, and when they are both greeted three times with the *Sree*, *Barandala Koolo*, water, plantain, betel and betel-nuts, as has been described before, by the bridegroom's mother, he, with his pair of nut-crackers in his right hand, throws over the ground a few grains of paddy from the *reck*, walks slowly over a new piece of red bordered cloth into a room, accompanied by his wife and preceded by other females, one of whom blows a conch and another sprinkles water,—both tokens of an auspicious event.

When all are properly seated upon bedding spread on the floor, the bridegroom and the bride play again the game of *jatook* with cowries (shells)† as before. They afterwards receive the usual *asseerbad* (blessing) in paddy, doovgrass and money. The mother-in-law in order to ensure the permanent submissiveness of the bride puts honey into her ears and sugar into her mouth that she may receive her commands and execute them like a sweet obedient girl. Some females then, placing a male child on the thigh of the

* The use of an iron bangle or bracelet has a deep meaning, it outlasts gold and silver ones. A girl may wear gold ornaments set in precious stones to the value of ten or fifteen thousand Rupees, but an *iron* bangle worth a pice,—a veritable insignia of *ayestreehood* opposed to widowhood—is indispensable to a married woman for its comparatively durable quality. A young widow may wear gold bangles till her twentieth year, but she is not privileged to put on an iron bangle after the death of her husband.

† In the early part of the British Government in Bengal, *cowries* were the common currency of the Province in the ordinary transactions of life. People used to make their *hautbazar* (market) with *cowries*, and a family that made a daily bazar with sixteen or eighteen *kahuns* of cowries, equal to one rupee or so, was reckoned a very respectable family. The prices of provisions ranged nearly one-third of what they now are. Even the revenues of Government were sometimes paid in cowries in the Eastern districts, namely, Assam, Sylhet, &c.

bridegroom, desire him to hand it to the bride. According to prescribed custom, the mother-in-law, on first seeing the face of her daughter-in-law, presents her with a pair of gold bangles. Other near female relatives, following her example, present her severally with a pair of gold armlets, a pearl necklace, a set of gold *pitjhapa*, or an ornament for the back, jingling as the girl moves, a pair of diamond cut gold earrings set in precious stones, and so on. To account for the common desire of the Hindoos to give a profusion of jewels to their females, Menu, their great fountain of authority, enjoins "let women be constantly supplied with ornaments at festivals and jubilees, for if the wife be not elegantly attired, she will not exhilarate her husband. A wife gaily adorned, the whole house is embellished."

She is next taken into the kitchen, where all sorts of cooked victuals, except meat, are prepared in great abundance. She is desired to look at them and pray to God that her father-in-law may always enjoy plenty. Returning from the cook-room, the bridegroom gives into her hands an embroidered Benares *saree* as also a brass *thala*, (plate) with a few *batees* (cups) containing boiled rice, *dhall*, and all the prepared curries, vegetables, and fish, frumenty, &c., and addresses her, declaring that from this day forward he undertakes to support her with food and clothes. He then partakes of the dinner and retires, while the bride is made to share the residue.* She is thus taught, from the moment of her union at the Hymeneal altar, her fundamental duty of absolute submission to, and utter dependence on, her husband. Should she be of dark complexion and her features not beautiful, the bridegroom is thus twitted by his elder brothers' wives: "you all along dis-

* There is a custom amongst the Hindoos that a married woman considers it no disgrace but rather an act of merit to eat the residue of her husband's meal in his absence; so great is the respect in which a husband is held, and so warm the sympathy existing between them. Even an elderly woman, the mother of five or six children, cheerfully partakes of the residue, as if it were the orts of gods.

liked a *kalo* (black) girl, now what will you do, *thacoorpo?* Surely you cannot forsake her, we will see by-and-bye you shall have to wash her feet." Words like these pierce the heart of the bridegroom, but politeness forbids him to reply. As regards the power of woman, the same lawgiver says—"a female is able to draw from the right path in this life, not a fool only, but even a sage, and can lead him in subjection to desire or to wrath."

The nearest relatives and friends of the family are invited to partake of the *Bowbhát* or bridal dinner consisting of boiled rice, dhall, fish and vegetable curries, frumenty, *polowya*, &c., served to the guests by the bride's own hands, which is tantamount to her recognition as one of the members of the family. To eat *unna* (boiled rice) is one thing and to eat *jalpan* (loochees and sweetmeats) is quite another. A Hindoo can take the latter at the house of one of inferior caste, but he would lose his caste if he were to eat the former at the same place. Even among equals of the same caste, and much more among inferiors, boiled rice is not taken without mature consideration, and some sort of compensation from the inferior to the superior for condescending to eat the same. The compensation is made in money and clothes according to the rank of the *Koolins.* Before departing, the guests invited to the *Bowbhát* at which they eat boiled *rice* from the hands of the bride, give her one, two, or more Rupees each.

The day following is a very interesting day or rather night, being the night of *Foolsajya** or flowery bed. At about eight o'clock in the evening the father of the bride sends to

---

* It is a noteworthy fact that in contracting matrimonial alliances, some families placed in mediocre circumstances are satisfied with taking a certain sum of money in lieu of the presents mentioned, partly because the articles are mostly of a perishable nature, and partly because the making presents of money to numerous servants for their trouble and feeding them, is regarded more as a tax than anything else. They prefer utility to show. Even in such cases of verbal contract, the father of the bride must send at least thirty servants with presents, besides 100 or 150 Rupees in cash as is stipulated before.

his son-in-law ample presents of all sorts of fruits in or out of season, home and bazar made sweetmeats, some in the shape of men, women, fishes, birds, carriages, horses, elephants, &c., &c., each weighing from 6 to 10 lbs., sweet and sour milk *(bátásá,)* a kind of sweet cakes, *chineere moorkey*, paddy, fried and sugared comfits, spices of all sorts, betel and prepared betel-nuts, sets of ornaments and toys made of cutch, representing railway carriages, gardens, house, dancing girls, &c., imitation pearl necklaces made of rice, imitation gold necklace made of paddy, colored imitation fruits made of curd *, butter, sugar, sugar-candy, *chána* (coagulated milk), otto of rose, rose-water, chaplets of flowers and flower ornaments, in great variety, Dacca and embroidered Benares *dhooty* and *saree* for the boy and the girl, clothes for all the elderly females, couch-cot, beddings, sets of silver and brass utensils, carpet, embroidered shoes, gold watch and chain, &c., &c. Between 125 and 150 servants, male and female, carry these articles, some in banghy, some in baskets, and some in large brass *thálás* or trays. These presents being properly arranged in the *Thácoor-dállán* the male friends of the family are invited to come down and see them, some praising the choice assortment and large variety, as well as the taste of the father of the bride, while others more calculating make an estimate as to the probable cost of the whole. These articles are then removed into the inner apartment, where the females, naturally loquacious, criticise them according to their judgment; the simple and the good-natured say they are good and satisfactory, others more fastidious find fault with them. They are, however, soon silenced by the prudent remarks of the adult male members of the family. The servants are next fed and dismissed with presents of money, some receiving one Rupee each being the

* In making the above imitations, Hindoo females exhibit an astonishing degree of skill and ingenuity which, if directed by the hand of an expert, is capable of still further improvement. Naturally and instinctively they evince a great aptitude for learning all sorts of handiwork.

servants of the bride's family, some half a Rupee being the servants of other families. They then take back all the brass *thálás* and trays, leaving the baskets behind.

Here we come to the climax of interest. The bridegroom and the bride, adorned with a wealth of flower wreaths, and dressed in red-bordered Dacca clothes, with sandal paste on their foreheads, and sitting side by side in the presence of females whose husbands are alive, are desired to eat even a small portion of the articles of food that have been presented, and what is the most interesting feature in the scene, is that the former helps the latter and the latter helps the former, both throwing aside for the first time the restraint which modesty naturally imposes on such an occasion. To be more explicit, the boy eats one half of a sweetmeat and gives the other half to the girl, and the girl in her turn is constrained to follow the same example, though with a blushing countenance and a veiled face. Female modesty predominates in this isolated instance. If the boy give blushingly, the girl gives shyly and tremulously; in spite of her best efforts, she cannot consistently make up her mind to lift up her right hand and stretch it towards the mouth of her husband, but is after all helped to do so by a woman, whose husband is alive. This process of eating* and mutual help, when three days have scarcely passed over their heads, naturally gives rise to joy, merriment and laughter among the females; and one amongst them exclaims; "look, look, *Soudaminey*, how our new *Rádha* and *Krishna* are sitting side by side and eating together; may they live long and sport thus." The mother of the boy watches the progress of the interesting scene, and

* It is perhaps not generally known that the dinner of a native, Hindoo or Mussulman, male or female, is not considered complete, until he chews his *pan beera* or betel. The bridegroom after eating and washing his mouth chews his usual *pan*, and is asked to give a portion thereof to the bride; he hesitates at first, but consents at length to give it into the right hand of his elder brother's wife, who forcibly thrusts the same into the mouth of the bride, observing at the same time that their mutual repugnance on this score will soon be overcome when their incipient affection grows into true love.

in transports of joy wishes for their continued felicity. The young and sprightly, who have once passed through the same process, and whose hearts are enlivened by the reminiscences of past occurrences, too recent to be forgotten, tarry in the room to the last moment, till sleep weighing down the eyelids of the happy pair, the mother of the bridegroom gently calls them aside, and leaves them to rest undisturbed. In accordance with the old established custom, their bed is strewn with flowers and their bodies perfumed with otto of rose. This is not enough for the sprightly ladies, the complement of whose amusement and merriment is not yet full. Even if the night be a chilly one, regardless of the effects of exposure, they must *aripato*, or jealously watch through the crevices of windows, whether or not the boy talks to the girl, and if he do, what is the nature of the talk. Thus they pass the whole night prying and laughing, chatting with each other on subjects suited to their taste and mode of thought, When morning dawns, the boy opening the door goes outside, and the girl slowly walks to her maid-servants, who accompanied her from her father's house. Her whole desire is to get back to her mother and sisters; nothing can reconcile her to her new home; novelty has no charms for her except in her paternal domicile. She repeatedly asks her maid-servants as to when the *Palkee* will come, and what is the time fixed for her *jattra*, (departure); the maid-servants, consoling her, induce her to wash her mouth and break her fast with a few sweetmeats. In obedience to the kind instruction of her mother, she sits closely veiled and talks little, if at all, even to young girls of her tender age. She next takes her *vojan*, or dinner, and to while away time, little girls try to amuse her with toys or a game at cards; at length the time comes for the toilet work, and the arrival of the covered *Mohapaya* is announced. She again takes a few sweetmeats, and making a *pronam* (bow) to all her superiors, is helped into the Palkee by her mother-in-law, a female having previously washed her feet. The usual benediction on such an occasion is, "may you continue to live under the roof of your father-in-law in the enjoyment of conjugal bliss."

On the arrival of the Mahápáyá at her father's house, almost all the females come out for a moment, taking care previously to have the suddur door bolted and the Palkee bearers removed. They cheerfully welcome the return of the girl home. Her mother, unveiling her face and taking her in her arms, thus affectionately addresses her, "my *Bacha*, (child) my *sonarchand* (golden moon) where have you been? Did not your heart mourn for us?" Our house looked *khakha* (desolate) in your absence. "What did they (bridegroom's family) say about our *dayway thowya* (presents)? Did they express any *nindya*, (dissatisfaction)? How have the women behaved towards you? How are your *sassooree* and *sasoor* (mother-in-law and father-in-law,)?" Thus interrogating, they all walk inside and, making the girl change her silk clothes and sit near them, begin to examine and criticise the ornaments given her by her father-in-law. "Let us see the pearl necklace *first*," says Bhoopada? The pearls are not smooth and round, what may be its value?" *Geeri Balla*, taking her own pearl necklace from off her neck, compares the one with the other. They unanimously pronounce the latter to be more costly than the former; be that as it may, its value cannot be less than Rupees 500. They next take in hand the *pitjapa*, ornament for the back, looking at it for a few minutes they pass their opinion, saying it is heavier and better made than that of *Geeri Balla*. The *Sita haur*, or *Jarawya* * (gold necklace) afterwards attracts their attention, and they roughly estimate its price at Rupees 350. It is not a little surprising that though these women are never

* *Jorawya* jewellery is set in precious stones, the value of which it is not easy to estimate.

permitted to go beyond the precincts of the zenana, yet their valuation of ornaments, unless it be a *jarawya bijoutry* of enormous cost, such as is worn on grand occasions by the wife of a "*big swell*," often bears the nearest approximation to the intrinsic worth of an article. Thus almost every ornament, one after another, forms the subject of their criticism. When their discussion is over, the girl is desired to take the greater portion of her ornaments off her body—save a pair of gold *balla* * on her hands and a necklace on her neck—and leave them to the care of her mother. She then mixes in the company of other little girls of her tender age, some married, some unmarried; who curiously ask her all about her new friends, until their talk resumes its usual childish topics. She passes the day among them very pleasantly, so much so that when her mother calls her to take her luncheon, she stays back and says only "*jachee, jachee*," (coming, coming,) her mind being so much absorbed in her juvenile sports.

The next day is again a day of trial for her, she has to go for *gharbasath* † to her father-in-law's house. On awaking, she remembers where she will have to go in course of the day; a sensation bordering on sulkiness almost unconsciously steals upon her, and as time passes it increases in intensity. About four in the afternoon the arrival of the *Mahápáyá* is announced, her sister combs her hair and

---

* A Hindoo *Ayistree* female, *i. e.*, one whose husband is alive, whether young or old, is religiously forbidden to take off *balla* (bangle) from her hands, if is a badge of *Ayistreeism*, even when dead red thread is substituted in the place of the *balla*, so great is the importance attached to it by *Ayistree* females. When the *balla* is not seen on the hand, it is called the *raur hatha*, or the hand of a widow, than which there could not be a more reproachful term.

† *Gharbasath* implies dwelling in a father-in-law's house. If the bride do not go there within eight days from the date of marriage, she could not do so for one year, but after *gharbasath* she can go and come back any time when necessary. The object is to impress on her mind that her father-in-law's house is her future home. It is on this occasion that the worship of *Shoobachini* already described is performed, and both the bridegroom and bride are taken to *Kally Ghat* to sanctify the hallowed union and obtain the blessings of the goddess.

adorns her person with all the ornaments she has lately received. Dressed in her bridal silk *saree*, her eyes seem charged with tears, and symptoms of reluctance are visible in every step; but go she must; no alternative is left her. So her mother helps her into the *Mahápáyá* and orders a durwan and two maid-servants to accompany her, not forgetting to assure her that she is to be brought back the next day. Despite this assurance, she whimpers and weeps, and is consoled on the way by her maid-servants. At her father-in-law's, young girls of her age being impatient to receive her, are seen moving backwards and forwards to get a glimpse of the *Mahápáyá*, the arrival of which is a signal for almost all the ladies to come out and greet the object of their affection. Her mother-in-law steps forward, and taking up the girl in her arms walks inside, followed by a train of other ladies, whose hearts are exhilarated again at the prospect of merriment at the expense of the married pair. When the time comes round for them to retire, the same scene of *arepáta* is re-enacted by the mirth-loving ladies, with all their "quips and cranks and wanton wiles." At day-break, the girl, as must naturally be expected, quietly walks to her confidential maidservant, and whispers her to go and tell her mother to send the *Mahápáyá* Palkee as early as possible. Bearing her message, one of them goes for the purpose but the mother replies, How can she send the Palkee except at the lucky hour after dinner? When this reply is communicated to the girl, she sits sulkily aloof, until her mother-in-law cajoles her and offers for her breakfast a few sweetmeats with milk. After a great deal of hesitation she complies with her request, which, to be effective, is always accompanied by a threat of not allowing her to return to her father's in the event of a refusal. About ten o'clock she takes her regular breakfast as described before, but she does not eat with zest, for whatever delicacy may be offered her, it palls upon her taste; continually brooding on the idea of a return home. This is the day when the bridegroom and the bride untie from each other's hand the yellow home-spun *charka* thread with which they were entwined on the day of marriage, as a mark of their indissoluble union. At length the lucky hour arrives, and with it the *Mahápáyá* comes. The very announcement of the fact revives the drooping spirits of the bride. After going through the usual toilet work and a slight repast, she gets into the covered conveyance, assisted by her mother-in-law and other ladies. When she returns home, she changes her bridal silk garment and strips herself of the greater portion of her ornaments. Now uncontrolled and unreserved, she breathes a free, genial, atmosphere; her mother and sisters welcome her with their heartfelt congratulations, and she moves about with her wonted buoyancy of spirit. Throwing aside her sulkiness, she commingles readily in conversation with all around her. She praises the amiable qualities of her father-in-law and mother-in-law, and the very kind treatment she has had while under their roof, but she keeps her reserve when even the slightest allusion is made to her husband, because this is to her young mind forbidden ground on which she cannot venture to tread without violating the sacred rules of conventionalism.

At the marriages of rich families, as will be understood from our description, vast sums of money are expended. The greatest expense is incurred in purchasing jewels and making presents of brass utensils, shawls, clothes, sweetmeats. &c., to Brahmins, Koolins, *Ghatacks* and numerous friends, relatives and acquaintances, besides illuminations, fireworks and all the pageantry of a pompous procession. In and about Calcutta, the Rajahs of Shobabazar, the Dey family, the Mullick family, the Tagore family, the Dutt family, the Ghosal family, and others, are reported to have spent from fifty thousand rupees to two lakhs (£5,000 to £20,000) and upwards in the marriages of their sons. Whilst writing this I am told Maharajah Jotendro Mohun Tagore is said to have expended about two lakhs of rupees in the marriage of his nephew. The most interesting feature in the extraordinary munificence of the Moharajah is, as I have learnt, his princely contribution io the " District Charitable Society,"—an act of benevolence which has shewn, in a very conspicuous manner, not only his good sense, but his warm sympathy with the cause of sufferrng humanity. It were to be wished that his noble example would exercise some influence on other Hindoo millionaires. If a tithe of such marriage expenses were devoted to Public Charity, the poor and helpless would ceaselessly chant the names of such donors, and the reward would be something better than the transient admiration of the idle populace.

For one or two years after marriage, the girl generally remains under the paternal roof, occasionally paying a visit to her father-in-law's as need be. As she advances in years, her repugnance—the effect of early marriage—to live with her husband is gradually overcome, till time and circumstances completely reconcile her to her future home. Her affection grows, and she learns to appreciate the grave meaning of a married life. She is still, however, but a girl, in habit and ideas, when the real union of wedded life or the second marriage takes place, which is solemnised when she arrives at the age of puberty, say at her twelvth or thirteenth year. There is a popular belief, whether erroneous or not it is not for me to decide, that in this country heat accelerates growth, and hence the Hindoo Shasturs enjoin the necessity of early marriage,the injurious consequences of which are chiefly seen in the weak constitution of the offspring, and the premature decay of the mother.

So abominable are some of the ceremonies connected with this event in the life of a female that to describe them fully would be an outrage on common decency.* I will, therefore, confine myself to a description of the ceremonies, entirely abstaining from an allusion to the abominations connected therewith. A general depravity of manners can only account for the prevalence of this obnoxious institution, in the eradication of which every Hindoo whose moral sense is not entirely blunted ought to co-operate. As the delay of the union is in the belief of a Hindoo an unpardonable sin, the fact referred to is announced by the sound of a conch, and the bodies of all the females are smeared with turmeric water,—an unmistakable evidence of joy. The news is also conveyed to the nearest relatives by the family barber who receives presents of clothes and money. It is quite evident from the silence of the Hindoo Shastur on the subject that the origin of the female rites is comparatively recent. Irrespective of the religious observances, it affords an opportunity to the zenana females to indulge in obscene depravities, the outcome of vitiated feeling.

The poor girl is placed on this occasion in the corner of a dark, dingy room, with a small round pebble before her, shut out from the gaze of men, and surrounded on four sides by four pieces of slender split bamboos about one yard long fastened by a piece of thread. This is called the *teerghur* mentioned before. Being regarded as unclean, she remains in this room for four days without a bedding or a musquito curtain, and no one touches her, not even her sisters. She is forbidden to see the sun, her diet is confined to boiled rice, milk, sugar, curd, and tamarind without salt. On the morning of the fifth day, she is taken to a neighbouring tank, accompanied by five women whose husbands are alive. Smeared

* It is perhaps not generally known that some women, not from any malicious design but rather from the ennui of a monotonous life, as well as for the sake of amusement in which they might participate, make a secret combination, and invent some artificial means to prematurely drag the girl—the poor victim of superstition—into the *Teerghur* before she actually arrives at the age of puberty.

with turmeric water, they all bathe and return home, throwing away the mat and other things that were in the room. She then sits in another room, and a very low caste woman, in the presence of five other respectable females (not widows), performs a series of what is vulgarly called *Nith Kith*,* purely female rites, which are exceedingly indecent and immoral, so much so that a woman who has any sense of shame feels quite disgusted. During the day, according to previous invitations, numerous female guests assemble and partake of a good dinner provided for the occasion. They are also entertained with songs, dancing and music, all done by professional females. When the guests retire, they congratulate the girl with the usual benediction to the effect,—"may you be blessed with a male child."

After a day or two the religious part of the ceremony is performed, which is free from obscenity. On this occasion, the officiating priest reading, and the bridegroom repeating the service after him, presents offerings of rice, sweetmeats, plantain, clothes, doovgrass, fruits and flowers to the following gods and goddesses, *viz.*, *Shasthi*, *Márcando*, *Soorja*, *Soobhachini*, *Gannesh*, and the nine planets, much in the same way as when the nuptial rites were formally solemnized. After this the hands of the bridegroom and the bride are joined together, and the priest repeating certain formulas, the bridegroom then causes a ring to slide between the bride's silk garment and her waist. Twenty-one small images (twenty male and one female) made of pounded rice are placed before the happy pair, and the priest feeds the bride with sugar, clarified butter,

* This part of the rite is called *Kádá* or mire. A small pool is dug in the court-yard and some water thrown into it;—two women, the one personating a Rajah (King) and the other, a Ranee (Queen) feign to bathe in the pool, change their clothes, put on straw ornaments and dine on the refuse of vegetables, while the songstress recites all sorts of obscene songs and the females hide their faces through shame. This loose and ludicrous representation proves nauseating even to those for whose amusement it is performed. We cannot regard in any other light than as a relic of unmitigated barbarism.

milk, and the urine and dung of a calf to ensure the purity of the offspring. They then partake of a good dinner, the bride taking the residue of the bridegroom's meal. The twenty-one images are put into the room of the pair as a token of happy offspring, and the proportion of the males to the females, shews the premium and discount at which they are respectively held. The bride now takes up her permanent residence in the house of her father-in-law and becomes one of his family.

For one twelve month after the marriage, the parents of the bridegroom and the bride have to make exchanges of suitable presents to one another at all the grand festivals. At the *first tatto* or present, besides clothes, heaps of fruits, sweetmeats, English toys and sundries, the father of the youth gives one complete set of miniature silver and brass utensils to the girl, while in return the father of the girl sends such presents as a table, chair, writing desk, silver inkstand, gold and silver pencil cases, stationery, perfumery, &c, in addition to an equally large quantity of choice eatables of all kinds too numerous to be detailed. The most expensive presents are two, namely, the *sittory* or winter present and the Doorga Poojah present, the former requiring a Cashmere shawl, *choga* and sundry other articles of use, and the latter, fine Dacca and silk clothes to the whole family, including men, women and children.

It is a lamentable fact that though a Hindoo bears a great love and affection to his wife while she lives, yet in the event of her death, the effects of these amiable qualities are too soon effaced by the strong influence of a new passion, and another union is very speedily formed. Even during the period of his mourning, which lasts one month, proposals for a second marriage are entertained, if not by the husband himself, by his father or elder brother. When the remembrance of this heavy domestic bereavement is so very fresh in the memory, it is highly unbecoming and ungenerous to open or enter into a matrimonial negotiation, and have it consummated immediately after the *asúchi* or mourning is over. A wife is certainly not a beast of burden that is no sooner removed by death than it may be replaced by another. She is a being whose joy and sorrow, happiness and misery, should be identical with her husband's, and he is a savage in the widest sense of the word who does not cherish a sacred regard for her memory after her death. In regard to the whole conduct and relations of the married life, Hindoos cannot have the golden rule too strongly impressed: 'Let every one of you in particular so love his wife, even as himself; and let the wife see that she reverence her husband."

VI.

THE BROTHER FESTIVAL.

ANY social institution that has a tendency to promote the growth of genuine love and affection between man and woman, is naturally conducive to the happiness of both. In this sublunary vale of tears, where unalloyed felicity is but transient and short lived, even a temporary exemption from the cares and anxieties of the world adds at least some moments of pleasure to life. The *Bhratridvitiya*, or *fraternal* rite of the Hindoos, is an institution of this nature, being admirably calculated to cement the natural bond of union between brothers and sisters of the same family. Bhratridvitiya, as the name imports, takes place on the second day of the new moon immediately following the Kali Poojah or Dewali. On the morning of this day, a brother comes to the house of a sister, and receives from her hand the usual benedictive present of unhusked rice, doova-grass and sandal, with a wealth of good wishes for his long, prosperous life, and the happy commemoration of the event from year to year. The brother in return reciprocates, and putting a Rupee or two into her hands, expresses a similar good wish, with the addition that she may long continue to enjoy the blessings of a conjugal life,—a benediction which she values over every other worldly advantage. The main object of this festival is to renovate and intensify the warmth of affection between kith and kin of both sexes by blessing each other on a particular day of the year. It is a sort of family reunion, pre-eminently calculated to recall the early reminiscences of life, and to freshen up fraternal and sisterly love. No ritualistic rite or priestly interposition is necessary for the purpose, it being a purely social institution, originating in the love that sweetens life.

After interchanging salutations, the sister who has every thing ready thrice invokes a blessing upon the brother in a Bengali verse, and marks his forehead thrice with sandal paste by the tip of her little finger. She then serves him with the provisions provided for the festive occasion. Here genuine love and true affection almost spontaneously gush forth from the heart of the sister towards one who is united to her by the nearest tie of consanguinity and tenderest remembrances. If the brother be not inclined to relish or taste a particular dish, how affectionately does she cajole him to try it, adding at the same time that it has been prepared by her own hand with the greatest care. Any little dislike evinced by the brother instantly bathes her eyes in tears, and disposes her to exclaim somewhat in the following strain: "Why is this slight towards a poor sister who has been up till twelve o'clock last night to prepare for you the *chunderpooley* and *Khirarchách* (two sorts of home-made sweetmeats) regardless of the cries of *Khoká* (the baby). Such a pathetic, tender expression bursting from the lips of a loving sister cannot fail to melt a brother's heart, and overcome his dislike.

About four o'clock in the afternoon, the sister sends, as tangible memorials of her affection, presents of clothes and sweetmeats to the house of the brother, fondly indulging in the hope that they may be acceptable to him. On this particular day, Hindoo homes as well as the streets of Calcutta in the native part of the town, present the lively appearance of a national jubilee. Each of the brothers of the family visits each of the sisters in turn. Hundreds of male and female servants are busily engaged in carrying presents, and return home quite delighted. On such occasions the heart of a Hindoo female, naturally soft and tender, becomes doubly expansive when the outflow of love and affection on her part is fully reciprocated by the effusion of good wishes on the part of her brother.

VII.

THE SON-IN-LAW FESTIVAL.

IF not precisely analogous in all its prominent features to the popular festival described in the preceding Chapter, the following bears a striking resemblance to it, in its adaptation to promote domestic happiness. The festival familiarly known in Bengal by the name of "*Jamai Shasthi*" is an entertainment given in honor of a son-in-law, in order to bind him more closely to his wife's family.

Nothing better illustrates the manners and usages of a nation from a social and religious standpoint than the festivals and ceremonies which are observed by it. They form the essential parts of what DeQuincey calls the equipage of life. As a nation, the Hindoos are proverbially fond of festivals, which are engrafted, as it were, on their peculiar domestic and social economy. A designing priesthood had concocted an almost endless round of superstitious rites with the view of acquiring power, and looking for permanent reverence to the credulity of the blind devotees. Such foolish rites are eventually destined to fall into desuetude, as popular enlightenment progresses, but those which are free from the taint of priestcraft by reason of their being interwoven into the social amenities of life, are likely to prevail long after the subversion of priestly ascendency. And *Jamai Shasthi* is a festival of this unobjectionable type. No superstitious element enters into its observance.

It invariably takes place on the sixth day* of the increase

* It appears to me rather anomalous, as far as Hindoo astrology is concerned, that such a national jubilee is fixed to be celebrated on this particular day, which is specially marked as an unlucky day for any good work. The Hindoo almanac places *Shasthi*, the sixth day of the moon, as *dugdhá* or destructive of any good thing in popular estimation. A Hindoo is religiously forbidden to commence any important work or set out on a journey on this day. It portends evil.

of the moon in the Bengali month of May, when ripe mangoes —the prince of Indian fruits—are in full season. Then all the mothers-in-law in Bengal are actually on the *qui vive* to welcome their sons-in-law and turn a new leaf in the chapter of their joys. A good son-in-law is emphatically the most darling object of a Hindoo mother-in-law. She spares no possible pains to please and satisfy him, even calling to her aid the supernatural agency of charms. Ostensibly and even practically a Hindoo mother-in-law loves her son-in-law more than her son, simply because the son can shift for himself even if turned adrift in the wide world, but the daughter is absolutely helpless, and the cruel institution of perpetual widowhood, with its appalling amount of misery and risk, renders her tenfold more so.

On this festive occasion, the son-in-law is invited to spend the day and night at his father-in-law's house. No pains or expense is spared to entertain him. When he comes in the morning, the first thing he has to do is to go into the female apartment, bow his head down in honor of his mother-in-law, and put on the floor a few Rupees, say five or ten, sometimes more if newly married. The food consists of all the delicacies of the season, and both the quantity and variety are often too great to be done justice to. The perfection of Hindoo culinary art is unreservedly brought into requisition on such occasions. Surrounded by a galaxy of beauty, the youthful son-in-law is restrained by a sense of shame from freely partaking of the feast specially provided for him. The earnest importunity of the females urges the bashful youth to eat more and more. If this be his first visit as son-in-law he finds himself quite bewildered in the midst of superfluity

---

Respectable Hindoo females who have children do not eat boiled rice on this particular day for fear of becoming Rakhasses, or cannibals prone to destroy their own offspring. The goddess Shasthi is the protectress of children. She is worshipped by all the women of Bengal six times in the year, except such as are barren or ill-fated enough to become virgin-widows.

and superabundance of preparations. Many are the tricks employed to outwit him. With all his natural shrewdness, and forewarned by the females of his own family, he is no match for either the playful humor and frolics of the young, sprightly ladies. Sham articles of food cleverly dressed in close imitation of fruits and sweetmeats are offered him without detection in the full blaze of day, and the attempt to partake of them excites bursts of laughter and merriment. The utmost female ingenuity is here brought into play to call forth amusement at the expense of the duped youth. In their own way, the good-natured females are mistresses of jokes and jests, and nothing pleases them better than to find the youthful new comer completely nonplused. This forms the favorite subject of their talk long after the event. Shut up in the cage of a secluded zenana, quite beyond the influence of the outside world, it is no wonder that their minds and thoughts do not rise above the trifles of their own narrow circle.

As in the case of the "Brother" festival, ample presents of clothes, fruits, and sweetmeats are sent to the house of the son-in-law, and every lane and street of Calcutta is thronged with male and female servants trudging along with their loads in full hopes of getting their share of eatables and a Rupee or a half Rupee each into the bargain.

VIII.

THE DOORGA POOJAH FESTIVAL.

BY far the most popular religious festival of the present day among the Hindoos of Bengal, is the *Doorga Poojah*, which in the North-Western and Central Provinces is called the *Dusserah* festival. It is believed that the worship of the goddess Doorgah has been performed from time out of mind. The following is a description of the image of the goddess which is set up for worship: "In one of her right hands is a spear, with which she is piercing the giant, Mohishasur; with one of the left, she holds the tail of a serpent and the hair of the giant, whose breast the serpent is biting. Her other hands are all stretched behind her head and filled with different instruments of war. Against her right leg leans a lion, and against her left, the above giant. The images of Luckee, Saraswathi, Kartick and Gannesh are very frequently made and placed by the side of the goddess." The majestic deportment of the goddess, with her three eyes and ten arms, the warlike attitude in which she is represented, her sanguinary character, which was the terror of all other gods, and the mighty exploits (far surpassing in feats of strength, courage and heroism, those of the Greek Hercules,) all combine to give her an importance in the eyes of the people, which is seldom vouchsafed to any other deity. Even *Bramah*, *Vishnoo* and *Shiva* the Creator, Preserver and Destroyer of the world, were said to have propitiated her, and *Ram Chunder*, the deified hero, invoked her aid in his contest with *Ravana*, and as he worshipped her in the month of October, her Poojah has, from that particular circumstance, been ever after appointed to take place in that period of the year.* A short description of this festival, the preliminary rites with which it is associated, and the national excitement and hilarity which its periodical return produces among the people, will not be altogether uninteresting to European readers.†

Twenty-one days before the commencement of the Doorga Poojah festival, a preliminary rite, by way of purifying the body and soul by means of ablution, is performed. The rite is called the "*Aapar pakhaya tarpan*" so called from its taking place on the first day of *Pratipad* and ending on the fifteenth day of *Amábashya*, an entire fortnight, immediately preceding the *Debipakhya* during which the Poojah is celebrated. It generally falls between the fifteenth of September, and the fifteenth of October. As already observed, this popular festival, called Doorga Poojah in Bengal and Dussera "or the tenth" in the North-West, although entirely military in its origin is universally respected. It is commemorative of the day on which the god Rám Chunder first marched against his enemy, Rávana, in *Lanka* or Ceylon for the restoration of his wife, Seeta,‡ who was deservedly regarded as the best model of devotion, resignation and love, as is so beautifully painted by the poet:

"A woman's bliss is found, not in the smile
Of father, mother, friend, nor in herself:
Her husband is her only portion here,
Her heaven hereafter. If thou indeed
Depart this day into the forest drear,
I will precede, and smooth the thorny way."

* Doorga is also worshipped in the month of April, in the time of the vernal equinox, but very few then offer her their devotion, though this celebration claims priority of origin.

† For some general remarks on the religion of the Hindoos, see Note C.

‡ "In this ancient story" says Tod, "we are made acquainted with the distant maritime wars which the princes of India carried on. Even supposing Ravana's abode to be the insular Ceylon, he must have been a very powerful prince to equip an armament sufficiently numerous to carry off from the remote kingdom of *Kousula* the wife of the great king of the Suryas. It is most improbable that a petty king of Ceylon could wage equal war with a potentate who held the chief dominion of India; whose father, *Dosaratha* drove his victorious car (*ratha*) over every region (*desa*) and whose intercourse with the countries beyond the Bramaputra is distinctly to be traced in the *Ramayana*."

In the mornings of *Apar pakhaya*, for fifteen days continually, those who live near the sacred stream go thither with a small copper-pan and some teel seeds, which they sprinkle on the water at short intervals, while repeating the formulæ in a state of half immersion. To a foreigner quite unacquainted with the meaning of these rites, the scene is well calculated to impress the mind with an idea of the exceeding devotedness of the Hindoos in observing their religious ordinances. The holy water and teel seeds which are sprinkled are intended as offerings to the manes of ancestors for fourteen generations, that their souls may continue to enjoy repose to all eternity. The women, though some of them are in the habit of bathing in the holy stream every morning, are, however, precluded by their sex from taking a part in this ceremony. Precisely on the last day of the fortnight, *i. e.*, on the *Amabáshya*, as if the object were attained, the rite of ablution ends, followed by another of a more comprehensive character. On this particular day, which is called *Moháloyá*,* the living again pay their homage to the memory of the fourteen generations of their ancestors by making them offerings of rice, fruits, sweetmeats, clothes, curded milk, and repeating the incantations said by the priest, at the conclusion of which he takes away all the articles presented and receives his *dakshiná* of one Rupee for his trouble. Apart from their superstitious tendency, these anniversaries, are not without their beneficial effects. They tend, in no small degree, to inspire the mind with a religious veneration for the memory of the departed worthies, and by the law of the association of ideas not unfrequently bring to recollection their distinctive features and individual characteristics.

Some aristocratic families that have been observing this festival for a long series of years, begin their *Kalpa* or preli-

* This is also the day which is vulgarly called the *Kalá kátá amabáshay* when unripe plantain fruits are cut in immense quantities for offerings to Doorga.

minary rite on the ninth day of the decrease of the moon, when an earthen water pot called *ghat** is placed in a room called *bodanghur*, duly consecrated by the officiating priest, who, assisted by two other Brahmins, invokes the blessing of the deity by reading a Sanskrit work, called *Chundee*, which relates the numerous deeds and exploits of the goddess. It is a noteworthy fact that the Brahmin, who repeats the name of the god, *Modosoodun*, seems, to all appearance, to be absorbed in mental abstraction. With closed eyes and moving fingers, not unlike the *Rishis* of old, he, as it were, disdains to look at the external world. From early in the morning till 10 o'clock the worship before the earthen pot is continued, and the officiating priests† are strictly prohibited from using *sidha*, (rice) taking more than one meal a day, or sleeping with their wives, as if that would be an act of unpardonable profanation. This strict *regime* is to be observed by them until the whole of the ceremonial is completed, on the tenth day of the new moon. It should be mentioned here that the majority of the Hindoos begin their *kalpa*, or preliminary rite, on *pratipad*, or the beginning of the new moon, when almost every town and village resounds with the sound of conch, bell and gong, awakening latent religious emotions, and evoking *agamaney*, (songs or inaugural invocations) which deeply affect the hearts of Doorga's devout followers. Some of these rhythmic effusions are exceedingly pathetic. I wish I could give a specimen here of these songs divested of their idolatrous tinge, but I am afraid of offending the ears of my European readers.

The Brahmins‡ as a rule, commence their *kalpa* on the sixth day or one day only previous to the beginning of the

* This sacred jar is marked with two combined triangles, denoting the union of the two deities, Siva and Doorga,—the worshippers of the *Sakti*, female energy, mark the jar with another triangle.

† The day before the *Kalpa* begins, these priests receive new clothes, comprising a *dhootie* and *dubja*, and some money for *habishay*, or food destitute of fish. Very few, however, abide by the rules enjoined in the holy writings.

‡ Even in the observance of this religious preliminary, the Brahmins take advantage of their superior caste, and curtail five days out of six in order to save expense. Every thing is allowable in their case, because they assume to be the oracles between the god and man.

grand poojah on the seventh day of the new moon. From the commencement of the initial rite, what thrilling sensations of delight are awakened in the bosom of the young boys and girls! Every morning and evening while the ceremony is being solemnized, they scramble with each other to get striking the gong and *Kasur* which produces a harsh, deafening sound. Their excitement increases in proportion to the nearer approach of the festival, and the impression which they thus receive in their early days is not entirely effaced even after their minds are regenerated by the irresistible light of truth. The females, too, manifest mingled sensations of delight and reverence. If they are incapable of striking the gongs, they are susceptible of deep devotional feelings which the solemnity of the occasion naturally inspires. The encircling of their neck with the end of their *saree* or garment, expressive of humility, the solemn attitude in which they pose, their inaudible muttering of the name of the goddess, and their prostrating themselves before the consecrated pot in a spirit of perfect resignation, denote a state of mind full of religious fervour, or, more properly speaking, of superstitious awe, which goes with them to their final resting place. On the night of the sixth day (Shashti) after the increase of the moon, another rite is performed, which is termed *Uddhibassey*, its object being to welcome the advent of the visible goddess with all necessary paraphernalia. Another sacred earthen pot is placed in the outer temple of the goddess, and a young plantain tree, with a couple of wood apples intended for the breast, is trimmed for the next morning's ablution. This plantain tree, called *kalabhoye*, is designed as a personification of Doorga in another shape. It is dressed in a silk *saree*, its head is daubed with vermilion *

* The vermilion is used by a Hindoo female whose husband is *alive*, the privilege of putting it on the forehead is considered a sign of great merit and virtue.

and is placed by the side of Gannesh. Musicians with their ponderous *dhak* and *dhole* and *sannai* (flutes) are retained from this day for five days at 12 or 16 Rupees for the occasion.* That music imparts a solemnity to religious service is admitted by all, but its harmony may be taken as an indication of the degree of excellence and refinement to which a nation has attained in the scale of civilization. What with the sonorous sound of *dhak* and *dhole*, *sannai*, conch and gong, the effect cannot fail to be impressive to a devout Hindoo mind. Except Brahmins, no one is allowed to touch the idol from this night, after the *bellbarun*, when it is supposed life and animation is imparted into it. By the marvellous repetition of a few incantations a perfectly inanimate object stuffed only with clay and straw, and painted, varnished and ornamented in all the tawdriness of oriental fashion, is suddenly metamorphosed into a living divinity. Can religious jugglery, and blind credulity go farther?

It will not be out of place to say a few words here about the embellishments of the images. As a refined taste is being cultivated, a growing desire is manifested to decorate the idols with splendid tinsel and gewgaws, which are admirably calculated to heighten the magnificence of the scene in popular estimation. Apart from the feast of colors presented to public view, the idols are adorned with tinsel ornaments, which, to an untutored mind, are in the highest degree captivating. Some families that are placed in affluent circumstances, literally rack their brains to discover new and more gaudy embellishments which, when compared with those of their neighbours, might carry off the bubble reputation. It is, perhaps, not generally known that a certain class of men—chiefly drawn from the lower strata of society—

* There is a singular coincidence between the Hindoos and the ancient heathen nations in regard to music. In both it is used as an indispensable accompaniment to religious worship.

subsist on this trade; they prepare a magnificent stock of tinsel wares for a twelve month, and supply the entire Hindoo community, from Calcutta to the remotest provinces and villages. Indeed so great is the rage for novelty and so strong the influence of vanity, that not content with costly home made ornaments, some of the Baboos send their orders to England for new patterns, designs and devices, that they may be able to make an impression on the popular mind; and as English taste is incomparably superior to native taste, both in the excellence and finish of workmanship as well as in neatness and elegance, the images that shine in new fashioned English embellishments * are sure to challenge the admiration of the populace. On the day of *Nirunjun*, or *Vhasan* as it is vulgarly called, countless myriads of people throng the principal streets of Calcutta, to catch a glimpse of the celebrated *pritimas*, or images, and carry the information home to their absent friends in the villages.

Before sunrise on *Saptami*, or the seventh day of the bright phase of the moon, the officiating priest, accompanied by bands of musicians and a few other members of the family, proceeds barefooted to the river side bearing on his shoulder the *kalabhoye* or plantain tree described above with an air of gravity as if he had charge of a treasure chest of great value. These processions are conducted with a degree of pomp corresponding with the other extraneous splendours of the festival. In Calcutta, bands of English musicians, and numbers of staff holders with high flying colors, give an importance to the scene, which is not ill suited to satisfy the vulgar taste. After performing some minor ceremonies on

* It is no less strange than surprising that ornamental articles prepared by the hands of European artisans who are accustomed to eat beef and pork, the very mention, and much more, the touch of which contaminates the purity of religion, are put on the bodies and heads of Hindoo gods without the least religious scruple, simply for the gratification of vanity. So much for the consistent and immaculate character of the Hindoo creed!

the banks of the river, and bathing the plantain tree, the procession returns home, escorting the officiating priest with his precious charge in the same way in which he was conveyed to the Ghât. On reaching home, the priest, washing his feet, proceeds to rebathe the plantain tree, rubbing on its body all kinds of scented oils * as if to prepare it for a gay, convivial party. This part of the ceremony, with appropriate incantations, being gone through, the plantain tree is placed again by the side of the image of Gannesh, who being the eldest son of Doorga, must be worshipped *first*. Thus the right of precedence of rank is in full force even among the Hindoo gods and goddesses.

Previous to the commencement of the *Saptami*, or first Pooja, the officiating priest again consecrates the goddess Doorga, somewhat in the following manner: "Oh, goddess, come and dwell in this image, and bless him that worships you," naming the person, male or female, who is to reap the benefit of the meritorious act. Thus, the business of giving life and eyes to the gods being finished, the priest, with two forefingers of his right hand, touches the forehead, cheeks, eyes, breast and other parts of the image, repeating all the, while the prescribed incantation: "May the soul of Doorga long continue to dwell in this image." This part of the ceremony, which is accompanied with music, being performed, offerings are made to all the gods and goddesses, as well as to the companions of Doorga in her wars, which are painted in variegated colors on the *chall* or shed over the goddess in the form of a crescent. The offerings consist principally of small pieces of gold and silver, rice, fruits, sweetmeats, cloths, brass utensils and a few other things. These are arranged in large round wooden or brass plates, and a bit of flower or *bell* leaf

* These scented oils are mostly prepared by Mussulmans, whose very touch is enough to desecrate a thing; the Brahmins knowing this fact unhesitatingly use them for religious purposes. Thus we see in almost every sphere of social and domestic life the fundamental rules of religious purity are shamefully violated.

is cast upon them to guard against their being desecrated by the demon Ravana, who is supposed to take delight in insulting the gods and goddesses; the officiating priest then consecrates them all by repeating a short mantra and sprinkling flowers and *bell* leaves on them, particular regard being had to the worship of the whole host of deities according to their respective position in the Hindoo pantheon. Even the most subordinate and insignificant gods or companions of Doorga must be propitiated by small bits of plantain and a few grains of rice, which are afterwards given to the idol makers and painters of the gods and goddesses. More valuable offerings form the portion of the Brahmins, who look upon and claim these as their birthright. In the evening, as in the morning, the goddess is again worshipped, and while the service is being held the musicians are called to play their musical instruments with a view to add to the solemnity of the occasion. In the morning, some persons sacrifice goats and fruits, such as pumpkin, sugar-cane, &c., before the goddess. In the present day, many respectable families have discontinued the practice from a feeling of compassion towards the dumb animals, though express injunctions are laid down in the Shasters in its favor. It is a remarkable fact that the idea of sacrifice as a religious institution tending to effect the remission of sin was almost co-existent with the first dawn of human knowledge. The Reverend Dr. K. M. Banerjea thus writes: "Of the inscrutable Will of the Almighty, that without shedding of blood there is no remission of sin, this, too, appears imbedded in ancient Ayrian tradition in the *sruti* or hearings of our ancestors." Next to the Jews, this religious duty was scrupulously observed by the Brahmins. Names of priests, words for fire, for those on whose behalf the sacrifices were performed, for the materials with which they were performed, abound in language etymologically derived from words implying sacrifice. No literature contains so many vocables relating to sacrificial ceremonies as Sanskrit. Katyayana says, "that heaven and all other happiness are the results of sacrificial ceremonies. And it was a stereotyped idea with the founders of Hindooism that animals were created for sacrifices. Nor were these in olden days considered mere offerings of meat to certain carnivorous deities, followed by the sacrificers themselves feasting on the same, as the practice of the day represents the idea. The various nature of the sacrifices appears to have been substantially comprehended by the promoters of the institution in India. The sacrificer believed himself to be redeemed by means of the sacrifice. The animal sacrificed was itself called the sacrifice, because it was the ransom for the soul." If we leave India and go back to the tradition and history of the other ancient nations, we shall find many instances, proving the existence among them of the sacrificial rite for the remission of sin and the propitiation of the Deity. The hecatombs of Greece, and the memorable dedication of the temple of Solomon when 20,000 oxen* and 100,000 sheep were slain before the altar, are too well known to need any comment.

In these later ages, when degeneracy has made rapid strides amongst the people of the country, the original intention of the founder of the institution being lost sight of, a

* It is deserving of notice that the slaughter of oxen, cows or calves is most religiously forbidden in the Hindoo Shaster. Divine honors are paid to the species. The cow is regarded as a form of Doorga and called Bhuggobutty. The husband of Doorga, Shiva, rides naked on an ox. The very *dung* of a cow purifies all unclean things in a Hindoo household, and possesses the property of a disinfectant. The milk of a cow assuredly affords the best nourishment to the young and the old, hence the species was deified by the Hindoo sages. Even after the advent of the English into this country for above two centuries, an orthodox Hindoo is apt to exclaim "what impious times!" whenever he happens to see a Mussulman butcher carry a cow or calf in the street for slaughtering purposes. Not a few wonder how the English power continues to prosper amidst the daily perpetration of such irreligious acts. By way of derision, the English are called *gokháduk* or beef-eaters and the *goylás* (milkmen) *Kásays* or butchers. If such Hindoos had power enough they would certainly have delivered their country from the grasp of these beef-eaters and placed it above the reach of sacrilligious hands. But alas! in the present *Kaliyaga* or iron age, both they and their gods are alike impotent.

perverted taste has given it an essentially sensual character. Instead of offering sacrifice from purely religious motives, it is now made for the gratification of carnivorous appetite. The late King of Nuddea, Rajah Kristo Chunder Roy, though an orthodox Hindoo of the truest type, was said to have offered at one of these festivals a very large number of goats and sheep to the goddess Doorga. "He began," says Ward, "with one, and, doubling the number each day, continued it for sixteen days. On the last day, he killed 33,168, and on the whole he slaughtered 65,535 animals. He loaded boats with the bodies and sent them to the neighbouring Brahmins, but they could not devour them fast enough, and great numbers were thrown away. Let no one, after this, tell us of the scruples of the Brahmins about destroying animal life and eating animal food."

About twelve o'clock in the day, when the morning service is over, the male members of the family make their *poospaunjooley* or offerings of flowers to the images, repeating an incantation recited by the priest, for all kinds of worldly blessings, such as health, wealth, fame, long age, children, &c. The women come in afterwards for the same hallowed purpose, and inaudibly recite the incantation repeated by the priest inside the screen. The very sight of the images gladdens their hearts and quickens their throbs. Though fasting, they feel an extreme reluctance to leave the shrine and the divinities, declaring that their hunger and thirst are gone not from actual excess in eating and drinking but from their fullness of heart at the presence of *Ma Doorga.* But go they must to make way for the servants to remove the offerings, distribute them among the Brahmins, and clean the temple for the evening service, at the close of which Brahmins and other guests begin to come in and partake of the entertainment* provided for the occasion.

* It is generally known that except the Brahmins, who are proverbially noted for their eating propensities, scarcely any respectable Hindoo condescends to sit

On the second day of the Poojah, offerings and sacrifices are made in the same manner as on the first day, but this is considered a specially holy day, being the day, as is generally supposed, when the mighty goddess is expected to come down from the mount Himalaya, and cast a twinkling of her eye upon the divers offerings of her devotees in the terrestrial world. This day is called *Moha Ustamy*, being the eighth day of the increase of the moon, and is religiously observed throughout Bengal. In Calcutta, this is the day when thousands and tens of thousands of Hindoos, who have had no Poojah in their houses, proceed to Kalyghât in the suburbs, and do not break their fast before making suitable offerings to the goddess Kali, who, according to Hindoo mythology, is but another incarnation of the goddess, Doorga. Except little children, almost all the members of a family, male and female, together with the priest, fast all day, and, if the combination of stars require it, almost the whole night. Elderly men of the orthodox type devote the precious time to religious contemplation. Until the *Moha Ustamy*, and its necessary adjunct *Shundya Poojah*, is finished, all are on the *qui vive*. It generally happens that this service is fixed by astrologers to take place before night's midmost stillest hour is past, when nature seems to repose in a state of perfect quiescence, and to call forth the religious fervour of the devotees. As the

---

down to a regular *jalpán* dinner at this popular festival. He comes, gives his usual *pranámy* of one Rupee to the goddess in the *thácoordállán*, talks with the owner of the house for a few minutes, is presented by way of compliment with otto of roses and pan, and then goes away, making the stereotyped plea that he has many other places to go to. Besides this, every man is expected to provide himself at home with a good stock of choice eatables on this festive occasion. The prices of sweetmeats, already too high, are nearly doubled at this time, because of the large demand and small supply. From 32 Rupees a maund (82 lbs) the normal price of *sundesh* in ordinary times, it rises to 60 or 70 Rupees in the Poojah time. Milk sells at four annas a pound, and without milk no *sundesh* could be made. It is the most expensive article of food among the Hindoos of Bengal, when well made with fresh *channa* (curded milk) it has a fine taste, but is entirely destitute of nutritive property. The Hindoos of the Upper Provinces, however, do not regard the preparation as *pure*, and consequently do not use it, because of its admixture with curded milk.

edge of hunger is sharpened, a Hindoo most anxiously looks at his watch or clock as to when the precious moment should arrive, and as the hour draws near, men, women and children are all hushed into silence. Not a whisper nor a buzzing sound is to be heard. All is anxeity, suspense and expectation, as if the arrival of the exact time would herald the advent of a true Saviour into the world. Amid perfect silence and stillness, all ears are stretched to catch the sound of the gun* which announces the *precise minute* when this most important of all Poojahs is to begin. As soon as the announcement is made by the firing of a gun, the priest in all haste enters on the work of worship, and invokes the blessings of the goddess on himself and the family. When the time of sacrifice arrives, which is made known by the sound of another gun, all the living souls in the house are bade to stand aloof, the priest with trembling hands and in a state of trepidation consecrates the *Kharra*, or scimitar, with which the sacrifice is to be made, and placing the *Khaparer sara* by the side of the *haureekat*, (the sacrificial log of wood) bids the blacksmith finish off his bloody job. Should the latter cut the head of a goat off at one stroke, all eyes are turned towards him with joy. The priest, the master, and the inmates of the house, who are all this while under the influence of mental agitation, now begin to congratulate each other on their good luck, praying for the return of the goddess every year.

Nor must I omit to mention the other secondary rites which are performed on the second day of the Poojah. Besides absolute fasting, the females of the household actually undergo a fiery ordeal. About one in the afternoon, when the tumult and bustle have subsided a little, all males being told to go away, the women unveiling their faces, and holding in each hand a *sara* or earthen plate of rosin, squat down

---

* Rich men are in the habit of firing guns for the guidance of the people.

before the shrine of the goddess, and in the posture of quasi-penitent sinners, implore in a fervent spirit the benediction of the goddess on behalf of their sons, while the rosin continues to burn in slow fire. As if dead to a sense of consciousness, they remain in that trying state for more than half an hour, absorbed, as it were, in holy meditation, repeating in their minds, at the same time, the names of their guardian deities. Towards the close of this penitent service, a son is asked to sit on the lap of his mother. Barren women to whom Providence has denied this inestimable blessing must go without this domestic felicity resulting in religious consolation, and not only mourn their present forlorn condition, but pray for a happier one at next birth. A few puncture their breasts with a slender iron *naroon* or nail cutter, and offer a few drops of blood to the goddess, under a delusion that the severer the penance the greater the merlt. Many women still go through this truly revolting ordeal at Kali Ghât, in fulfilment of vows made in times of sickness.

Another ceremony which is performed by the females on this particular day is their worship of living Brahmin *Komarees* (virgins) and matrons (*sodhavas*). After washing and wiping the feet of the objects of their worship, with folded hands, and, with the end of their *sari* round their necks, in a reverential mood, they fall prostrate before the Brahmin women, and crave blessings, which, when graciously vouchsafed, are followed by offerings of sweetmeats, clothes and rupees. The purpose of this ceremony is to obtain exemption from the indescribable misery of widowhood, and ensure the enjoyment of domestic happiness,

On the third or last day of the Poojah, being the ninth day of the increase of the moon, the prescribed ritualistic ceremonies having been performed, the officiating priests make the *hoam* and *dhukinanto*, a rite, the meaning of which is to present farewell offerings to the goddess for one year, adding in a suitable prayer that she will be graciously pleased to forgive the present shortcomings on the part of her devotees, and vouchsafe to them her blessings in this world as well as in the world to come. This is a very critical time for the priests, because the finale of the ceremony involves the important question of their respective gains. Weak and selfish as human nature assuredly is, each of them (generally three in number) fights for his own individual interest, justifying his claim on the score of the religious austerities he has had to undergo, and the devotional fervour with which his sacred duties have been discharged. Until this knotty question is satisfactorily solved, they forbear pronouncing the last *munter* or prayer. It is necessary to add here that the presents of rupees which the numerous guests offered to the goddess during the three days of the Poojah, go to swell the fund of the priest, to which the worshipper of the idol must add a separate sum, without which this act of merit loses its final reward in a future state. The devotee must satisfy the cupidity of the priests or run the risk of forfeiting divine mercy. When the problem is ultimately solved in favor of the officiating priest who actually makes the Poojah, and sums of money are put into the hands of the Brahmins, the last prayer is read. It is not perhaps generally known that the income the Indian ecclesiastics thus derive from this source supports them for the greater part of the year, with a little gain in money or kind from the land they own.

The last day of the Poojah is attended with many offerings of goats, sheep, buffaloes* and fruits. The area before the shrine becomes a sort of slaughter house, slippery with gore and mire, and resounding with the cries of the dying victims, and the still more vociferous shouts of "*Ma, Ma,*"

* The flesh of buffaloes is used only by sweepers, shoemakers, &c., who sometimes quarrel for the possession of the slaughtered animals. The meat with country liquor ends in drunken feasts.

uttered by the rabble amidst the discordant sound of gongs and drums. Some of the deluded devotees, losing all sense of shame and decency, smear their bodies from head to foot with this bloody mire, and begin to dance before the goddess and the assembled multitude like wild furies. In this state of bestial fanaticism, utterly ignoring the ordinary rules of public decorum, and literally intoxicated with the glory of the meritorious act, the deluded mob, preceded by musicians, proceed from one house to another in the neighbourhood where the image has been set up, sing obscene songs, and otherwise make indecent gestures which are alike an outrage on public morals and common decency. When quite exhausted by these abominable orgies, they go and bathe in a river or a tank, and return home, thinking how to make the most of the last night. Should any sober-minded person remonstrate with them on their foolish conduct, the stereotyped reply is—"this is *Mohamayer Bazar* and the last day of the Poojah, when all sorts of tomfoolery and revelry are justifiable." The sensible portion of the community, it must be mentioned, keep quite aloof from such immoral exhibitions.

However great may have been the veneration or the depth of devotional feeling in which the Doorga Poojah was held among the Hindoos of bygone ages, it is certain that in the lapse of time this and all other national festivals have lost their original religious character, and in the majority of cases degenerated into profanities and impure orgies, which renew the periodical license for the unrestrained indulgence of sensuality, not to speak of the dissipation and debauchery which it usually brings in its train. Except a few patriarchal Hindoos, whose minds are deeply imbued with religious pre-possessions as well as traditional proclivities, the generality celebrate the Poojah for the sake of name and fame, no less than for the purposes of amusement, and for the satisfaction of the women and children, who still retain, and will continue to do so for a long time to come, a profound veneration for the old *Doorga Uttsob.* Apart from the children, whose minds are susceptible of any impression in their nascent state, the women are the main prop of the idolatrous institutions and of the colossal superstructure of Hindoo superstition. If I am not much mistaken, it was to satisfy them that such distinguished Hindoo Reformers as the late Baboos Dwarkeynauth Tagore, Prosonocoomar Tagore, Romanauth Tagore, Ram Gopal Ghose, Digumber Mitter and others celebrated this Poojah in their family dwelling houses. How far they were morally justified in countenancing this popular festival, it is not for me to say. The fact speaks for itself. Even in the present time, when Hindoo society is being profoundly convulsed by heterodox opinions, not a few of my enlightened countrymen observe this religious festival, and spend thousands of rupees on its celebration. There are, however, a few redeeming features in connection with this annual demonstration, which ought to be prominently noticed. First and foremost, it affords an excellent opportunity for the exercise of benevolent feelings ;* secondly, it materially contributes to the promotion of annual reunions, brotherly fraternization, and to the general encouragement of trade throughout Bengal.

The very great interest which Hindoo females feel in the periodical return of this grand festival, is known to every one who is at all conversant with the existing state of things in

---

* The late Rajah Rajkissen Bahadoor, Baboos Santiram Sing, Ramdoolal Dey, Shibnarain Ghose, Prankissen Holdar, the Mullick family, the Ghosal family of Bhookoylash and others, spent large sums of money from year to year in giving clothes, food and money to a very large number of poor men, and liberating prisoners from jail on payment of their debts. Any relief to suffering humanity is certainly an act of great merit for which the donors deserve well of the community. In our days there are several Baboos who do the same on a limited scale, but the name of Baboo Tarucknauth Puramanick of Kassiriparrah deserves a special notice. Naturally unassuming and unambitious, his character is as irreproachable as his large-heartedness is conspicuous. On every anniversary of the Doorga Poojah, and on almost every religious celebration, he gives alms to huudreds and thousands of poor people without distinction of caste or creed. On the occasion

this country. In the numerous districts and villages of Bengal inaugural preparations are made for the celebration of this anniversary rite precisely from the day on which the Juggernauth car is drawn in *Assar*, from the date of the festival of Ruth Jattra, that is for about four months before the date of the Doorga Poojah. While the *koomar*, or the image maker, is engaged in making the Bamboo frame-work for the images, the women in the villages devote their time to cleaning and storing the rice, paddy, different kinds of pulse, cocoanuts, and other products of the farm, all which are required for the service of the goddess. Ten times a day they will go to the temple to see what the Koomar is doing. Not capable of writing, nor having any idea of 'Letts' Diaries,' they note down in their minds the daily progress of work, and feel an ineffable pleasure in communicating the glad tidings to each other. When day by day the straw forms are converted into clay figures, and they are for the first time plastered over with chalk and then painted with variegated colors, the hearts of the females leap with joy, and again when the completed images are being decorated with *dack* ornaments or tinsel ware, their exhilaration knows no bounds. In the fulness of anxiety, the mistress of the house directing her attention to what more is yet wanted for the due completion of the Poojah, rebukes the master for his apparent neglect somewhat in the following manner: "Where is the *dome sujah*, (basketware)? Where is the *koomar sujah*, (pottery)? Where are the spices and clothes? Where are the *sidoorchupry* and sundry other things for the *Barandalla*?" Adding that there is no time to

of the Doorga Poojah festival he would not break his fast until midnight, when he is assured that all the poor people who came to his door have been duly provided with food and coppers. For three nights this distribution of alms continues. The public road before his house is closed by order of the police for the accommodation of beggars. Five or six times in a month he feeds all the poor people that come to his house, hence the fame of his generosity is spread far and wide, and he is surnamed Taruck Baboo, "the *datta*" or charitable—a distinction which the more opulent of his countrymen (and there are not a few) should seek to covet.

be lost, the Poojah is near at hand. The husband acquiescing in what the wife says assures her that everything shall be procured by Saturday or Sunday next.

On the first day of the new moon, when every Hindoo in the city becomes more or less busy on account of his official, domestic and religious engagements, the lady of the house is chiefly occupied with making suitable arrangements for *tutwa* or presents, first to her son-in-law and then to her other relatives, a subject on which I shall have to say a few words in its proper place. On the eve of the sixth day of the new moon, when the grand Poojah may be said to commence, the females, consigning all their past sorrows to oblivion, feel a sort of elasticity, hopefulness and confidence which almost involuntarily draw forth from the depths of their hearts, feelings of joy and ecstacy. Even a virgin widow, whose grief is yet fresh, forgets her miseries for awhile, and cheerfully mingles in the jubilee. She forms part and parcel of the domestic sisterhood, and for the five days of her life at least, her settled sadness gives way to pleasing sensations, and though forbidden by a cruel priesthood to lend her hand to the ceremonial, she nevertheless goes up to the goddess and prays in a devotional spirit for a better future. Amidst such a scene of universal hilarity, supplemented by a confident hope of eternal beatitude, it is quite natural that Hindoo females, socially divorced from every other innocent amusement, should feel a deep, sincere and intense interest in such a national festival which possesses the twofold advantages of a religious ceremony and a social demonstration. None but the most callous hearted can remain indifferent. Men, women and children, believers and unbelievers, are alike overcome by the force of this religious anniversary. The females go to the temple at all hours of the day, and feast their eyes upon the captivating figure of mighty Doorga and her glorious satellites. Nor do they stare at her with a vacant mind; each has her grievance to represent, her wish to express; prayer in a fervent spirit is offered to the goddess for the redress of the one and the consummation of the other. Should a son die prematurely, should a husband suffer from any difficulty, should a son-in-law be not true to his wife, should a daughter be doomed to widowhood, the females wrestle hard in prayer for relief and amelioration. On the fourth or Bijoya day, when the image is to be consigned to the river, one takes away a bit of the consecrated *urghy**; a second, the *khappurer sara*, or the sacrificial earthen plate; a third, the crushed betel; a fourth, the sacred *billaw* leaves, and so on; each forms a sacred trust, and all are preserved with the greatest possible care, as the priceless heirloom of a benignant goddess.

Having briefly described the main features of this religious festival, I will now endeavour to give a short account of the other circumstances connected with it. In the house of a Brahmin, *Khichree*, rice, dhall, fish and vegetable curries, together with sweetmeats and sour milk, are given to the guests, chiefly in the day time during the three Pooja days. Many Hindoos, whose religious scruples will not allow them to kill a goat themselves, generally go to the house of a Brahmin—but not without an eight anna piece or a Rupee—to satisfy their carnivorous appetite during the Poojah. It is very creditable to the women of the sacerdotal class that three or four of them undertake the duty of the *cuisine*, and feed from six to eight hundred persons for three days successively. As fish is not acceptable to Doorga, neither cooked goat's and sheep's flesh, a separate kitchen is set apart for the purpose of cooking meat of sacrificed annimals. Brahmin

* An *Urghy* is a bunch of doorva grass tied up at the last, either with red cotton or a slip of plaintain leaf. Two or three of such bundles are made, one is placed on the crown of the goddess and two on her two feet. It is usually stuffed with paddy and besmeared with sandal wood water and vemillion. It is a sacred offering and consequently preserved for solemn occassions.

women, as a rule, cook remarkably well. Their long experience in the culinary art, their habitual cleanliness, their undivided attention to their duty, and above all, the religious awe with which they prepare food for the goddess, give quite a relish to every thing they make. Nor is this all. Their devotion and earnestness is so great that they cannot be persuaded to eat any thing until all the guests are fully satisfied, and what is still more commendable, they look to no other reward for their trouble than the fancied approbation of the goddess, and the satisfaction of the guests. It is not before nine o'clock at night that they become disengaged, after which they bathe again, change clothes, say their prayers to the goddess, and then think of appeasing their hunger. Simple and unartifical as they naturally are, they, being mostly widows, are quite content with *habishi unno*, which was of yore the food of the Hindoo *rishis* or saints. It consists of *autob* rice, or rice from unboiled paddy, green plaintain and dhall, all boiled in the same pot. Of course a large quantity of ghee is added to it, and at the time of eating milk is taken. These Brahmin women are, indeed, mistresses of the culinary art, if the bill of fare is not long, yet the dishes they make are generally very palatable. The truth is, they practically follow the trite saying, "what is worth doing at all, is worth doing well." Their simple recipes always produce appetising and wholesome dishes, they are thrifty housewives. It must be admitted that simplicity is not meanness, nor thriftiness a fault.

In the house of a *Kayasta* or *Sudra*, whose female members, it must be observed, are generally more indolently inclined, and whose style of living is consequently more luxurious, the food offered to the guests consists chiefly of different kinds of sweetmeats, fruits, *lochees*, vegetable curries, &c. Four or five days before the Poojah begins, professional Brahmin sweetmeat-makers are employed to make the necessary arrangements at home, the principal ingredients required being flour, *soojee*, *chattoo*, (gram fried and powdered) *safeyda* (pounded rice) sugar, spices, almonds, raisins, &c. Not a soul is permitted, not even the master of the house, to touch and much less taste these articles* before they are religiously offered to the goddess in the first instance and afterwards to the Brahmins. In these "feast days" of the Poojah in and about Calcutta, where nearly five hundred *pratimas* or images are set up, every respectable Hindoo, as has been observed before, is previously provided at home with an adequate supply of all the necessaries and luxuries of life that would last about a month or so, it being considered unpropitious then to be wanting in any store, save fruit and fish. This accounts for a general disinclination on the part of the well-to-do Baboos to partake of any ordinary entertainment when visiting the goddess at a friend's house, but to the Brahmins and the poverty-stricken classes this is a glorious opportunity for "gorging." The despicable practice to which I have alluded elsewhere of carrying a portion of the *jalpan* (food) home is largely resorted to on this occasion. It is certainly a relic of barbarism, which the growing good sense of the people ought to eschew.

The night of the ninth day of the increase of the moon is a grand night in Bengal. It is the *nabamee ratree*, and modesty is put to the blush by the revelry of the hour. The houses of the rich become as bright as the day, costly chandeliers, hanging lamps and wall lights burning with gas, brilliantly illuminate the whole mansion, while the walls of the *Boytuckhana* or sitting room are profusely adorned with English and French paintings and engravings, exhibiting certainly not the best specimens of artistic skill, but sin-

* Home made things are, in the long run, cheaper and more preferable to the questionable products of the market, which are not only inferior in quality but are more or less subject to defilement, being exposed for sale to people of all castes. This detracts from the absolute purity of the preparation.

gularly calculated to extort the plaudits of the illiterate, because engravings and pictures are the books of the unlearned, who are more easily impressed through the eye than the ear. All the rooms and antechambers are frequently furnished in European style. Splendid Brussels or Agra carpets are spread on the floors of the rooms, a few of which, as if by way of contrast, have the ordinary white cloth spread on them. Nor are hanging Punkhas wanting. In one of the spacious halls sits the Baboo of the house, surrounded by courtiers pandering to his vanity. Indolently reclining on a bolster, and leisurely smoking his *albollah* with a long winding *nal* or pipe, half dizzy from the effects of last night's revelry, he feels loath to speak much. Like an opium eater, he falls into a siesta, whilst the Punkah is moving incessantly. If an orthodox Hindoo, freed from the besetting vice of drinking, and awake to all that is going on around him, before him are placed the Dacca silver filagree worked *atterdan* and *golappass*, as well as the *pandan* with lots of spices and betel in it. On entering the room, the olfactory nerves of a visitor are sure to be regaled with fragrant odours. At intervals rose water is sprinkled on the bodies of the guests, and weak spiced tobacco is served them every fifteen minutes, the current topics of the day forming the subject of conversation. All this is surely vain ostentation and superfluity. So far the arrangements and reception of friends are essentially *oriental*, the manner of sitting, the mode of conversation, and the way in which otto of roses, rose water and betel are given to guests are Mahomedan and Hindoo-like, but there is something beyond this; here orthodoxy is virtually proscribed and heterodoxy practically proclaimed. While the officiating priests and the female devotees are offering their prayers to the presiding goddess, the Baboo, a liberal Hindoo, longs to retire to his *private* room, perhaps on the third storey, at the entrance of which a guard is placed to keep off unwelcome visitors, that he might partake of refreshments supplied by an English Purveying Establishment with a few select friends. The room is furnished after European fashion, chairs, tables, sofas, cheffoniers, cheval glass, sideboard, pictures, glass and silver and plated ware, knives, forks and spoons, and I know not what more, are all arranged in proper order, and friends of congenial tastes have free access. First class wines and viands, such as Giesler's champagne, Heatly's Port and Sherry, Exshaw's Brandy No. 1. Crabbie's Ginger wine, Bass's best bottled beer, soda water, lemonade, ice, Huntley and Palmer's mixed biscuits, manilla cigars, cakes and fruits in heaps, *poloway*, *kurma*, *kupta*, *kallya*, roast fowl, cutlets, mutton chop and fowl curry,* are at your service, and an English visitor is not an unwelcome guest. *Loochee*, *Sundesh mittoye*, *burfi*, *rasagullah*, *sittavog*, &c., the ordinary food of the Hindoos on festive days, are at a discount. The Great Eastern Hotel Company should be thankful for the large orders which the Hindoo aristocracy of Calcutta and its suburbs favor them with during this grand festival. The taste for the English style of living is not a plant of recent

* It would not be out of place to observe here that liberal Hindoos as a body are not beef-eaters as is vulgarly supposed. They are content with fowls, goat, sheep and fish. About forty years ago before the Calcutta University was founded, the late Baboo Isser Chunder Goopto, the editor of *Pravakur*, a vernacular news paper, very cleverly hit off and satirised in popular ballads the then growing desire of the young Hindoo reformers to adopt a European style of eating. He commenced with Rammohun Roy—the pioneer of Hindoo reformation—and thus sarcastically described his public career. Addressing *Saraswattee* the Hindoo goddess of learning, he thus laments: "Oh goddess! in vain have you established schools in Calcutta, look at the end of that Roy (Rammohun Roy); profound learning had wafted him over the waters to a distant region (England), and never brought him back again." As regards the young alumni, he makes a wife thus accost her husband: "*Pran*, *Pran*, my heart, my heart, you go to society and lectures every day, and when the Examination is held at the Town Hall you get prizes, heaps and heaps of books you read and always remain outside. Is it written in the books that you should never touch the body of a female? What sort of a *gooroo* (master) is your Sahib? he is a regular *garu* (bull) if he give you such lessons. You dislike *loochee* and *mundá* (Hindoo sweetmeats) but you get *gunda* and *gunda* of fowl eggs and satisfy your hunger, and for you all there is an end of cows and calves." But this is an exaggeration about the eating of beef by the educated Hindoos. Except a few medical students, who have, in a great measure, overcome their prejudices by the constant handling of dead bodies, the rest still feel a sort of natural repugnance to eating beef. This is, perhaps, the

growth. It has been germinating since the days of John Company, when India merchantmen enjoyed the monopoly of the foreign trade of the country, when the highest authorities of the land had no religious scruples as Christians to be present at a Hindoo festival, when, in fact, Hindoo millionaires were wont to indulge in lavish expenditure* for the purpose of pleasing their new European masters. Leaving aside the dignity and gravity of the clerical profession for a while, the Reverend Mr. Ward was induced out of curiosity to pay a visit to the palatial mansion of the Shoba Bazar Rajahs of Calcutta on the last night of the Poojah.

"In the year 1806," says he, "I was present at the worship of this goddess, as performed at the house of Rajah Rajkishnu at Calcutta. The buildings where the festival was held were on four sides, leaving an area in the middle. The room to the east contained wine, English sweetmeats, &c.,

---

effect of early impressions produced by the religious veneration in which a cow is held among the Hindoos. "The superstitious reverence," says an eminent writer, "for the ox, points doubtless to a period when that useful animal was first naturalized in India and protected by a law for its preservation and encouragement, which, now that the original intention is lost sight of in the lapse of ages, has invested the cattle with a religious character, and, indeed, it is not 200 years since the Emperor Jehangir was obliged once to prohibit the slaughter of kine for a term of years, as a measure absolutely required to prevent the ruin of agriculture." It is a striking fact that that loathsome disease, leprosy, is very common among the lower orders of Mussulmans who use this meat freely. Perhaps it is more suited to the inhabitants of milder regions than those of a tropical climate.

* So great was the mania for entravagant, ostentations show, that instances were not wanting in which a lakh of Rupees was freely spent on this grand occasion. The late Prankissen Holdar, of Chinsurah, in the neighbourhood of Calcutta, expended annually for three or four years the above sum in furnishing his house without stint of cost in truly oriental style, giving rich entertainments to Europeans and Natives, and distributing alms among the poor. There was no Railway then, and consequently the boat hire alone from Calcutta to Chinsurah for English and Native grandees might have cost four to five thousand Rupees. The very invitation cards written in golden letters with gold fringes cost eight to ten Rupees each. For the entertainment of his English friends he used to give ten thousand Rupees to Messrs. Gunter and Hooper, the then public Purveyors of Calcutta. First class wines and provisions were procured in abundance, and arranged in the corridor under European and Mahomedan stewards, while one hundred Brahmins were engaged in prayers, reciting *Chundee* and repeating the name of the god, Modosoodun, for the propitiation of the goddess and the interests of the family. It sometimes so happened that the clang of knives, forks and spoons was simultaneous with the sound of the holy bell and conch, the one neutralising what the other was supposed to produce in a religious point of view.

for the entertainment of English guests, with a native Portuguese or two to wait on the visitors. In the opposite room was placed the image, with vast heaps of all kinds of offerings before it. In the two side rooms, were the native guests, and in the area groups of Hindoo dancing women, finely dressed, singing, and dancing with sleepy steps, surrounded with Europeans who were sitting on chairs and couches. One or two groups of Mussulman-men singers entertaincd the company at intervals with Hindoosthanee songs, and ludicrous tricks. Before two o'clock the place was cleared of the dancing girls, and of all the Europeans except ourselves, and almost all the lights were extinguished, except in front of the goddess,—when the doors of the area were thrown open, and a vast crowd of natives rushed in, almost treading one upon another, among whom were the vocal singers, having on long caps like sugar loaves. The area might be about fifty cubits long and thirty wide. When the crowd had sat down, they were so wedged together as to present the appearance of a solid pavement of heads, a small space only being left immediately before the image for the motions of the singers, who all stood up. Four sets of singers were present on this occasion, the first consisting of Brahmins, *(Huru Thacoor)*, the next of bankers, *(Bhuvanundu)*, the next of boeshnuvus, *(Nitaee)*, and the last of weavers, *(Lukshmee)*, who entertained their guests with filthy songs and danced in indecent attitudes before the goddess, holding up their hands, turning round, putting forward their heads towards the image, every now and then bending their bodies, and almost tearing their throats with their vociferations. The whole scene produced on my mind sensations of the greatest horror. The dress of the singers, their indecent gestures, the abominable nature of the songs, (especially *khayoor*) the horrid din of their miserable drum, the lateness of the hour, the darkness of the place, with the reflection that I was standing in an idol temple, and that this immense multitude of rational and immortal creatures, capable of superior joys, were in the very act of worship, perpetrating a crime of high treason against the God of heaven, while they themselves believed they were performing an act of merit, excited ideas and feelings in my mind which time can never obliterate. I would have given in this place a specimen of the songs sung before the image, but found them so full of broad obscenity that I could not copy a single line. All those actions which a sense of decency keeps out of the most indecent English songs, are here detailed, sung, and laughed at, without the least sense of shame. A poor ballad singer in England would be sent to the house of correction, and flogged, for performing the *meritorious actions* of these wretched idolaters.* The singing is continued for three days from two o'clock in the morning till nine."

It is a noteworthy fact that in those days when Bengal was in the zenith of its prosperity and splendour, the Governor-General, the members of the Council, the judges of the Supreme Court, and distinguished officers and merchants, did not think it derogatory to their dignity, or at all calculated to compromise their character as Christians, to honor the Rajahs with their presence during this festival, but since the days of Daniel Wilson, the highly venerated Lord Bishop of Calcutta, who must have expressed his strong disapprobation of this practice, these great men have ceased to attend. At present but a few young officers, captains of ships in the port and East Indians may be seen to go to these nautches, and as a necessary consequence of this withdrawal of countenance, the outward splendour of the festival has of late considerably diminished. Seeing the apparent approval of idolatrous

---

* "The reader will recollect that the festivals of Bacchus and Cybele were equally noted for the indecencies practised by the worshippers both in their words and actions."

ceremonies by some Europeans, a conscientious Christian once exclaimed: "I am not ashamed to confess that I fear more for the continuance of the British power in India, from the encouragement which Englishmen have given to the idolatry of the Hindoos, than from any other quarter whatever." *

As regards the other amusements at this popular festival, a few words about the Indian *nautch* (dancing) girls may not be out of place here. These women have no social status, their principles are as loose as their character is immoral. They are brought up to this disreputable profession from their infancy. They have no husbands, and many of them are never married. The Native Princes, and chiefs, rich zemindars and persons in affluent circumstances, the capacity of whose intellect is as stinted as its culture is scanty, have been their great patrons. Devoid of a taste for reading and writing, they managed to drive the ennui of their lives by the songs of these dancing girls. Great were the rewards which they sometimes received at the hands of the Native

* The Reverend Mr. Maurice, a pious clergyman, who had never seen these ceremonies, attempted to paint them in the most captivating terms. Should he think that Hindoo idolatry is capable of exciting the most elevated conceptions about the godhead and leading the mind to the true path of righteousness, let him come and join the Brahmins and their numerous devotees in crying "Huree Bole! Hurree Bole! Joy Doorga! Joy Kally!" "Mr. Forbes, of Stanmore Hill, in his elegant museum of Indian rarities, numbers two of the bells that have been used in devotion by the Brahmins. They are great curiosities, and one of them in particular appears to be of very high antiquity, in form very much resembling the cup of the lotus, and the tune of it is uncommonly soft and melodious. I could not avoid being deeply affected with the sound of an instrument which had been actually employed to kindle the flame of that superstition which I have attempted so extensively to unfold. My transported thoughts travelled back to the remote period when Brahmin religion blazed forth in all its splendour in the caverns of Elephanta: I was, for a moment, entranced, and caught the odour of enthusiasm. A tribe of venerable priests, arrayed in flowing stoles, and decorated with high tiaras, seemed assembled around me, the mystic song of initiation vibrated in my ear; I breathed an air fragrant with the richest perfumes, and contemplated the deity in the fire that symbolized him." And again, in another place, "She, (the Hindoo religion) wears the similitude of a beautiful and radiant cherub from Heaven, bearing on his persuasive lips the accents of pardon and peace, and on his silken wings benefaction and blessing." What strange hallucinations some of these Christian ministers labour under in attempting to reconcile the ideas of idolatry with those of the True and Living God!

kings in their palmy days. When a Principality groaned under extravagance and financial embarrassment, these bewitching girls were entertained at considerable expense to drown the cares of state-craft and king-craft. Even the most astute prince was not free from this courtly profligacy. Though these girls often basked in the sunshine of royal favor, yet there was not a single *Jenny Lind* among them either in grace or accomplishment. As regards their income, a girl has been known to refuse ten thousand Rupees for performing three nights at the Nazim's Court. When Rajah Rajkissen of Sobha Bazar, the Singhee family of Jorasanko, and the Dey family of Simla, celebrated these Poojahs with great pomp, dancing girls of repute were retained a month previous to the festival at great cost, varying from 500 to 1000 Rupees each for three nights. Now that those prosperous days are gone by, and the big English officials do not condescend to attend the nautch, the amount has been reduced to fifty Rupees or a little more. Their general attire and gestures, as well as the nature and tendency of their songs, are by no means unexceptionable. These auxiliaries to sensual gratification, combined with the allurements of Bacchus, even in the presence of a deity, are the least of all fitted to animate or quicken devotional feelings and prayerful thoughts.

Theatrical performances from the popular dramas of the Indian poets, and amateur *jattras*, pantomimical exhibitions, also contribute largely to the amusement of the people. The old *Bidday Soonder*, *Maunvunjun*, *Dukha Juggo*, and others of a similar character are still relished by pleasure-seekers and holiday-makers. It is, however, one of the healthy signs of the times that native gentlemen of histrionic taste have recently got up amateur performances, which bear a somewhat close approximation to the English tragedics and comedies.

Having previously described all the important circumstances and details, religious and social, connected with this popular festival, I will now give a short account of the Bhásán or *Nirunjun* which takes place on the tenth day of the new moon, or in the fourth day of the Poojah. It is also called *Bijoyá*, because the end of a ceremonial is always attended with melancholy feelings. This is the day when the image is consigned to water either of a river or tank. Apart from its religious significance, the day is an important one to English and Native merchants alike. Although all the public offices, Government and mercantile, are absolutely closed for twelve days, agents of Manchester and Glasgow firms must open their places of business on this particular day, which to native merchants and dealers is an auspicious day when large bargains of Piece Goods for present and forward delivery are made. Ten to fifteen lakhs of Rupees worth of articles are sold this day in three or four hours, the general impression being that such bargains bring good luck both to the buyer and the seller.

About eight o'clock in the morning, the officiating priest begins the service, and in half an hour it is over. Music, the indispensable accompaniment of Hindoo Poojahs, must attend every such service. A small looking-glass is placed on a pan of Ganges water and every inmate of the family, male or female, is invited to see the shadow or rather the reflex of the goddess on its surface. Deeply imbued as the minds of the votaries are with religious ideas, every individual looks on the mirror with a sort of devotional feeling, and expresses his or her conviction as to the reality of the representation. The children, more from amusement than faith, hang about the place, but the females steadfastly cling to the panoramic view, quite unwilling to leave it. Though totally ignorant of the philosophical theory of the association or suggestion of ideas, the scene naturally presents to their mind's eye the emotions they feel when leaving the paternal roof for the father-in-law's house. "*Ma Doorga* is going to her father-in-law's and will not return for another twelve month," exclaims one. "Look at her eyes, her sorrowful countenance," ejaculates another. "The temple will look wild and desolate when *Ma Doorga* goes away," adds a third. To console them, the mistress of the house exhorts all to offer their prayers to the goddess, beseeching that she may continue to vouchsafe her blessings from year to year, and give prolonged life and happiness to all concerned. With this solemn invocation, they, each and every one, fall down on their knees before the goddess, whose spirit had departed on the day previous, and in a contemplative mood implore her benediction. Before retiring, however, every one takes with her some precious relic of the offerings (flowers or *billaputtra*) made to Doorga when her spirit was present, and preserves it with all the care of a divine gift, using it religiously in cases of sickness and calamity.

About three in the afternoon, after washing their bodies and putting on new clothes and ornaments, the females make preparations for performing the last and farewell ceremony in honor of the goddess. The *sudder* (main) door is closed, musicians are ordered to go out in the streets, the Doorga with all her satellites is brought out into the area of the temple, the *baranddálláh* with all its sundries is produced, and the females whose husbands are alive begin to turn round the images and touch the forehead of each and every one of the deities with the *baranddálláh*, repeating their prayers for lasting blessings on the family. To the inexpressible grief of the widows, who are present on the occasion, a cruel institution has long since debarred them from assisting in this holy work. These ill-fated creatures are doomed only to stare at the images, but are not permitted to take an active part in the ceremonial. Is it possible to conceive a more gloomy picture of society than that which absolutely expunges from a human breast all traces of a religious privilege the exercise of which, though under a mistaken faith, tends to sweeten a wretched life? The miserable widows of India are unhappily destined to pine away their existence until greater leaders of native reforms arise and deliver them from the galling fetters of superstition.

The epilogue which closes the parting ceremony is called the *kanakánjally*, which consists in a woman (not a widow) taking a small brass plate of paddy and *doova* grass with a Rupee dyed in red lead in it, and throwing it from the fore part of the image right over its head into the cloth of a man who stands behind for the purpose of receiving it. This last offering, it is needless to say, is preserved with the greatest care. The female who performs the rite is an object of envy. This rite being performed, the females take each a bit of the sweetmeat and betel which has been *last* offered to *Ma Doorga*. A sudden reaction of feeling takes place, all hearts are grieved, and some actually shed tears. Two sensations, though not exactly analogous, arise in their minds; first the religious part of the festival, and the consequent arousal of a devotional spirit, vividly reminding one of the unceasing round of ritualistic ceremonies as well as festivity and gaiety that the presence of the goddess naturally enough produced, and which are about to vanish and disappear in an hour by the immersion of the goddess in the river or pond; and second, a worldly one, the recurrence of the idea when a mother sends her daughter to the house of her father-in-law. In either case, the tender heart of a Hindoo female easily breaks down under the pressure of grief.

The goddess is afterwards brought out and placed on a Bamboo stage borne on the shoulders of a set of coolies, all he flowers and *billáputtrá* offered her during the past three days are also put in a basket and taken to the riverside. The procession moves slowly forward, preceded by bands of English and Native musicians, and the necessary retinue of servants and guards, while from within the house, the women, not satiated with the sight of the goddess for one long month, stretch their eyes as far as their visual organs can extend to catch a last farewell glimpse of her. The streets of Calcutta, the English part of the town excepted, become literally crammed and almost impassable on such a day. Groups of Police constables are posted here and there with a view to maintain peace and order, the streets become a pavement of heads. At the lowest calculation, there cannot be less than 100,000 sight-seers abroad. Men, women and children of all classes and ranks come from a great distance to have a sight of the image. The tops of houses, the verandahs, the main roads, nay the unfrequented corners present a thick mass of living creatures, all anxious to feast their eyes upon the matchless grandeur of the scene. A foreigner, unaccustomed to such a magnificent spectacle, is apt to overrate the wealth and prosperity of the people on such a day. The number of images, the dazzling and costly embellishments with which they are decorated, the rich livery of some of the servants, the bands of musicians preceding the procession, the letting off of red and blue lights at intervals, the gala dress of the multitude, and last but not least, the elegant carriages of the big "swells," and the still more elegant attire of their owners, who loll back on the cushion of the carriages, diffusing fragrant odours as they pass, cannot fail to produce an imposing effect. Here a gaily clad Baboo with his patent Japan leather shoes; there a Hindoosthanee dandy with his massive gold necklace and valuable pearls hanging down his ears; here a proud Mogul in all the bravery of cloth of gold; there a frowning Mussulman with his dazzling cap and gossamer *chápkán* (tunic), and ivory mounted stick, all combine to present a motley group of characters, national in their costumes, and unique in appearance. The poor country woman, her lord and children, though not favored by fortune, still cut a figure far above their normal condition.

Those Hindoos, who adorn their images without stint of cost, parade them through the most densely crowded streets till eight in the evening—vanity being the chief motive of action—while those who move in humbler spheres of life take them to boats on the river hired for the purpose, and throw them into the water amidst shouts of exultation. The mob of course sing obscene songs and dance indecently, all which is tolerated for the occasion. The growing sense of the people—the result of English education—has now-a-days greatly diminished the amount of indecency which was one of the distinguishing characteristics of former days on such an occasion.

Between seven and eight o'clock in the evening, the assembled crowd begins to disperse in joyous mood, talking all the way as to the respective superiority of such and such images. Amongst such a great number and variety, there is sure to be difference of opinion, but it is soon settled by the affirmation of a wise head that "the spirit of the goddess is the same in all the images; *Ma Doorga*, does not mind show."

When the worshippers and others return home, they go at once to the temple, where the officiating Brahmin waits for them to sprinkle on their bodies the sacred water; all are made to sit down on the floor with their feet covered with their clothes, lest a drop should fall upon them. The Brahmin with a small twig of mangoe leaves sprinkles the water, while repeating at the same time the usual incantation, the meaning of which is that health, wealth and prosperity may attend the votaries of *Doorga*, from year to year. After this they write on a piece of green plantain leaf the name of the goddess several times, and then clasp one another in their arms, and take the dust off the feet of all the seniors, with the mutual expression of good wishes for their worldly prosperity. An elderly man thus blesses a boy; "may you have long life, gold inkstand and gold pen, acquire profound learning and immense wealth, and support lakhs of men"; If a girl, he thus pronounces his benediction (there being no clasping of arms between man and woman nor between woman and woman), "may you enjoy all the blessings of a married life (*i. e.*, never become a widow) become the mother of a *rajah* (king), use vermillion on your grey head, continue to wear the iron bangle, get seven male children, and never know want." It is well known that no blessing is more acceptable to a Hindoo female than that she may never become a widow, because the intolerable miseries of widowhood are most piercing to her heart; nor can it be otherwise so long as human nature remains unaltered. This social institution of the Hindoos of cordially embracing each other and expressing all manner of good wishes on a particular day of the year, when all hearts are more or less affected with grief at the departure of the goddess, is a very commendable one. It has an excellent tendency to promote social reunion, good fellowship and brotherhood. Not only all the absent friends, relatives, acquaintances and neighbours, male and female, join in this annual greeting, but even strangers and the most menial servants are not forgotten on the occasion. Every heart rejoices, every tongue blesses, every acrimonious feeling is consigned to oblivion. This is a "quiet interval at least between storm and storm; *interspaces* of sunlight between the breadths of gloom, a glad voice on summer holidays, happy in unselfish friendships, in generous impulses, in strong health, in the freedom from all cares, in the confidence of all hopes." During such a happy period "it is a luxury to breathe the breath of life."

To drown their sorrows in forgetfulness, the Hindoos use a slight intoxicating beverage made of hemp leaves on this particular occasion. Every one that comes to visit—and there must be a social gathering—or is present, is treated with this diluted beverage and sweets. Even the most innocent and simple females for once in a year are tacitly allowed to use it, but very sparingly. One farthing's worth of hemp leaves, or about one ounce, suffices for fifty persons or more, so that it becomes almost harmless when so copiously diluted. But those who have imbibed a taste for English wines and spirits always indulge freely on this occasion, giving little heed to temperance rules and lectures. It is "*Bijoya*" and drinking to excess is justifiable.

It would not be proper to close this subject without saying a few words about the national excitement which the approach of this festival produces, and the powerful impetus it gives to trade in general. It has been roughly estimated that upwards of a crore of Rupees (£ 10,000,000) is spent every year in Bengal on account of this festival. Every family, from the aristocracy to the peasant, must have new clothes, new shoes, new every thing. Men, women, children, relatives, poor acquaintances and neighbours, nay beggars must have their holiday dress. Persons in straitened circumstances, who actually live from hand to mouth, deposit their hard-earned savings for a twelvemonth to be spent on this grand festival. Famished beggars who drag a miserable existence all their lives, and depend on precarious alms to keep their body and soul together all the year round, hopefully look forward to the return of this anniversary for at least a temporary change in their rags and tatters. Hungry Brahmins, whose daily avocation brings them only a scanty allowance of rice and plantain, cheerfully welcome the advent of

" *Ma Doorga*," and gratefully watch the day when their empty coffer shall be replenished. Cloth merchants, weavers, braziers, goldsmiths, embroiderers, lace-makers, mercers, haberdashers, carpenters, potters, basket-makers, painters, house-builders, English, Chinese and Native shoemakers, ghee, sugar and corn merchants, grocers, confectioners, dealers in silver and tinsel ware, songsters, songstresses, musicians, hackney carriage keepers, Oorya bearers, hawkers, pedlars and such dealers in miscellaneous wares, all look forward to the busy season when their whole year's hopes shall be realised by bringing lots of Rupees into the till. To a man of practical experience in business matters, as far as the metropolis of British India is concerned, it is perhaps well known that the "Trades" because of the Doorga Poojah make *more* in one month than they can possibly make in the remaining eleven months. From the first week in September to the middle of October, when the Poojah preparations are being actually made by the Hindoos, when they, frugal as they assuredly are, once in a twelvemonth, loosen their purse strings, when the accumulated interest on Government securities is drawn, when all the arrears of house rent are peremptorily demanded, when remittance from the distant parts of the country arrives, when in short, rupees, annas and pice, are the "Go" of the inhabitants, the shopkeepers make a display of their goods as best they can. From sunrise to ten o'clock at night the influx of customers continues unabated, extra shops are opened and extra assistants employed, the shopkeepers themselves have scarcely leisure enough to take a hasty meal a day, and each day's sales swell the heart of the owner. The thrifty and economical Provincial, who loves money as dearly as the blood that runs through his veins, leisurely makes his sundry purchases before the regular rush of customers begins to pour in. He has not only the choice of a large assortment, and the "pick," of a new investment, but gets the benefit of a reasonable price, because the shopkeeper is not hard and tenacious in the early stage of the Poojah sale. As each day passes, and novelties are exposed for public inspection, the shopkeeper raises his prices according to increasing demand. The effeminate and extravagant Baboo of the City, who does not worship Mammon half so devoutly as his country brother, does not mind paying a little too much for his "whistle," because he is large hearted and liberal minded. His more frequent intercourse with Englishmen has taught him to look upon money as "filthy lucre." He is not calculating, and hence he defers making his purchases till the eleventh hour, when, to use a native expression, "the shopkeeper cuts the neck with one stroke."

About one-fifth of the Hindoo population of Calcutta consists of people that are come from the contiguous villages and pergunnas of the Presidency Division; these men live in Calcutta solely for employment, keeping their families in the country where they have generally small farms of their own which yield them enough produce in the shape of rice, pulses, cereals, vegetables, &c., to last them throughout the year, leaving, in some instances, ample surplus stock, with which and a few milch cows as well as tanks, they husband their resources with the greatest frugality, and enjoy every domestic comfort and convenience. They do not care for Davie Wilson's biscuits and sponge-cakes, or a glass of raspberry ice-cream or Roman Punch on a summer day; their bill of fare is as short and simple as their taste is primitive. These men make their Poojah purchases much earlier than their brethren in the city, simply because they have to start for home as soon as the public holidays commence on the eve of the fourth day of the increase of the moon. If the Indian Railways have benefited one class of the people more than another, it is these men who should be thankful for the boon. If the East Indian and Eastern Bengal Railway Companies' coaching receipts are properly examined for two days, *viz.*, the fourth and fifth days of the new moon or the beginning of the Doorga Poojah holidays, they will certainly exhibit an incredibly large amount of receipts from third class carriages. Indeed it has been rather facetiously remarked by town's people that Calcutta becomes much lighter by reason of the exit of country people during the Doorga Poojah holidays, but then the return of the former to their home from the Moffussil should be also taken into the account. On a fair calculation, the outgoing number far exceeds the incoming proportion. It should also be observed that the list of purchases of the former embraces a greater variety of items than that of the latter. Their mothers, wives, daughters and sisters, not to speak of the male members of the family, being absent in the country-house, the want of each and every one must be supplied. Articles for domestic consumption in a Hindoo family are in the greatest requisition. Looking-glasses, combs, *áltá*, *sidoor* or China vermillion, *ghoomsi* (string round the loins), scented drugs for ladies' hair, black powder for the teeth, soap, pomatum, otto of rose, rose water, wax candles, *sidoorchoobry* (toilet box made of small shells), silk, thread, wool, carpets, spices of all sorts both for the betel and the kitchen, betel-nuts, cocoanut oil for ladies' hair, sugarcandy, almonds, raisins, Cabul pomegranates, Dacca, Santipore and English made *dhooties*, *oorunees* (sheets), *sarees* (lady's apparel), silk handkerchiefs, silk cloth, Benares embroidered cloth, satin and velvet caps, lace, hose, tinsel ornaments for the images, English shoes and sundries, constitute the catalogue of their purchases. This explains their going into the Bazar early and accounts for their extra expenditure on the score of luxuries and superfluities of life, but the reader should bear in mind that such extravagance is indulged in only once a year. Generally esteemed as these people are for their saving qualities, frugal, simple and abstemious habits, an annual departure from the established rule is not unjustifiable. The rich classes, as will be evident from what has been said, spend enormous sums in making their fashionable purchases on this occasion.

From the foregoing details it is easy to infer that the Doorga Poojah anniversary presses heavily on the limited resources of a Hindoo family. A rich man experiences little difficulty in meeting his expenses, but the middling and the humbler classes, who comprise nine-tenths of the population, are put to their wits' end to make both ends meet. They are sometimes obliged to solicit the pecuniary aid of their rich friends to enable them to get over the *Doorga* difficulty. It is, perhaps, not generally known that during this popular festival, or rather before it, when all Bengal is in a state of social and religious ferment, when money must be had by fair means or foul, not a few unfortunate men, chiefly libertines and rakes, deliberately commit frauds by forging cheques, drafts, and notes, which eventually lead them into the greatest distress and disgrace. Besides the high price of clothes and of all descriptions of eatables, every family must have a month's provision to carry them through the period during which no money is forthcoming.

I had almost forgotten to say anything about the annual gratuity which the Brahmins of Bengal obtain on the occasion of this festival. From time immemorial, when orthodox Hindooism was in the ascendant, the Brahmins not only advanced their claims, as now, to all the offerings made to gods or goddesses, small or great, but established a rule that every Hindoo, whose circumstances would permit it, should give them individually, one, two, four, or five Rupees at the return of this festival. Every respectable Hindoo family, even now-a-days when heterodoxy is rampant in all the great centres of education, has to give ten, fifteen, twenty-five, or fifty Rupees to Brahmins. Rich families give much more. So very tenacious are the Brahmins of this privilege that even if they earn one hundred Rupees a month by employment they will not forego a single Rupee once a year on this occasion, seeing they claim it as a birthright.

These men have studied human nature, but they have built their hopes of permanent gain on the baseless fabric of a hollow superstition, which is destined, through the progress of improvement, inevitably to fall into decay. It is too late to retrieve the huge blunder of laying a false foundation for their gains.

IX.

THE KALI POOJAH FESTIVAL.

IN Bengal, next to the Doorga Poojah in point of importance stands the Kali Poojah, which invariably takes place on the last night of the decrease of the moon, in the month of Kartik (between October and November). She is represented as standing on the breast of her husband, Shiva, with a tongue projecting to a great length. She has four arms, in one of which she holds a scimitar; in another, the head of a gaint whom she has killed in a fight, the third hand is spread out for the purpose of bestowing blessing, while by the fourth, she welcomes the blessed. She also wears a necklace of skulls and has a girdle of hands of giants round her loins. To add to the terrific character of the goddess, she is represented as a very black female with her locks hanging down to her heels. The reason ascribed for her standing on the breast of her husband, is the following: In a combat with a formidable giant called Ruckta Beeja, she became so elated with joy at her victory that she began to dance in the battle-field so frantically that all the gods trembled and deliberated what to do in order to restore peace to the earth, which, through her dancing was shaken to its foundation. After much consultation, it was decided that her husband should be asked to repair to the scene of action and persuade her to desist. Shiva, the husband, accordingly came down, but seeing the dreadful carnage and the infuriated countenance as well as the continued dancing of his wife, who could not in her frenzy recognise him, he threw himself among the dead bodies of the slain. The goddess was so transported with joy that in one of her dancing feats she chanced to step upon the breast of her husband, whereupon the body moved. Struck with amazement she stood motionless for a while, and fixing her gaze at length discovered that she had trampled on her husband. The sight at once restored her feminine modesty, and she stood aghast feeling shocked at the unhappy accident. To express her shame, she put out her tongue and in that posture she is worshipped by her followers.*

Her black features, the dark night in which she is worshipped, the bloody deeds with which her name is associated, the countless sacrifices relentlessly offered at her altar, the terrific form in which she is represented, the unfeminine and warlike posture in which she stands, and last but not least, the desperate character of some of her votaries, invest her name with a terror which is without a parallel in the mythological legends of the Hindoos. The authors of the Hindoo mythology could not have invented in their fertile imagination a sanguinary character more singularly calculated to inspire terror† and thereby extort the blind adoration of an ignorant populace. About seven hundred years ago, a devoted follower of this goddess, named Agum Bagish, proclaimed that her worship should be performed in the following manner: The image is to be made, set up, worshipped and destroyed on the same night. It is a *nishi* or midnight Poojah on the darkest night of the month, so that not a single soul from outside could know it. He strictly observed this rule while he was alive, and it was said that Rajah Krishnu Chunder Roy of Kishnaghur followed his example for some time. Baboo Obhoy Churn Mitter of Calcutta and Bhobaney Churn Mookerjee of Jessore also tried to observe the rule prescribed above, but as it has been alleged the spirit of secret devotion forsook them after a little while. They reverted to the general

* The Hindoos put out their tongues when they are shocked at anything.

† "The image of Minerva, it will be recollected, was that of a threatening goddess, exciting terror. On her shields she bore the head of a gorgon. Sir William Jones considers Kali as the Proserpine of the Greeks."

custom of worshipping the goddess on the darkest night in Kartik, inviting friends and making pantomimic exhibitions.

Though her Poojah lasts but one night, the sacrifices of goats, sheep and buffaloes are as numerous as those offered before the altar of Doorga. In former times, when idolatry prevailed universally throughout Bengal and religious belief of the people therein was firm and unshaken, the splendour with which the worship of this goddess was performed was second only, as I have remarked, to that of the Doorga. Both goddesses, however, still continue to count their votaries by millions. "The reader may form some idea," says Mr. Ward, "how much idolatry prevailed at the time when the Hindoo monarchy flourished from the following circumstance, which belongs to a modern period, when the Hindoo authority in Hindoosthan was almost extinct. Rajah Krishnu Chunder Roy, and his two immediate successors, in the month of Kartick, annually gave orders to all the people over whom they had a nominal authority to keep the *skyma* festival, and threatened every offender with the severest penalties on non-compliance. In consequence of these orders, in more than ten thousand houses in one night, in the Zillah of Kishnaghur, the worship of this goddess was celebrated. The number of animals destroyed could not have been less than ten thousand."

Kali, like Doorga, Siva, Vishnu and Krishna, is the guardian deity of many Hindoos, who daily offer their prayers to her both in the morning and evening. Several, who possess great wealth and know not how to employ it better, dedicate temples to her service and consecrate them with ample endowments. In the holy City of Benares, there still exists a Kalí shrine where hundreds of beggars are daily fed at the expense of the founder, the late Rani Bhobaney of Nattore. Nearly a hundred and fifty years ago, Raja Ramkrishna erected a temple at Burranagore, about six miles north of Calcutta, in honor of this goddess, and spent upwards of a lakh of Rupees when it was first consecrated. He endowed it with a large revenue for its permanent support, so that any number of religious mendicants who might come there daily could be easily fed. In his prosperous days, this rich zemindar paid an annual revenue of fifty-two lakhs of Rupees to the East India Company. Unfortunately the family has since been reduced to a state of poverty, and the temple is a heap of ruins. The endowment, like most other endowments of this nature, disappeared soon after the death of the founder. The Rajah of Burdwan's endowment of this kind still endures, and promises to enjoy a longer lease of life.

The name of Kali, be it observed, is more extensively used than either that of Doorga or Shiva. Whenever a Native Regiment is to march or set out on an expedition the stereotyped acclaim is,—"*Kali Maikey Jay,*" "victory to mother Kali." When the evening gun is fired in any of the military stations, the almost involuntary exclamation is, "*Jay Kali Calcutta Wallee.*" Nor is her worship less universal than her fame. On the last night of the decrease of the moon in Kartik, every family in Bengal must worship her though in a somewhat different shape. Every family, rich or poor, Brahmin or Soodar, must celebrate the Lucki or Kali Poojah before the sacred *Reck* of *dhán* or paddy, which in the estimation of a Hindoo is a valuable heritage.* Several incidents connected with this religious festival are worth recording. In the Upper and Central Provinces, as in the South of Hindoostan, it is called the *Dewallee* Festival. Though the image is not set up, yet the Hindoo and Parsi inhabitants observe the holiday by opening their new year's account on that day. Illuminations, fireworks and all sorts of festivities mark the day. To try their luck for the next year, almost all Hindoo merchants and bankers indulge

---

* A *Reck* is a small round basket, with which Natives measure rice, the staff of life in Bengal. Every family has its sacred *Reck* of paddy which is preserved with religious care and brought out on such special occasions.

in gambling that night, and large sums are sometimes at stake on the occasion. In Calcutta, where gambling is strictly prohibited, the law is shamefully violated on that dark night. This does not imply any reflection on the vigilance of the Police, because the game is carried on surreptitiously. The Parsi merchants who deal in wines and stores throw open their shops and trèat their European customers free of cost on that particular day. Their brethren in Bengal are, however, not so liberal to their customers, simply because it is not their new year's day. In Calcutta and all over Bengal the night is remarkable for illumination,* fireworks, feasting, carousing and gambling. There is a time-honored custom among the people to light bundles of *paycáttee* or faggots that night. As is naturally to be expected the children take a great delight in such pastimes. At the close of the Poojah a servant of the house takes a *Koolow* or winnowing fan and a stick with which he beats and sings "Bad luck out" and "Good luck in."†

Kali is also the guardian deity of thieves, robbers, *thugs* and such like desperate characters. Before starting on their diabolical work, they invoke her aid to protect them from detection and punishment. The supposed aid of the goddess arms them with courage and leads them to commit the most atrocious crimes. When successful they come and

---

* A superstitious idea prevails among the Hindoos that unless they illuminate their houses on this particular night, devils would come and take possession of them. In the Upper and Central Provinces it is customary with the Hindoo inhabitants not only to illuminate but whitewash their houses and decorate the doors and walls of shops with colored China paper so that every thing may look "*smart*" according to Native taste. In the Jubbulpore District I have seen the poorest laborer whitewash the mud walls of his tiled-hut with one farthing's worth of white earth called *Sewmattee* which is found in great abundance in that part of the country.

† One Joy Ghose, a notorious buffoon, was once asked by his old mother to perform the above rite. Joy, instead of reciting the motto in the right way, purposely inverted it just to irritate the old lady, and repeated the first last and the last first. The joke was too much for the sensitive mother; she wrung her breast, tore her hair, and refused to be consoled until the son repeated the song in proper order, *i. e.*, "bad luck out, good luck in." Trifling with *Luckee*, the goddess of prosperity, is the height of folly. It is punished with misery here and perdition hereafter.

offer sacrifices of goats, spirituous liquors and other things, under an impression that the superintending power of the goddess has shielded them from all harm. But the unbending rigor of the British law has almost entirely dissipated the delusion. Many an infamous dacoit in Bengal has confessed his guilt on the scaffold, lamenting that "*Ma Kali*" had not protected him in the hour of need. The notorious "Rugho Dacoit" of Hooghly, whose very name terrified a wayward child into sleep, made fearful disclosures as to the originating cause of his numerous crimes. Some forty years ago there lived in Calcutta a very respectable Hindoo gentleman, by name Rajkissore Dutt, who was a very great devotee of this goddess. Every month, on the last night of the decrease of the moon, he, it was said, used to set up an image of this goddess, and adorned her person with gold and silver ornaments to the value of about one thousand Rupees which were afterwards given to the officiating priest. On the annual return of this grand Poojah in the month of Kartik, he used to give the goddess a gold tongue, and decorate her four arms with divers gold ornaments to the cost of about three thousand Rupees, and his other expenses amounted to another six or seven thousand. For a number of years he continued to celebrate the Poojah in the above magnificent style, his veneration becoming more intensified as his wealth increased. He established a Bank in Calcutta called the "India Bank," which circulated notes of its own to a considerable amount. A combination was formed among a few influential Natives, whose names I am ashamed to mention, and a well concocted system of fraud was organised. Through one, Dwarkey Nath Mitter, a son-in-law of Rajkissore, Company's Paper or Government Securities to the amount of about twenty Lakhs of Rupees were forged and passed off as genuine on the public. But as fraud succeeds for a short while only, the gigantic scheme was soon discovered, and the delinquent was tried, convicted and sentenced to transportation for life to one of the Penal Settlements of the East India Company, where he lived for several years to rue the consequences of his iniquitous conduct. His eldest son told the writer that his father concealed in a wall of one of the rooms of his house Bank notes for upwards of a Lakh of Rupees. When the search of the Police was over he opened the part of the wall and to his utter disappointment found all the notes crumbled to pieces, and become a small bundle of rotten paper of no earthly use to any one. Thus was iniquity rightly punished. No wonder that the deep faith of Rajkissore in the goddess Kali did not avail him in the hour of danger. His flagitious career commenced by a blind dovotion to his guardian deity, culminated in a gigantic forgery, and closed with transportation and infamy.

It is generally known that there exists a temple of this goddess in the suburbs of Calcutta, which has long been celebrated for its sanctity. The place is called Kali Ghat, about four miles south of Government House. It is not exactly known when this temple was first built. The probable conjecture is that some three hundred years ago a shrewd and far-seeing member of the sacerdotal class, observing the great veneration in which the goddess was held among the Hindoos of those days, erected a temple to the image and gave the place a name after her, the renown of which, as Calcutta grew in importance, gradually spread far and wide. To perpetuate the holy character of the shrine, and to consecrate it by traditional sanctity, the following story was given out, in the truth of which the generality of the orthodox Hindoos have a firm belief. In time out of mind, when the Suttee (Doorga) destroyed herself on the *Trisool* (three edged weapon), one of her fingers was said to have fallen on the spot on which the temple now stands and in whose recess the priests pretend it is still preserved. Hence the sacred character of the shrine, which still attracts thousands of devotees every year from all parts. In popular estimation from a religious point of view she does not yield much to the Juggernauth of Orissa, the Bisseshur of Benares, the Krishna of Brindabun, the Gyasoor of Gya, and the Mahadeb of Buddinauth. Fortunately for the site of the temple, which is in close proximity to the metropolis of British India, and until recently was in the immediate neighbourhood of the highest Appellate Court (Suddur Dewanny Adawlut) independently of its bordering on the *Addigunga* (the original sacred stream of Ganges), it has always drawn the wealthiest and poorest portions of the Hindoo community. Had the offerings in gold, silver and in kind fallen to the share of one priest, it is not too much to say that he would long before this have been as rich as the Juggut Sett (Banker of the world) of Moorshedabad, who was reputed to have been worth upwards of fifteen *crores* of Rupees.

Wealthy Hindoos, when on a visit to Kali Ghat, expend from one to fifty thousand Rupees on the worship of this goddess, in the shape of valuable ornaments, silver plate, dishes &c., sweetmeats and food for a large number of Brahmins, and small presents to thousands of beggars, besides numerous sacrifices of goats, sheep and buffaloes, which make the space before the temple swim with blood. The flesh of goat, and sheep is freely used by the *saktá* class of Hindoos when offered to Kali and Doorga, but they would never use it without such an oblation. It is otherwise called *brithá* or unsanctified flesh, which is altogether quite unfit for the use of a religious Hindoo. But the progress of English education has made terrible inroads on the religious practices of the people, at least of the rising generation.* The following description of the Kali or *Shyma*

---

* Young Bengal is no longer satisfied with Kali Ghat meat; his taste being improved and his mind disabused, he must needs have kid and mutton from the new Municipal market, which is certainly superior in quality to that of Kali Ghat.

Poojah given by Mr. Ward will serve to convey to the reader some idea of the nature of the festival.

"A few years ago," says he, "I went to the house of Kali Sunkur Ghose at Calcutta, at the time of the Shyma festival, to see the animals sacrificed to Kali. The buildings where the worship was performed were raised on four sides, with an area in the middle. The image was placed at the north end with the face to the south; and the two side rooms, and one of the end rooms opposite the image, were filled with spectators: in the area were the animals devoted to sacrifice, and also the executioner, with Kali Sunkur, a few attendants, and about twenty persons to throw the animal down and hold it in the post, while the head was cut off. The goats were sacrificed first, then the buffaloes, and last of all, two or three rams. In order to secure the animals, ropes were fastened round their legs; they were then thrown down, and the neck placed in a piece of wood fastened into the ground and open at the top like the space betwixt the prongs of a fork. After the animal's neck was fastened in the wood by a peg which passed over it, the men who held it pulled forcibly at the heels, while the executioner, with a broad heavy axe cut off the head at one blow; the heads were carried in an elevated posture by an attendant, (dancing as he went) the blood running down him on all sides, into the presence of the goddess. Kali Sunkur, at the close, went up to the executioner, took him in his arms, and gave him several presents of cloth, &c. The heads and blood of the animals, as well as different meat offerings, are presented, with incantations, as a feast to the goddess, after which clarified butter is burnt on a prepared altar of sand. Never did I see men so eagerly enter into the shedding of blood, nor do I think any butchers could slaughter animals more expertly. The place literally swam with blood. The bleating of the animals, the numbers slain, and the ferocity of the people employed, actually made me unwell, and I returned about midnight, filled with horror and indignation." In the foregoing account, Mr. Ward has omitted to say anything about the nocturnal revelry with which the festival is in most instances accompanied. I have witnessed scenes on such occasions, which are too disgusting to be described. Not only the officiating priest and the spiritual guide, but all the members of the family and not a few of the guests partake of the spirituous liquors offered to the goddess, and in a state of intoxication sing *Ramprasadi* songs befitting the occasion. The festival closes with orgies such as are observed in the worship of Bacchus. There are, however, a few honorable exceptions to the rule, who, though they perform the worship of this goddess, yet altogether abstain from drinking. The goddess, Kali, is their guardian deity, they worship her daily, but are known never to touch a drop of wine. They attribute to her all the worldly prosperity they enjoy and look to her for everlasting blessedness. Such men have no faith in the common drunken motto, "*Bharey ma Bhobaney*," mother *Bhobaney* (another name of Kali) is in the cup." But the grand characteristic of this and similar festivals which are annually recurring is, as I have already mentioned, "the wine, the fruit and the lady fair."

"Even *bacchanalian* madness has its charms."

But to return to the priests of Kali Ghat.—As time rolled on, their descendants multiplied so rapidly that it soon became necessary to allot a few days only in the year to each of the families, and on grand occasions, which are not a few, the offertories are proportionately divided among the whole set of the sacerdotal class. Thus it has now become a case of what a Hindoo proverb so aptly expresses: "The flesh of a sparrow divided into a hundred parts," or infinite simal quantities.

God has so constituted man that he can find little or no enjoyment in a state of inactivity. The proper employment of time, therefore, is essentially necessary to the progressive development of our powers and faculties, the non exercise of which must needs induce idle and vicious habits. No bread is sweet unless it is earned by the sweat of our brow. The Haldars (priests) of Kali Ghaut having no healthy occupation in which to engage their minds, and depending for their sustenance on a means which requires neither physical nor mental labor, have inevitably been led to adopt the Epicurean mode of life, which says, "eat, drink and be merry." This habit is further confirmed by the peculiar nature of the religious principles which the worship of this goddess enjoins. Certain texts of the Tantra Shaster expressly inculcate that without drinking the mind is not properly prepared for religious exercise and contemplation. The pernicious effects of such a monstrous doctrine are sufficiently obvious. It has been said that not only the men but the women also are in the habit of drinking. As a necessary consequence the vicious practice has not only enervated their minds but made their "wealth small and their want great." Disputes often arise between the worshippers and the priests of the temple respecting the offerings and the proper division of the same, the latter often claiming the lion's share which the former are unwilling to submit to. Gross lies are sometimes told in the presence of the goddess in order to secure to the major portion of the offerings in the interests of the worshippers—an expedient which the notorious rapacity of the officiating Brahmins imperatively demands. Surrounded by an atmosphere densely impregnated with the miasm of a false religion and a corrupt morality, the ennobling thought of a true God and the moral accountability of man never enters their minds. The chief end and aim of their life is to impose on the credulity of their blind votaries, and thereby pander to their unhallowed desires and selfish gratification. Nor can they rise to a higher and purer sphere of life because from their childhood they are nurtured in the cradle of error, ignorance, indolence and profligacy. Who can contemplate the effects of their impure orgies on the eighth, ninth, fourteenth and fifteen nights of the increase and decrease of the moon without being reminded of the saturnalia of the Greeks?* If a sober-minded man were to visit the holy shrine of Kali Ghat on one of these nights, he would doubtless be shocked at the unrestrained debauchery that runs riot in the name of religion. The temple, no less than the private domicile of the priests, presents an uninterrupted scene of bacchanalian revelry, which is unspeakably abominable. Men deprived of a sense of shame, and women of decency and morality, mingle in the revels, and the result is that all the cherished notions of the better part of humanity are at once put to flight. It is painful to reflect that notwithstandings the progress of enlightenment in the great centre of Indian civilization, people still cling to the adoration of a blood-thirsty goddess, and to the support of a depraved class of priests. The sacrifices of goats that are daily offered before the altar of Kali being too numerous for local consumption, are sold to outside customers much in the same manner as fruits and vegetables are brought from the neighbouring villages into

---

* The writer in his younger days remembers to have been once taken up on a Kali Poojah night by a gang of infamous drunkards in the very heart of Calcutta. When he was returning home about midnight in company with some of his friends after seeing the *támáshá*, he being the youngest of the lot had necessarily lagged behind, when to his utter dismay he was suddenly laid hold of by a man who smelt strongly of liquor and carried him hurriedly into an empty house on the roadside. The first shout at the very threshold was,—" here we have got a *moori*", *i. e.* a victim; the ruffians, who had their faces covered with clothes, jumped up at the announcement, and one of them accosted him in the following manner—" what money and pice have you got? The writer replied a few an his pice only. No Rupees? asked another; whereupon they all fell to searching his person and stripped him of all his clothes, which consisted of a *dhooty*, a *chádur* and a *jamá*, and finally bade him go. As a matter of course he was obliged to return home almost in a state of nudity, one of his friends lending him a *chádur* on the occasion. In these days the introduction of gas light and the posting of constables on the highway have greatly checked such ruffianism.

the market. On Saturday the sale is larger than on the other week days, because that night is specially dedicated to the worship of Bacchus, Sunday affording a respite from work. But the sale of Kali Ghat goat meat has of late been much interfered with by the establishment of rival shrines in several parts of Calcutta, where a pound is to be had for three annas. The owners (mostly prostitutes and drunkards) of these pseudo-goddesses, vulgarly called *Kashdye* or butcher Kali, sacrifice one or two goats every morning without any ceremony, except on Saturday when the number is doubled to meet increased requirements. Thus a regular and profitable butcher's trade is openly carried on in the name of the goddess, and the generality of the *Sakta* Hindoos feel no religious scruples in using the meat which is thus sanctified. The comparative ease with which flesh is now obtained in Calcutta has tended, in no small degree, to encourage habits of drinking among a proverbially abstemious race of men; it being the popular impression that meat neutralises the effects of spirituous liquors.*

Many images of Kali which have from time to time been set up in and about Calcutta, ostensibly for religious but practically for secular purposes, in imitation of the unrivalled prototype at Kali Ghat, have acquired unenviable celebrity, and been made subservient as a source of income to the owner and the officiating priests, who fatten on the offerings made to the goddess in the shape of money and provisions. Thus, for instance, the *Sidhassurry* or Kali of Nimtollah obtains a few

---

* This idea is strengthened by the opinion of Native medical students, many of whom, it is a matter of regret, are not great advocates of temperance. Natives use liquor not for health but solely for intoxicating purposes. A very successful Native Practitioner to whom not only the writer but many of his respectable friends are under great obligation, not long ago fell a victim to the besetting vice of intemperance, and confessed his guilt like a penitent sinner in his dying moments. His reputation was so great at one time that it was said "patients felt half cured when he entered the room." In the beginning of his brilliant career, he was one of the most staunch advocates of temperance. How frail is human nature!

Rupees daily from such Hindoos as are carried to the river-side to breathe their last, independently of the small presents made at all hours of the day, especially in the mornings and evenings, when the crowd assembles. It is amusing to observe the complaisance with which a Brahmin gives a consecrated *Billaputtra* or flower to a devotee in return for a Rupee or so. A shrewd Brahmin, like the ancient Roman soothsayer, laughs in his sleeves at such stupidity.

A Sanskrit proverb says that a meritorious work endures. It keeps alive the name of the founder, and this vanity furnishes the strongest stimulus to the endowment of works of a religious character, and of public utility. It is, however, a painful fact that the nature and character of such endowments is, in most cases, lamentably wanting in the element of stability. Two or three generations after the death of the founder, the substance of the estate being impaired, the family is reduced to a state of poverty, the surviving members, often a set of demoralised idlers, depend for their support on the usufruct of the *Deybatra*, originally set apart for exclusively religious purposes, and placed beyond the reach of law. In these days the offshoots of many families are absolutely dependent on this sacred fund for their subsistence, and the consequence naturally is that the endowment is frittered away and the work itself inevitably falls into decay. Thus in process of time both the fund and the founder's name pass into utter oblivion.*

The following account given by Mr. Ward about the death of a devotee of this goddess will not be uninteresting. "In the year 1809, Trigonu Goswamee, a vyuktavudhootu, died at Kali Ghat in the following manner: Three days before his death, he dug a grave near his hut, in a place surrounded by three *vilwu* trees which he himself had planted. In the evening he placed a lamp in the grave, in which an offering

* For an account of the *Bamacharee* Sect, see note D.

of flesh, greens, rice, &c., to the shakals was made, repeating it the next evening. The following day he obtained from a rich native ten rupees worth of spirituous liquors, and invited a number of mendicants, who sat drinking with him till twelve at noon, when he asked among the spectators at what hour it would be full moon ; being informed, he went and sat in his grave, and continued drinking liquors. Just before the time for the full moon, he turned his head towards the temple of Kali, and informed the spectators that he had come to Kali Ghat with the hope of seeing the goddess, not the image in the temple. He had been frequently urged by different persons to visit the temple, but though he had not assigned a reason for his omission, he now asked what he was to go and see there : a temple? He could see that from where he was. A piece of stone made into a face, or the silver hands? He could see stones and silver any where else. He wished to see the goddess herself, but he had not, in this body, obtained the sight. However, he had still a mouth and a tongue, and he would again call upon her ; he then called out aloud twice, "Kali? Kali?" and almost immediately died ;—probably from excessive intoxication. The spectators, though Hindoos (who in general despise a drunkard), considered this man as a great saint, who had foreseen his own death, when in health. He had not less than four hundred disciples."

The various causes which have hitherto conspired to impart a sanctity to this famous temple are gradually waning in their influence, but it will be a very long time before the minds of the mass of the people are completely purified in the crucible of true Religion, before which superstition and priestcraft must vanish into air.

X.

THE SARASWATI POOJAH.

SARASWATI is the Hindoo goddess of learning. She is represented as seated in a water lily and playing on a lute. Throughout Bengal her worship is celebrated with more or less pomp on the fifth day of the increase of the moon, in the Bengali month of Magha or Falgoon (February). As the popular Shastras reckon the commencement of spring from this date, the people, especially the young and gay of both sexes, put on *basantee* or yellow garments, and indulge in all sorts of low merriment, manifesting a depraved and vitiated taste.

Every Hindoo, young or old, who is able to read and write, observes this ceremony with apparent solemnity, abstaining from the use of fish on that day as a mark of reverence to the goddess. The worship is performed either before an image of the goddess, or before a pen, ink-bottle and *pooti* (manuscript), which are symbolically regarded as an appropriate substitute for the image. The officiating priest, after reading the prescribed formula, and presenting rice, fruits, sweetmeats, flowers, &c., directs the votaries of the goddess to stand up with flowers in their hands and repeat the usual service, beseeching her to bestow on them the blessings of learning, health, wealth, good luck, longevity, fame, &c. Apart from its idolatrous feature, it is a rather strange sight to see a number of youths, after going through the process of ablution and changing their clothes, stand up before the goddess in a body, and in a devotional spirit address her in prayer for the blessings above enumerated. Even apart from its superstitious character, it is decidedly objectionable on the score of its purely secular tendency, as it makes no allusion whatever to the primary object of all prayer, *viz.*, the atonement and pardon of sin and the salvation of the soul—an element in which the religious ceremonies of the Hindoos are singularly deficient.

"Life is real, life is earnest,
And the grave is not its goal;
'Dust thou art, to dust returnest,'
Was not spoken of the soul."

It was reported of Sir William Jones that when he studied Sanscrit, he used to place on the table a metal image of this goddess, evidently to please his Pundit. Let it not be inferred from this that he advocated the continuance of idolatry; far from it, but even in appearance to acquiesce in homage to an idol made of clay and straw is to withhold from the Most High the reverence, gratitude and obedience due to Him alone. The early formation of a prayerful habit divested of any idolatrous feature will always exercise a healthy religious influence on the mind in maturer years.

In every *chatoospati* or school, the Brahmin Pundit and his pupils worship this goddess with religious strictness. The Pundit setting up an image, invites all his patrons, neighbouring friends and acquaintances on this occasion. Every one who attends must make a present of one or a half Rupee to the goddess, and returns home with the hollow benediction of the Brahmin. To so miserable a strait have the learned Pundits been reduced of late years, that they anxiously look forward to the anniversary of this festival as a small harvest of gain to them, as the authoritative ministers of the goddess. They make from fifty to one hundred Rupees a year by the celebration of this Poojah, which keeps them for six months; should any of their friends fail to make the usual present to the goddess, they are sure to come and demand it as a right.*

* A gift once made to a Brahmin must be continued from year to year till the donor dies; in some cases it is tenable from one generation to another.

Females are not allowed to take a part in the worship of this goddess, simply because the great lawgiver of the country has denied them this privilege. They, however, now-a-days read and write in spite of the traditional prohibition, but are religiously forbidden to say their prayer before the goddess, though she is herself an embodiment of their sex. It is quite obvious that feelings of lamentable debasement arise in their hearts at the annual recurrence of this festival, strongly reminding them of the unhealthy, unnatural ordinance of their great lawgiver.

The day following the Poojah, the women are not permitted to eat any *fresh* prepared article of food, but must be satisfied with stale, cold things, such as boiled rice and boiled pease with a few vegetables, totally abstaining from fish, which they cannot do without on any other day. Taking place on the sixth day of the increase of the moon, this part of the festival is called *Situl Shasthi* as enjoining the use of cold food.

As a mark of homage to the goddess, the Hindoos do not read or write on that day. Hence the day is observed as a holiday in public and mercantile offices where the clerks are mostly Hindoos. Should any necessity arise they write in red ink, as all the inkstands in the household are washed out and placed before the goddess for annual consecration. They are, however, not prevented from attending to secular business on this occasion. Unlike the sanguinary character of the Poojahs of Doorga and Kali, no bloody sacrifices are offered to this gentle goddess, but as regards rude merriment, the one in question does not form an exception to the others. Revelry and unbecoming mirth are the grand characteristics of this as indeed of almost every other Hindoo festival. It is sickening to reflect how indecency and immorality are thus unblushingly countenanced under the sacred name of religion.

Loose women celebrate this festival, and keep up dancing and singing all night in a bestial state of intoxication to the utter disgust of all sober-minded men. The Moharajah of Burdwan used to expend large sums of money on this occasion, engaging the best dancing girls of the metropolis and illuminating and ornamenting his palace in a splendid style, besides giving entertainment to his English and Native friends. Vast multitudes of people from Calcutta still resort to his palace and admire the profuse festoons of flowers and the yellow appearance of everything, indicative of the advent of spring,—a season which, according to popular notion, invites the mind to indulge in licentious mirth. It is needless to enumerate farther the many obscenities practised in songs and actions on this occasion.

XI.

THE FESTIVAL OF CAKES.

ON the annual commemoration of this popular festival in Bengal, which is analogous to the English "Harvest home," the people in general, and the agricultural classes in particular, manifest a gleeful appearance, indicative of national demonstrations of joy and mirth. It takes place in the Bengalee month of *Pous* or January, following immediately in the wake of the English Christmas and New year's day. With the exception of the upper ten thousand, almost all men, women and children alike participate in the festivities of the season, and for three succeeding days are occupied in rural pastimes and gastronomical enjoyment. The popular cry on this occasion, is—"*Awoynee, Bownee, teen deen, pittaey, bhat, khawnee,*" "the *Pous* or *Makar Sankranti* is come, let three days be passed in eating cakes and rice," accompanied by a supplementary invocation to the goddess of Prosperity (Lukshmee) that she may afford her votaries ample stores so that they may never know want. As the outward manifestation of this internal wish, they tie all their chests, boxes, beddings, the earthen cooking pots in the kitchen, as well as those in the store-house containing their food grains, and in fact every movable article in the house, with shreds of straw that they may always remain intact. The origin of this festival is involved in obscurity, but tradition says that it sprung from the general desire of the people engaged in agricultural pursuits to celebrate the last day of *Pous*, and two succeeding days, in eating what they most relish, cakes of all sorts, to their hearts' content, after having harvested and gathered their corn and other food grains, which form the main staff of their life. Whatever may have been the origin of this festival, it is evident that it does not owe its existence, like most other Hindoo festivals, to priest-craft. The idea is good and the tendency excellent. After harvesting and gathering the fruits of their labour, on which depend not only their individual subsistence throughout the year, but the general prosperity of the country by the development of its resources, the husbandmen are well entitled to lay aside, for a short while, the ploughshare, and taking three days rest, spend them in rural amusements and festivities amid their domestic circle. All this tends, in no small degree, to awaken and revive dormant feelings of love and friendliness by mutual exchange of invitations as well as of good fellowship. Their incessant toil in the field during the seven previous months, their intense anxiety on the score of weather, carefully noting, though not with the scientific precision of the meteorological reporter, deficient and plenteous rainfall, and apprehending the destructive October gale, when the ears of corn are almost fully developed, their constant watchfulness for the prevention of theft and the destruction of the crops by cattle, their unceasing weeding out of troublesome and useless plants and *cassay* grass, sometimes wading in marshy swamp or mire knee deep, and their incessant anxiety for the due payment of rent to the zemindar, or perhaps of interest to the relentless money lender, are sources of uneasiness that do not allow them a moment's peace of mind. Should they, by way of relaxation, cease to work for three days in the year, they are not to be blamed for laziness or supineness. The question of a good harvest is of such immense importance to an agricultural country like India, that when the god, Ram Chunder, the model king, visited his subjects in Oude, the first thing he asked them was about the state of the crops, and when the enquiry was favorably answered, his mind was set at rest, and he cheerfully unfolded to them the scheme of his future Government.* Physically and practically considered, temporary cessation from labor is indispensable to recruit the energy of the exhausted frame of body, and promote the normal vigor of mind. So in whatever light this national jubilee is regarded, socially, morally or scientifically, it is productive of beneficial results, ultimately contributing to the augmentation of the material prosperity of the land.

Some of my countrymen of a fastidious taste look upon this festival as a puerile and foolish entertainment, because it possesses no dignified feature to commend it to their attention, but they should consider that it is free from the idolatrous abominations and rank obscenity by which most of the Hindoo festivals are charaterised, independently of its having a tendency to promote the innocent mirth and general hilarity of the masses, whose contentment is the best test of a good government and of a generous landed aristocracy.

So popular is this festival amongst the people that the Mussulmans have a common saying to the effect, that their *Eed*, *Bakrid* and *Shub-i-Barat*—three of their greatest national festivals—are no match for the Hindoo *Pous Sakrad.*

Our children and women in the city, whose minds are so largely tinctured with an instinctive regard for all festivities, share in the general excitement. On this occasion, exchanges of presents of sweetmeats, cloths, jaggery, ghee, flour, oranges, cereals, cocoanuts, balls of concentrated milk, vegetables, spices, sugar, almonds, raisins, etc, are made between relatives in order

* Indeed, it has become a byword among the Natives in general that the compound word, "*Ram-Rajya*," or the empire of Ram is synonymous with a happy dynasty. There existed peace, union and harmony among the people in the infancy of society. Almost every family had its assigned plot of land which they cultivated, and the fruits of which they enjoyed without the incubus of a rack-renting system, because the virgin soil always afforded an abundant harvest. The wants of the people were few and those were easily supplied. In fact there was a complete identity of interests between the rulers and the ruled. The result was universal contentment and happiness. But unhappily the present advanced stage of social organisation has considerably impaired the relation.

that they may be enabled to solemnise the cake festival with the greatest *éclat*. In respectable families, the women cheerfully take the trouble of making these preparations, instead of trusting them to their female cooks, because male cooks are no adepts in the art. So nicely are these cakes made and in such variety, that the late Mr. Cockerell, a highly respected merchant of this City, used every year to get an assortment from his Baboo and invite his friends to partake of them; and notwithstanding the proverbial differences of taste, there are few who would not relish them.

The boys in the many pátshálás or primary schools around Calcutta, annually keep up this festival in a splendid style. The more advanced form themselves into a band of songsters, and, attended by bands of musicians with all the usual accompaniments of flags, staves, etc., proceed in procession from their respective schools to the bank of the river Bhagiruttee, singing rhythmically in a chorus all the way in praise of the holy stream, and of her powers of salvation in the present *Kali Yuga*, or iron age. When they reach their destination they pour forth their songs most vociferously. They afterwards perform the usual ablutions and return home in the same manner as they set out from the Pátshálá, regard ing the performance as an act of great merit.

XII.

THE HOLI FESTIVAL.

THE annual return of this festival in honor of the god Krishna, excites the religious feelings and superstitious frenzy of the Hindoos not only in Bengal but also in Orissa, Bombay, and in the Upper Provinces of India. From time immemorial, it has continued to exercise a very great influence over the minds of the people at large, so much so that what the Holi festival is in the Upper Provinces, the Doorga Poojah is in the Lower Provinces of Bengal, being by far the most popular and demonstrative in all their leading features. Though originally and essentially a Hindoo festival of a religious character, dedicated to the worship of a Hindoo god, it has subsequently assumed a jubilant phase, drawing the followers of a different creed to its ranks; hence not a few Mussulmans in Upper India observe it in a secular sense, quite distinct from its religious aspect or requirements.

In Bengal it is called *Dole Jattra*, or the rocking of the image of Krishna on its throne. It occurs on the day of the full moon in the Bengallee month of Falgoon or March, at the vernal equinox,—a season of the year when all the appetites, passions and desires of the people are supposed to be more or less inflamed, and they naturally seek outlets of gratification. In the Upper Provinces it is known by the name of *Holi*, or festival of scattering *fhag* or red powder among friends and others. On the previous night the people both here and in the Upper Provinces burn amidst music the effigy of an uncouth straw image of a giant named Maydhasoor, who caused great disturbance among the gods and goddesses in their hours of meditation and prayer. To put a stop to this unholy molestation the god Narayan or Krishna destroyed the giant by means of his matchless valor and skill, and thus restored peace in heaven as well as on earth. To commemorate this glorious achievement, the image of the above giant is annually burnt on the night previous to the *Holi* festival.

The religious part of the ceremony, irrespective of its idolatrous element, is performed in accordance with the original rules of the Hindoo ritual, which are free from all kinds of abominations. But the great body of the people, lacking the vital principle of a pure and true faith and following the impulse of unrestrained appetites, have gradually sunk into the depths of corruption,—the outcome of impure imaginations and of a vitiated taste. In Bengal, the observance of this festival is not characterised by anything that is violently opposed to the social amenities of life. Notwithstanding the many-featured phases and multitudinous requirements of the Hindoo creed, the peculiarities of this festival are mainly confined to the worship of the household image, and the entertainment of the Brahmins and friends. Daubing the bodies of the guests with red powder in an either dry or liquid state, and singing songs descriptive of the sports of Krishna with the milk-maids in the groves of Brindabun, form the constituent elements of the festival in Bengal. Offerings of rice, fruits and sweetmeats are made to the god, and its body is also smeared with red powder by the officiating priest, so as to render it one with that of its followers. At the close of the ceremony, the rite of purification is performed, which restores the image—either a piece of stone or metal—to its normal purity.

It is a noteworthy fact that in this festival, no *new* image made of clay and straw is either set up or thrown into the sacred stream, as is invariably the case with the other Hindoo gods and goddesses generally worshipped by the people of Bengal. Krishna, in whose honor this festival is celebrated, has many forms, one of which generally constitutes the household deity that is worshipped every morning and evening by the hereditary priest with all the solemnity of a religious service. A Hindoo who keeps an image of this god is esteemed more in a religious point of view than one who is without it. In the popular estimation he escapes many censures to which a godless Hindoo is often exposed. Nor is this at all singular. An orthodox Hindoo who offers up his daily prayer to his tutelar deity is at least more consistent in his principles, which, as Confucius very justly says, means Heaven, than one who is tossed about by a wavering faith in the indistinguishable whirl of life.

The festival of Dole Jattra or Holi in Bengal, commencing on the day of the full moon, varies, however, in its observance as to the day on which it is to be held. Some celebrate it on the first, some on the second, and some again on the third, fifth, seventh, ninth day of the dark phase of the moon. Generally Vaishnaws, or the followers of Krishna, observe it, though in some cases, the Saktos,—the followers of Doorga and Kalli—also celebrate it. No bloody sacrifices are offered on the occasion. Apart from the religious merit attributed to the ceremonial, it is comparatively a tame and undemonstrative affair in the Lower Provinces of Bengal when compared with the sensational excitement with which it is celebrated in the Upper Provinces. In Orissa too, it is kept up with great eclat before the shrine of Juggurnauth and its environs. Thousands and tens of thousands of pilgrims from a great distance congregate there on this occasion and offer their oblations to the "stumped" lord of the world. When the inhabitants of Bengal talk of their most popular festivals, they pronounce almost involuntarily the *Dole* and *Doorgutsub*, but the latter has long since completely eclipsed the former. Morally, socially and intellectually the enlightened Bengallees are assuredly the Athenians of Hindoostan. Their growing intelligence and refined taste,—the outcome of English education—have imbued them with a healthier ideal of moral excellence than any other section of the Indian population throughout the length and breadth of the land (the Parsis of Bombay excepted). It is owing to the influence of this superior moral sense that they do not abandon themselves to the general corruption of manners obtaining in Upper India during the *Holi* festival.

"Fools make a mock at sin" is a scriptural proverb which is especially applicable to the inhabitants of the Upper Provinces on the annual return of this festival. Unlike their brethren in Bengal they pay greater attention to the secular than to the religious part of the ceremony. A few days before the *Holi*, as if to enkindle the flame of a national demonstration of a sensational character, they return to the low, obscene old ballads which constitute a notable feature of the ceremonial. Week after week, day after day, and hour after hour, they pour them out almost as spontaneously as a bird, because they have a perverse propensity for the indulgence of impure thoughts, and rude, profane mirth, which is an outrage on common decency and a scandal to a rational being. Notwithstanding the vigilance of the Police and the stringency of the Penal Code, these ragamuffins stroll along the public streets in bands, dance antics and sing obscene songs with impunity, simply because the major portion of the Native constables come from the same lower strata of society. Of course before a European they dare not commit the same nuisance. Should a luckless female, even old and infirm, chance to come in their way, they unblushingly assail her with a volley of scurrilous and insulting epithets much too gross to be tolerated by a rational being having the smallest modicum of decorum about him. To give a specimen of the songs, vulgar as they unquestionably are, would be an act of unpardonable profanation. Even in the Burra Bazar of Calcutta, where the Up-country Hindoos mostly reside, excesses and enormities are committed, even in the full blaze of day, which alike belie reason and conscience, and ignore the divine part of humanity. Mirth, music and melody do not form the programme of their amusement, but a feverish excitement, originating in lust and leading to criminal excesses, is the characteristic of the scene. If a sober-minded man were permitted to examine the Cash Book of a country liquor shop, he would most assuredly be struck with the enormous receipts of the shopkeeper during the festive days on this occasion. Bacchanalianism in all its most detestable forms reigns rampant in almost every home and purlieu throughout the Upper Provinces. Every brothel, every toddykhannah, every grog shop, is crowded with customers from early morning to dewy evening and later on. An almost incessant volume of polluted and polluting outcries rises to the skies from these dens of sin, smirching and vulgarising the brilliant ideals of a holy festival. The endless chanting of obscene songs, the discordant notes of the inebriated songsters almost tearing their throats in excessive vociferations, the harsh din of music, their frightful gesticulations and contortions of the body, their frantic dance, their dithyrambic fanaticism in which every sense of decorum is lost, their horrid looks rendered tenfold more horrid by reason of their smearing their bodies with red powder, the pestiferous atmosphere by which they are encompassed, and their reeling posture and bestial intoxication, *all* conspire to make them "mock at sin."* Nor is this to be wondered at. The lives and examples of the Hindoo gods

* When the late Mr. Thomason, the Lieutenant-Governor of the North-Western Provinces, visited Benares, the far famed city of holy shrines and holy bulls, during this festival, he exclaimed in pious indignation, "what disgusting scenes are enacted and frightful crimes perpetrated in the name of religion by rational beings capable of purer and sublimer enjoyments. Surely the shameless ragamuffins are the fit subjects of a bedlam."

have, in a great measure, moulded the character of their followers: "Shiva is represented as declaring to Luckhee that he would part with the merit of his works for the gratification of a criminal passion; Brahma as burning with lust towards his own daughter; Krishna as living with the wife of another, murdering a washerman and stealing his clothes, and sending his friend Yoodhisthira to the regions of torment by causing him to utter a falsehood; Indra and Chundra are seen as the paramours of the wives of their spiritual guides." It is much to be lamented that the authors of the Hindoo mythology have unscrupulously held up the revels of their gods to the imitation of their followers.

It is but just to observe that the more respectable classes are restrained by a sense of honor from participating with the populace in the vicious pleasures of undisciplined passions. But their implied approval of such sensual gratifications tends, in no small degree, to fan the flame of superstitious frenzy. If they do not expose themselves in the highway, they betray their concupiscence within the confines of their own dwellings. They substitute opium and bhang (hemp) for spirituous liquors, and among the females of the house, some aunt or other is the butt of their rude, unseemly satire. Their lusts and want of inward discipline, stimulated by a false religion as well as by the demoralized rules of an abnormal conventionalism, have deadened, as it were, their finer sensibilities, and generations must pass away before they are enabled rightly to appreciate their social relations and their moral and religious duties.

XIII.

CASTE.

The distinction of caste is woven into the very texture of Hindoo society. In whatever light it is considered, religiously, morally, or socially, it must be admitted that this abnormal system is calculated to perpetuate the ignorance and degradation of the race among which it prevails. It is useless to enquire when and by whom it was founded. The Hindoo Shastras do not agree as to this point, but it is obvious to conclude that it must have originated in a dark age when a proud and selfish priesthood, in the exercise of its sacerdotal functions, imposed on the people this galling yoke of religious and social servitude. Even the rulers of the land were not exempt from its baneful influence. They were as much subject to the prescribed rules of their order as the common people. Calculating on the implicit and unquestioning obedience of men to their authoritative injunctions, a scheming hierarchy. established a universal system, the demoralizing effects of which are perhaps without a parallel in the annals of human society. The capacity and culture of man's intellect was shamefully under-estimated when it was expected that such an artificial order, so preposterously unsuited to the interests of humanity and to the advancement of civilization, should for ever continue to influence the life and destiny of unborn generations.

"The distinctions of rank in Europe" says Mr. Ward, "are founded upon civic merit or learning, and answer very important ends in the social union ; but this system commences with an act of the most consummate injustice that was ever perpetrated ; binds in chains of adamant nine-tenths of the people, debars them for ever from all access to a higher state, whatever their merits may be; puts a lock upon the whole intellect of three of the four orders, and branding their very birth with infamy, and rivetting their chains for ever, says to millions and millions of mankind,—'you proceeded from the feet of Brahma, you were created for servitude.'"

History furnishes no parallel to such an audacious declaration, made in utter defiance of the fundamental principles of humanity. The onward march of intellect can never be checked, even when fenced in by the strongest of artificial barriers. Still will that "grey spirit" rise and chase away the errors which age has accumulated and superstition cherished.

> "That grey spirit yearning in desire
> To follow knowledge, like a sinking star,
> Beyond the utmost bound of human thought."

The distinction of caste, it is obvious, was originally instituted to secure to the hierarchy all the superior advantages of a privileged class, and to condemn all other orders to follow menial occupations such as the trades of the country could furnish. They kept the key of knowledge in their own hands, and thus exercised a domineering influence over the mass of the people, imagining that their exclusive privileges should have endless duration. This power in their hands was "either a treasury chest or a rod of iron." The mind recoils from contemplating what would have been the state of the country, the extent of her hopelessness and helplessness, if the light of European knowledge had not dawned and penetrated the Hindoo mind, and thereby introduced a healthier state of things. Eighty years back this system was at the zenith of its splendour; men clung to it with all the tenacity of a natural institution, and proscribed those who ventured to break through its fetters. It was a terrible thing then to depart from the established order of social union; the least whisper of a deviation and the slightest violation of its rules were visited with social persecution of the worst type. I cannot do better than give a few instances, illustrating the nature of the punishments to which a Hindoo was subjected in that period of terror, when caste-mania raged most furiously.

"After the establishment of the English power in Bengal, the caste of a Brahmin of Calcutta was destroyed by a European who forced into his mouth flesh, spirits, &c. After remaining three years an outcast, great efforts were made, at an expense of eighty thousand rupees, to restore him to the pale of his caste, but in vain, as many Brahmins of the same order refused to associate with him as one of their own. After this, an expense of two lacks of Rupees more was incurred, when he was re-admitted to the privileges of his caste. About the year 1802, a person in Calcutta expended in feasting and presents to Brahmins fifty thousand Rupees to be re-admitted into the ring of his caste from which he had been excluded for eating with a Brahmin of the *Peeralee* caste. Not long after this, two *Peeralee* Brahmins of Calcutta made an effort to wipe out the opprobrium of *Peeralism*, but were disappointed, though they had expended a very large sum of money.

"Ghunusyamu, a Brahmin, about thirty-five years ago, went to England and was excommunicated. Gocool, another Brahmin, about the same time went to Madras, and was renounced by his relatives; but after incurring some expense in feasting Brahmins, he was received back. In the year 1808, a blacksmith of Serampore returned from Madras and was disowned by his fellow caste men, but after expending two thousand Rupees amongst the Brahmins, he was restored to his family and friends. In the same year the mother of Kali Prosaud Ghose, a rich *Kayusto* of Benares, who had lost caste by intercourse with Mussulmans and was called a *Peeralee*, died. Kali Prosaud was much concerned on account of the rites required to be performed in honor of the manes of his deceased parent, but no Brahmin would officiate at the ceremony; after much entreaty and promise of rewards, he prevailed at last upon eleven Brahmins to perform the necessary ceremonies at night. A person who had a dispute with these Brahmins informed against them, and they were immediately abandoned by their friends. After waiting several days in vain, hoping that his friends would relent, one of these Brahmins, tying himself to a jar of water, drowned himself in the Ganges. Some years ago, Ram, a Brahmin of Tribany, having, by mistake, married his son to a *Peeralee* girl, and being abandoned by his friends, died of a broken heart. In the year 1803, Shibu Ghose, a *Kayusto*, married a *Peeralee* girl, and was not restored to his caste till after seven years, and after he had expended seven thousand Rupees for the expiation of his offence. About the same period, a Brahmin woman of Velupookuria, having been defloured, and in consequence outcasted, put an end to her existence by voluntary starvation. In the village of Buj Buj, some years ago, a young man who had lost his caste through the criminal intrigues of his mother, a widow, in a state of frenzy poisoned himself, and his two surviving brothers abandoned the country. Gooroopraṣaud, a Brahmin of Churna, in Burdwan, not many years ago, through fear of losing caste, in consequence of the infidelity of his wife, left his home and died of grief at Benares. About the year 1800, a Brahmin lady of Santipore murdered her illegitimate child, to prevent discovery and loss of caste. In the year 1807, a Brahmin of Tribany murdered his wife by strangling her to avert loss of caste through her criminal intrigues. About the year 1790, Kalidass, a Brahmin, who had been inveigled into marrying a washerman's daughter, was obliged to flee the country to Benares, where being discovered, he sold all his property and fled, and his wife became a maniac. In the time of Rajah Krishna Chunder Roy, a Brahmin of Santipore was found to have a criminal intrigue with the daughter of a shoemaker:

the Rajah forbade the barber of the village to shave the family or the washerman to wash for them: in this distress they applied to the Rajah and afterwards to the Nawab for restoration, but in vain. After having been despoiled of their resources by the false promises of pretended friends, the Rajah relented and removed the ban, but the family have not obtained to this day their pristine position.*

"Numbers of outcasts abandon their homes and wander about till death. Many other instances might be given in which the fear of losing caste had led to the perpetration of the most shocking murders, which in this country are easily concealed, and thousands of children are murdered in the womb, to prevent discovery and the consequent loss of caste, particularly in the houses of the Koolin Brahmins."

The inveterate tenacity with which the rites and privileges of caste are clung to is a prominent feature of the Hindoo character, showing, like many other facts, that as a nation—the Rajpoots excepted—they fear the sword-blade, but can meet death with calmness and fortitude when they apprehend any danger to the purity of caste. In the year 1777, a Mussulman nobleman forcibly seized the daughters of three Brahmins. They complained to the judge of the district, but obtaining no redress, they committed suicide by poison under the nose of the unrighteous judge. "When, about a century since, a body of sepoys were being brought from Madras to Calcutta, the provisions ran short, till at last the only food consisted of salted beef and pork. Though a few submitted to the necessity of circumstances and defiled themselves, many preferred a languishing death by famine to a life polluted by tasting

* Rajah Kissen Chunder Roy, in the latter end of the 18th century, used to restore persons and families who had forfeited their caste by their laches by recovering from them a heavy fine for which there used to be much higgling. This fine was in addition to the expenses incidental to the ceremony of *Prayischittra*. Many heads of *Dalls* or parties of our day follow the same practice.

forbidden food. The Mussulman Governors often took advantage of this prejudice, when their exchequers were empty The Hindoo would submit to the most excruciating tortures rather than disclose his hoard, but the moment his religious purity was threatened, he complied with any demand, if the sum asked for was within his means ; if not, the man being linked to his caste fellows, the latter raised the required sum by subscription."

In a moral point of view, the effects of this distinction are equally mischievous. Far from promoting a spirit of benevolence and good fellowship between man and man, it has a natural tendency to engender hostile feelings, which cannot fail to militate against the best interests of humanity. Should a Hindoo of inferior caste happen to touch one of superior caste, while the latter is cooking or eating, he throws away everything as defiled. Even in cases of extreme sickness, the one will seldom condescend to drink water out of the hands of the other. There are also instances on record in which two Hindoos of the same caste refuse to eat together, simply because they belong to two several *dalls* or parties ; in the villages especially this partisan feeling is sometimes carried to so great a length that no party will scruple to blast the fair fame of their antagonists by scandalous accusations and uncalled-for slanders. Thousands and thousands of Rupees are spent in securing the favors or alliance of the *Koolins*—the great arbiters of caste,—and he who by the power of his purse can enlist on his side a larger numbers of these pampered *Koolins*, generally takes away the palm. The hard struggle for the attainment of this hollow, ephemeral distinction, instead of stimulating any noble desire or laudable ambition, almost invariably terminates in fostering an antagonistic spirit, which is decidedly opposed to the laws of good fellowship and the general brotherhood of mankind. Genuine charity can never exist in such an unexpansive state of society, and mutual love is torn in shreds. If the original founder of the system had calmly and soberly considered, apart from selfish motives, a tithe of the evils which the caste system was calculated to inflict on society, he would, I make no doubt, have paused before imposing on Hindoo society the fetters of caste servitude.

It has been urged by the advocates of the system that it is designed to confer a great boon on society by confining each trade or occupation to one particular class, and thereby securing perfection in that line; but the argument is as fallacious as the result is disappointing. Experience and observation sufficiently prove that the Hindoo artisans use almost the same tools and implements which their predecessors used centuries ago. They work with the same loom and spindle, the same plough, the same spade, the same scythe, the same threshing machine, and the same everything that were in vogue at the time of *Vicramadyatta* in the sixteenth century, and if any improvement has been effected, it is owing to the superior skill of the foreigners. It is, however, creditable to the native artisans to say that they evince a great aptitude for learning and imitating what they see. Native carpenters, shoemakers, tailors, engravers, lithographers, printers, gold and silver-smiths, &c., now-a-days turn out articles which in point of workmanship are not very much inferior to those imported from Europe. Of course they are materially indebted to Europeans for this improvement.

The circumstances which cause the loss of caste are the following: The abandonment of the Hindoo religion, journey to foreign countries which involves the eating of forbidden food, the eating of food cooked by one of inferior caste or of food forbidden to the Hindoos, female unchastity in a family, the cohabiting with women of a lower caste, or with those of foreign, nations and the non-performance of religious rites prescribed in the Shastras.* There are other circumstances which detract from the dignity of a family, but they are of secondary importance. These causes were in full operation some seventy or eighty years ago. The unanimous voice of the neighbours denounced a Hindu as an outcast if he were found guilty of any of the above transgressions. Purity of caste was then watched with greater solicitude than purity of conscience and character. The magnates of the land spared neither expense nor pains to preserve inviolate the outward purity of their caste. The popular shastras of the Hindoos are certainly very convenient and accommodating in every respect; the sins of a life-time, nay of ten lives, may be washed away by an ablution in the sacred stream of the Ganges on the occasion of certain *holy days* called *yogas;* so requisite provision is made in them for the atonement of the loss of caste by performing certain religious rites and feasting, and making suitable presents to Brahmins in money and kind. But it has always been a matter of wonder to many that the *Peeralees* or the Tagores of Calcutta, alike noted for their wealth and liberality, have not as yet been able to regain their caste or their original position in Hindu society. The obvious reason appears to be that they are not desirous of a restoration by submitting to any kind of humiliating atonement. They have shown their wisdom in pursuing such an independent and manly course. The history of *Peeralee* is thus given by Mr. Ward: "A Nabob of the name of *Peeralee* is charged with having destroyed the rank of many Hindus, Brahmins and others; and from these persons have descended a very considerable number of families scattered over the country, who have been branded with the name of their oppressor. These persons practise all the ceremonies of the Hindu religion, but are carefully avoided by other

* The non-performance of religious rites does not now, however, entail forfeiture of caste. Hindu society is getting lax in our days.

Hindus as outcasts. It is supposed that not less than fifty families live in Calcutta, who employ Brahmin priests to perform the ceremonies of the Hindu religion for them. It is said that Rajah Krishna Chunder Roy was promised five lacks of Rupees by a *Peeralee*, if he would only honor him with a visit of a few moments, but he refused." Such was the virulence with which the caste mania raged when Hindu bigotry had reached its culminating point. Rajah Krishna Chunder Roy of Kishnaghur, about 100 miles north of Calcutta, was otherwise reputed to have been a very generous-hearted man, a great patron of learning and learned men, but he was so blindly led away by the impulse of bigotry that he unhesitatingly declined to assist a brother countryman of his who had been subjected to social ostracism through mere accident. But the Rajah's grandson, if I am rightly informed, when he had occasion to come down to Calcutta a few years back, unscrupulously took up his quarters at Spence's Hotel, and freely enjoyed the company of his European friends, indicating a healthy change in the social economy of the people, the result solely of intellectual expansion, and of the inauguration of a better era through the rapid diffusion of western knowledge.*

The *Peeralee* or the Tagore family of Calcutta, be it recorded to their honor, have long been eminently distinguished by their liberality, manly independence, enlightened principles and enterprising spirit. Some of the members of this family occupy the foremost rank amongst the friends of native improvement. The late Baboo Dwarkey Nath Tagore set a noble example to his contrymen by his disinterested exertions in the cause of native education and public charities. Several of his European friends were under deep obligations to him for his unbounded liberality under peculiarly

---

* I am inclined to believe that what the late Nuddea Raja did was his individual act; as the head of the Hindus of Bengal, the Rajah of Nuddea would strictly follow the pratices of his great ancestor even to this day.

embarrassed circumstances ;* the length of his purse was equalled by the breadth of his views. His object in proceeding to England was mainly to extend his knowledge by a closer and more familiar intercourse with Europeans. He was the right hand of the illustrious Hindoo reformer, the late Raja Rammohun Roy. His magnanimous mind, his enlightened views, his engaging manners, his amiable qualities both in public and private life, and his indomitable zeal in endeavouring to elevate his country in the scale of civilization, gave him an influence in English society never before or after enjoyed by any Hindoo gentleman. His worthy relative and coadjutor, the late Baboo Prosono Coomar Tagore, C. S. I., who has left a princely fortune, was no less distinguished for his enlarged views and liberal sentiments. His rich endowment of the Tagore Law Lecturship in connection with the Calcutta University has substantially established his claim on the gratitude of his countrymen. It was he that first started the native English Paper called the "Reformer," which not only opened the eyes of the Hindoos to the errors of the antiquated system under which they lived, but diffused a healthy taste for the cultivation of English literature among the rising generation of his countrymen, and thereby paved the way for the development of advanced thought and intelligent opinion on the practical enunciation and appreciation of which mainly depends the future advancement of the nation. The late Moha Rajah Ramanauth Tagore, C. S. I., another member of the Tagore family, was deservedly esteemed for his liberal sentiments, his high sense of honor, his scrupulous fidelity and his unblemished character. Baboo Debendernath Tagore, the son of the late Baboo Dwarkeynauth Tagore, bears a highly exemplary character. His uncompromising straightforwardness, his sincerity and piety, his high integrity,

* To one friend alone he gave two lacs of Rupees without any security, showing a degree of magnanimity seldom to be met with among the millionaires of the present day.

his devotedness to the cause of religion, his unassuming habits, the suavity of his disposition, and his utter contempt for worldly enjoyments, have shed an unfading lustre around his name. Well may India be proud of such a worthy son. Moha Raja Jotendeımohun Tagore, C. S. I., Raja Sourendermohun Tagore, his brother, and Baboo Gynendermohun Tagore, the son of the late Baboo Prosonocoomar Tagore, also belong to this family: all of them bear a very high character for intelligence, integrity, and sound moral principles.

All these distinguished individuals are descended from *Peeralee* ancestors. Few have more deservedly merited the respect and esteem of their countrymen, or better vindicated their rightful claim to the honors bestowed on some of them. If they are denounced as outcasts, such outcasts are the ornaments of the country. If they are far in the rear of caste they are assuredly far in the van of intelligence, ability, mental activity, refinement and honesty. If to be a *Peeralee* were an indelible stigma, it is certainly a glory to the whole nation that such a noble and stainless character as Baboo Debendernauth Tagore is a member of the same family. We would search in vain among the countless myriads of India for such a meek, spotless, but bright and glorious model.

It is, moreever, to the *Peeralee* or Tagore family that the enlightened Hindoo community of Calcutta is principally indebted for its refined taste and elevated ideas. May they continue to shed their benign influence not only on the rising but unborn generations of their countrymen, and carry on the work of reformation, not with the impetuosity of rash innovators, but with the cool deliberation of reflecting minds.

The rules of caste are not now strictly observed, and their observance is scarcely compatible with the spirit of the age, and in one sense we have scarcely a Hindoo in Bengal, especially amongst those who live in the Presidency town and the district towns.

The distinction of caste is more honored in the breach than in the observance of it.* As English schools and colleges are multiplying in every nook and corner of the empire, more liberal ideas and principles are being imbibed by the Hindoo youths, which bid fair in process of time to exercise a regenerating influence on the habits of the people. Idolatry, and its necessary concomitant, priestcraft, is fast losing its hold on their minds; a new phase of life indicates the near approach of an improved order of things; ideas which had for ages been pent up in the dark, dreary cell of ignorance now find a free outlet, and the recipients of knowledge breathe a purer atmosphere, clear of the hazy mists that had hitherto clouded their intellect. To a philanthropist such a forecast is in the highest degree encouraging. The distinction of caste has also received a fatal blow by the frequent visits of young and aspiring native gentlemen to England for the purpose of completing their education there. This growing desire among the rising generation should be encouraged as it has an excellent tendency to promote the moral and intellectual improvement of the nation.

The late Baboo Ramdoolal Dey,† of Calcutta, who was a self-made man and a millionaire, was a Dullaputty or head

* The young members of a family have no hesitation in partaking of food cooked by Mussulmans and forbidden in the Hindoo Shasters. On holidays or on special occasions, they send orders to the "Great Eastern Hotel," and get supplies of English delicacies such as they have a liking for. It is a well-known fact that almost every rich family in Calcutta and its suburbs (the orthodox members excepted) recognised as the head of the Hindoo community, patronise the English Hotel-keepers. Mr. D. Wilson, the famous purveyor in Government Place, seeing the great rush of native gentlemen into his shop on a Christmas eve, was said to have remarked that the Baboos were amongst his best customers. The great purveyor was right, because the Baboos give large orders and pay regularly for fear of exposure. Such of them as are placed in mediocre circumstances arrange with their Mussulman syces and get fowl curry or roast as often as they choose. There are indeed a few honorable exceptions, who on principle do not encourage the English style of eating and drinking. A very little reflection will convince any one that the English mode of living is ill suited to the Natives. It not only leads a man into extravagance, but what is more reprehensible, begets a habit of drinking, which, I need hardly say, has been the ruin of many a promising young Baboo.

† This gentleman was a Banian to several American and English firms, which used to deal largely in cow and other hides. From religious scruples he refused

of a party. When the subject of caste was discussed, he emphatically said, that "the caste was in his iron chest," the meaning of which was that money has the power of restoring caste.

The late Baboo Ram Gopal Ghose, a distingushed merchant and reformer of this City, had a country residence at Bagati, near Tribani, in the Hooghly district, about 100 miles east of Calcutta. He had a mother who was, as might be expected, a superstitious old lady. Baboo Ram Gopal on principle never wounded her feelings by interfering with her religious belief. On the occasion of the Doorga Poojah at his country house, his mother as usual directed the servants to distribute the *noybidhi*, or offerings, consisting of rice, fruits and sweetmeats, among the Brahmins of the neighbourhood; but they all, to a man, refused to accept the same, on the ground that Ram Gopal was not a *Hindoo*, which was tantamount to declaring that he had no faith in Hindooism, and was an outcast from Hindooism. On seeing the offerings brought back, his mother's lamentations knew no bounds, because the refusal of the Brahmins to accept the offerings was a dishonor, and involved the question of the loss of caste. Apprehending the dreadful consequences of such a refusal, especially in a village where bigotry reigned supreme, the old lady became quite disconsolate. Ram Gopal, who with strong common sense combined the benefit of a liberal English education, thought of the following expedient: He at once suggested that every *noybidhi* (offering) should be accompanied by a sum of five Rupees. The temptation was too great to be resisted, the very Brahmins who, two hours back, openly refused to take the offerings, now came running in numbers to Ram Gopal's house for their share, and regularly

---

to accept the usual commission on such articles by which he might have obtained at least forty thousand Rupees per annum. In these days no Baboo declines to take the usual commission, but on the contrary, many are engaged in the trade, which is a sacrilegious act in the eye of the Hindoo Shaster.

scrambled for the thing. In fact, he had more demands than he could meet. Thus a few Rupees had the marvellous effect of turning a *Sahib* into a pure Hindoo, fully illustrating the truth of Ramdoolal Dey's saying, that "Caste was in his iron chest." Examples of this nature may be multiplied to any extent, but they are not necessary. Thus we see the decadence of this artificial system is inevitable, as indeed of every other unhealthy institution opposed to the best interests of humanity.

I cannot close this chapter without drawing the attention of my readers to the gross inconsistency of the conduct of the caste apologists. Thousands and tens of thousands of the most orthodox Hindoos daily violate the rules of caste by using the *shidho chàll*, (rice produced from boiled paddy) which is often prepared by Mussalmans and other low caste husbandmen, whose very touch is pollution to the food of the Hindoo. It is a notorious fact that nine-tenths of the Hindoos of Bengal, including the Brahmin class, are in the habit of eating *shidho chàll*, which is the prime staff of their lives, simply because the other kind of rice, *àtab chàll* (rice produced from sun-dried paddy), contains too much starch or nutritive property and is difficult of digestion by *bhayto* or rice-fed Bengallees who are, with a few exceptions, constitutionally weak from a variety of causes enumerated before. In the North-West Provinces, people never use *shidho* rice owing to its being boiled in an unhusked state.

The Hindoos of our day often consume sugar refined with the dust of charcoal bones. The universal use of *shidho* rice and sweetmeats which contain refined sugar leads the Hindoos to break the rules of caste almost every hour of their lives. Besides these two chief articles of food, there are several other things made by Mussulmans, such as rose-water, *kaywra àrauk*, and the like, the general use of which is a direct violation of the rules of caste. A Hindoo female, when she becomes a widow at an advanced period of life, sometimes takes to *átab* rice because it is not produced from boiled paddy which makes it impure, but from sun-dried paddy, and here the members of the Tagore family are more strict in their *regime* than any other class of Hindoos in Bengal. There are, however, yet a few orthodox Hindoos, who, though they eat *shidho* rice, nevertheless abstain from using bazar-made sweetmeats and Municipal pipe water because the engines of the latter are said to be greased and worked by Mussalman and Christian hands. Such men make their own sweetmeats at home with Benares sugar and drink Ganges water, but the younger members of their family, if not without their approval at least with their partial cognisance, daily make the greatest inroads on this institution without having the moral courage to avow their acts. They eat and drink in the European fashion, and preserve their castes intact by a positive and emphatic disclaimer. So much for the consistency of their character. When the orthodox heads of Hindoo families are gathered unto their fathers, the key-note of the present or rising generation will be—"perish caste with all its monstrous evils."

XIV.

A BRAHMIN.

A Brahmin of the present iron age is quite a different ecclesiastic from what he was in the past golden age. He is a metamorphosed being. Believing in the doctrine of metempsychosis, he claims to have descended from the mouth of the Supreme Brahmá, the Creator according to the Hindoo triad. In the lapse of time, his physical organisation, his traditional reputation as a saint and sage, his thorough devotion to his religious duties, his mental abstraction, his logical acumen, the purity of his character, his habitude and mode of living, have all undergone a radical change, unequivocally indicating the gradual declension of corporeal strength, of intellectual vigor, as well as of moral worth. In former times he was popularly regarded as the visible embodiment of the Creator, and the delegated exponent of all knowledge, revealed or acquired. The old and venerable Munis and Rishis, and their philosophical dissertations, their theological controversies and their religious and ethical disquisitions, evoked the admiration of the world in the dark ages before the Christain era. Almost all of them lived in a state of asceticism, and devoted their lives to religious contemplation, renouncing all the pleasures, passions and desires of the mundane world. The longevity of their lives in their sequestered retreat, the perfect purity of their manners, the simplicity of their habits, and their elevated conception of the immutable attributes of God, inspired the people with a profound reverence for their precepts and principles. The prince and the peasant alike paid their homage to the sacerdotal class, whose doctrines had, in the primitive state of society, the authority of religion and law.

The power of the Brahmins penetrated every class of the people, and by way of eminence they called themselves *Dvija*, *i. e.*, the regenerated or the twice born—a term which should only be applied to the really inspired sons of God. Since the promulgation of the Institutes of Manu they obtained that prominent rank among the Hindoos which they have retained unimpaired amidst all dynastic changes. Keeping the key of all knowledge in their exclusive custody, their functions were originally confined to the performance of religious ceremonies and the promulgation of laws. In all the affairs of the state or religion, the fiat of their ordinances had all the weight of a sacred command. Even the order of a mighty potentate was held in subordination to their injunctions. They were enjoined to worship their guardian deity three times a day, and were strictly prohibited from engaging in any secular occupation. They practised all manner of austerities tending to beget a contempt for all worldly enjoyments, and paved the way by religious meditation for ultimate absorption into the divine essence,—an ideal of the sublimity of which we can have no conception in the present degenerate age.

The complete monopoly of religious and legal knowledge which the Brahmins enjoyed for a very considerable period after the first dawn of learning in the East anterior to the Christian era, enabled them to put forth their very great influence upon the spiritual and temporal concerns of the three other orders of the Hindoo population, who implicitly accorded to them all the valuable rights of a privileged class, superior to all earthly power whatsoever. It has been expressly declared in the Institutes of Manu that Hindoo Law was a direct emanation from God. "That Immutable Power," says Manu, "having enacted this Code of Laws, himself taught it fully to me in the beginning; afterwards I taught Marichi and the nine other holy sages." It is believed that in the tenth century, B. C. "the complete fusion of Hindoo law and religion," was effected, and that both were administered by the Brahmins, until some mighty kings arose in Rajpootana, who curtailing their supreme influence reduced them to a secondary position. Thenceforward their ascendency gradually began to decline, till at length through succeeding generations it dwindled into comparative insignificance.* In process of time, the four grand original classes slowly multiplied, which is not to be wondered at in a great community split into divisions and subdivisions, separated from each other by different creeds, manners, customs and modes of life. These ramifications necessarily involved diversities of religious, moral and legal opinions and doctrines more or less fatal to the unquestioned authority of the Brahmins, who seeing in the progress and revolution of society the inevitable decay of their hitherto undisputed influence, abandoned the traditional and prescribed path of religious life and betook themselves to secular pursuit of gain for their subsistence. The necessary consequence now is that in almost every sphere of life, in every profession or calling, the Brahmins of the present day are extensively engaged. And their cupidity is so great, that every principle of law and morality is shamefully compromised in their dealings with mankind. A Brahmin is no longer typical of either religious purity or moral excellence. His profound erudition, his logical subtlety in spinning into niceties the most commonplace distinctions, his spirit of deep research and his illimitable power of polemical discussion, have all forsaken him, and from an inspired priest he has degenerated into a mercenary *purohit.* He no longer wears on his forehead the frontlet of righteousness, his whole heart, his whole soul is

---

* As the natural consequence of this declension of supremacy, Brahminical learning, from this and other analogous circumstances, slept a winter sleep, occasionally disturbed and broken by brilliant coruscations of light thrown upon it by Western researches, contemporaneously sustained by the faint efforts of learned Pundits.

impregnated with corruption. In a fervent spirit, he no longer says to his followers—"let us meditate on the adorable light of the Divine Ruler; may it guide our intellects." His sacred *poita* (Brahminical thread) his divine *gayútree* (prayer) his holy *basil* (bead roll), his three daily services with the sacred water of the Ganges, no longer inspire the minds of his votaries with awe, obedience and homage. From the worship of the only Living and True God he has descended to the worship of 330 millions of gods and of goddesses. Human numeration reels at the list. The individuality of the godhead is lost in the never ending cycles of deified objects, animate and inanimate. We no longer recognise in the Brahminical character and life an unsullied image of godlike purity, holiness and sublimity. His ministrations no longer fill us with joyful and exhilarating hopes which extend beyond the grave and promise to lead us to the safe anchorage of everlasting bliss. They no longer stir up in our breasts during each hour of life's waning lustre "a sublimer faith, a brighter prospect, a kinder sympathy, a gentler resignation." I ask every Hindoo to look into his heart honestly and answer frankly whether a Brahmin of the present day is a true embodiment, a glorious display, a veritable representative of Brahma, the Creator. Has he not long since sacrificed his traditional pure faith on the altar of selfishness and concupiscence and committed a deliberate suicide of his moral and spiritual faculty? We blush to answer the question in the affirmative.

I now purpose to give a short account of the ceremonies connected with the investiture of the *poita*, the sacred thread of a Brahmin, on the strength of which he assumes the highest ecclesiastical honors and privileges. According to the Hindoo almanac, an auspicious day is fixed for this important ceremonial, which opens a new chapter in the life of a Brahmin especially intended to ensure him all the rare benefits of a full-blown *Dwija*, or the twice-born. In celebrating the rite, particular regard is had to the state of the weather; should any atmospheric disturbance occur, the ceremony is postponed to the next clear day. The age assigned for the investiture is between nine and fifteen years. The occasion is accompanied in many cases by the preparation of *ananunda naru*, a kind of sweetmeat made of powdered rice, treacle, cocoanut and gingelly seeds rolled up into small round balls and fried in mustard oil. This particular sort of Hindoo confectionery, evidently a relic of primitive preparations, is manufactured on all occasions indicative of domestic rejoicing, hence the significance of the name given above. Before the appointed day, the boy is enjoined to abstain from the use of fish and oil, and on the morning of the ceremony, having been shaved, he is made to bathe, and put on red clothes, and when the rite of investiture commences wears a conical shaped tinsel hat, while the priest reads certain incantations and worships Narayan or Vishnoo, represented by a small round stone called *Saligram Sulu*, the ordinary household god of all Hindoos. A piece of cloth is held over his head, that he may not see or be seen by any of the non Brahminical caste. He then assumes the *dunda*, or the staff of an ascetical mendicant, which is represented by the branch of a *vilwa* tree held in his right hand, at the top of which is tied a knot with a bit of dyed cloth. An initiatory *poita* made of twisted *khoosh* grass, to which is fastened a piece of deer's skin, is next placed over the boy's left shoulder during the repetition of the prescribed incantations. The father then repeats to his son, in a low voice, lest a Soodra should hear, the sacred *gayútree* three times, which he tries his best to commit to memory. The *khoosh* grass *poita* is here removed, and a real thread *poita* spun by Brahmin women* which

* To so miserable a strait are some of them reduced that they actually strive to get a living by making these sacred thread poitas and strings for loins, indicating the pinching poverty and repulsive squalor in which they pine away their wretched existence. Indeed not

he is to wear ever afterwards, is substituted in its place. The boy now puts on his shoes and holds an umbrella in his hand while the priest reads and the father repeats the usual incantations, tending to awaken in the boy a sense of the grave responsibility he assumes. Thus dressed as a *Brahmacharee* (a religious mendicant), with a staff upon his shoulder and a beggar's wallet hanging by his side, he goes to his mother, father and other relatives and begs alms, repeating at the same time a certain word in Sanskrit. They give him each a small quantity of rice, a few *poitas* and a few Rupees, amounting in some cases to two or three hundred. The boy then squats down while the father offers a burnt sacrifice and repeats the customary incantations. After the performance of these ceremonies, the boy in his *Brahmacharee* attire suddenly rises up in a fit of pretended ecstacy and declares before the company that he is determined in future to lead the life of a religious mendicant. The announcement of this resolution instantly evokes the sympathy of the father, mother and other relatives, and they all persuade him to change his mind and adopt a secular life, citing instances that that life is favourable to the cultivation and growth of domestic and social affections as well as religious principles of the highest order. The holy Shastra expressly inculcates that a clean heart and a righteous spirit make men happy even amid the sorrows of earth, and that the sackcloth of mendicancy is not essential to righteousness if we earnestly and sincerely ask God to give us His true riches. Thus

---

a few of these widows are left "to the cold pity and grudging charity of a frosty world." They might almost sing and sigh with the poet as he sat in deep dejection on the shore.

> "Alas! I have nor hope, nor health,
> Nor peace within, nor calm around;
> Nor that content, surpassing wealth,
> The sage in contemplation found;
> *   *   *   *
>
> Others I see whom these surround,
> Smiling they live, and call life pleasure;
> To me that cup hath been dealt in another measure."

admonished, he with apparent reluctance abandons his pre-concerted design, which is a mere sham, and assumes the *rôle* of secularism. Certain formulas are now repeated, after which the boy leaves his *vilwa* staff, and takes in hand a thin Bamboo staff, which he throws over his shoulder. Other ritualistic rites are then performed, at the close of which the priest receives his fee for the trouble and departs home with the offerings. The boy next walks into a room, a woman pouring out water as he goes. He is then taught to commit to memory his daily service, called *sundhya*, after the repetition of which he eats the *charú* made of milk, sugar and rice boiled together.

For three days after being investited with the *poita* the boy is enjoined to sleep either on a carpet or a deer's skin, without a mattress or a musquito curtain. His food consists of boiled rice, ghee, milk and sugar, etc., only once a day, without oil and salt. He is strictly prohibited to see the sun or the face of a soodra, and is constantly employed in learning the sacred *gayútree* and the forms of the daily service which should be repeated thrice in a day. On the morning of the fourth day, he goes to the sacred stream of the Ganges, throws the two staves into the water, bathes, repeats his prayers, returns home, and again enters on the performance of his ordinary secular duties. During the day, a few Brahmins are fed according to the circumstances of the family. Thus the ceremony of investiture is closed, and the boy being purified and regenerated is elevated to the rank of a *Dwija* or twice born. How easily does the Brahminical Shastra make a change for the better in a religious sense in a youth quite incapable of forming adequate conceptions of a spiritual regeneration by the mere administration of a single rite!

Having endeavoured to give thus a short account of the ceremonies connected with the investiture of the sacred thread of a Brahmin, it remains to be seen how far his present position, character and conduct harmonise with the reputed sanctity of his regenerated nature. Great blame is laid at the door of the British Government, because it does not accord that high respect to the sacerdotal class which their own Rajahs had shewn them in the halcyon days of Hindooism. Before the advent of the British to India, the doctrines of the Brahminical creed, as indicated above, were in full force. Every Hindoo king used to enforce on all classes of the people high or low, a strict observance of the idolatrous ceremonies prescribed in the Hindoo Shastra. In the dark ages scarcely any nation in the world was hemmed in by such a close ring of religious ceremonials as the people of this country. Almost every commonplace occurrence had its peculiar rites which required the interposition of the sacerdotal class. On occasions of prosperity or adversity, of rejoicing or calamity, their ministration was alike needed. These formed their ordinary sources of gain, but the greatest means of support consisted in the grants of lands, including sometimes houses, tanks, gardens, etc., given in perpetuity to gods or the priests. These grants are called, as I have already stated, the *Debatras* and *Brahmatras*. Among others, the Rajahs of Burdwan, Kishnaghur, and Tipperah made the greatest gifts, and their names are still remembered with gratitude by many a Brahmin in Bengal. But the Law authorizing the resumption of rent-free tenures has, as must naturally be expected, made the English Government obnoxious, and it is denounced in no measured terms for the sacrilegious act. If Manu were to visit Bengal now, his indignation and amazement would know no bounds in witnessing the sacerdotal class reduced to the humiliating position of a servile, cringing and mercenary crowd of men. Their original prestige has suffered a total shipwreck. Generally speaking, a Brahmin of the present day is practically a

Soodra (the most inferior class) of the past age, irretrievably sunk in honor and dignity. Indeed it was one of the curses of the Vedic period that to be a Brahmin of the present *Kali yagu* would be an impersonation of corruption, baseness and venality.

There is a common saying amongst the Natives that a Brahmin is a beggar even if he were possessed of a lakh of Rupees (£10,000.) It is a lamentable fact that impecuniosity is the common lot of the class. In ordinary conversation, when the question of the comparative fortunes of the different classes is introduced, a Brahmin is often heard to lament his most impecunious lot. The gains of the sacerdotal class of the present day have been reduced to the lowest scale imaginable. If an officiating priest can make ten Rupees a month, he considers himself very well off. He can no longer plume himself on his religious purity and mental superiority, once so pre-eminently characteristic of the order. The spread of English education has sounded the death-knell of his spiritual ascendancy. In short, his fate is doomed; he must bear or must forbear, as seems to him best. The tide of improvement will continue to roll on uninterruptedly, in spite of every "freezing and blighting influence," and we heartily rejoice to discover already that the "tender blade is grown into the green ear, and from the green ear to the rich and ripened corn."

When, a few years ago, Sir Richard Temple carefully examined the Criminal Statistics of Bengal, he was most deeply concerned to find that the proportion of the Brahmin criminals in the jails of the Province far outnumbered that of any other caste. This is an astounding fact, bearing the most unimpeachable testimony to the very lamentable deterioration of the Hindoo ecclesiastical class in our days. To expatiate on the subject would be unpalatable. But we believe we can point with a degree of pardonable pride to a past period when nine men of literary genius, among whom the renowned Kalidas, the Indian Shakespeare, was the most brilliant, flourished in the Court of Vikramaditya in Ougein; but dynastic changes were simultaneously accompanied by the rapid decline of learning as well as of religious purity.

The English rule, though most fiercely denounced by selfish, narrow-minded men, has nevertheless been productive of the most beneficial results even as far as the sacerdotal class is concerned. Every encouragement is now-a-days afforded to the cultivation of the classical language of India —Sanskrit—and not only are suitable employments provided for the most learned Pundits* in all the Government, Missonary and private educational Institutions throughout the country, but the University degrees conferred on the most successful students, tend to stimulate them to further laudable exertions in the study of the sacred language, which, but for this renewed attempt at cultivation and improvement, would have been very much neglected.

Independently of the above consideration, it is no less gratifying than certain that the progress of education has produced men, sprung from the sacerdotal class, whose eminent scholarly attainments, high moral principles and unblemished character, as well as a practical useful career, have raised them to the foremost ranks of Hindoo society. Rammohun Roy, Dr. K. M. Banerjea, Pundit Isser Chunder Vidyasager, Baboo Bhoodeb Mookerjee, and others of equal

* However learned a Pundit might be in philology, philosophy, logic and theology, he is lamentably deficient in scientific knowledge, notably in geography and ethnology. With a view to test the knowledge of his Pundit on those two subjects, Bishop Middleton was said to have once asked him two very simple questions, (1) whence are the English come? (2) what is their origin? The reply of the Pundit was somewhat to the following effect: The English are come somewhere from Lunka or Ceylon (the imaginary land of cannibals), and they are of mixed origin, sprung from monkey and cannibal, because they jabber like monkeys, and sit like them on chairs with their legs hanging down,—an attitude pecular to the monkey species,—and they eat like cannibals half-boiled beef, pork, mutton, &c. Childish as the reply was, the pious Bishop, however, with his wonted benignity, smiled and corrected his error.

mental calibre, are names deservedly enshrined in the grateful memory of their countrymen. If Western knowledge had not been introduced into India, men of such high culture and moral excellence would have passed away unnoticed and unrecognised in the republic of letters, and the fruits of their literary labors, instead of being regarded as a valuable contribution to our stock of knowledge, would have been buried in obscurity. To study the lives of such distinguished pioneers of Hindoo enlightenment, "is to stir up our breasts to an exhilarating pursuit of high and ever-growing attainments in intellect and virtue."

XV.

THE BENGALEE BABOO.

THIS is an euphonious oriental title, suggestive of some amiable qualities which are eminently calculated to adorn and elevate human life. A Bengalee Baboo of the present age, however, is a curious product composed of very heterogeneous elements. The importation of Western knowledge has imbued him with new fangled ideas, and shallow draughts have made him conceited and supercilious, disdaining almost everything Indian, and affecting a love of European æsthetics. The humourous performance of Dave Carson, and the caustic remarks of Sir Ali Baba, give graphic representations of his anglicised taste, habits and bearing. Any thing affected or imitated is apt to nauseate when contrasted with the genuine and natural.

The anglicised Baboos are certainly well-meaning men, instinctively disposed to move within the groove traditionally prescribed for them, but the scintillation of European ideas and a servile imitation of Western manners have played sad havoc with their original tendencies. Ambitious of being considered enlightened and elevated above the common herd, their improved taste and inclination almost unconsciously relegate them to the enchanted dream-land of European refinement, amidst the ridicule of the wise and the discerning. Society now-a-days is a quick-shifting panorama. Old scenes and associations rapidly pass away to make room for new ones, and prescriptive usages fall into oblivion. A new order of things springs up, and new actors replace the old ones. The influence of the aged is diminished, and the young and impulsive seize with avidity the prizes of life, forgetting in their wild precipitancy the unerring dictates of cool deliberation. "The hurried, bustling, tumultuous, feverish Present swallows up men's thoughts," and the momentous interests of society looming in the Future are almost entirely disregarded. The result necessarily carries them wide of the great object of human life. They forfeit the regard and sympathy of their fellow countrymen whose moral and intellectual advancement they should gradually strive to promote by winning their love and confidence.

As a man of fashion he cuts a burlesque figure by adopting partly Mussulman and partly European dress, and imitating the European style of living, as if modern civilization could be brought about by wearing tight pantaloons, tight shirts and black coats of alpaca or broadcloth. He culminates in a coquettish embossed cap or thin-folded shawl turban, with perhaps a shawl neckcloth in winter. He eats mutton chops and fowl curry, drinks Brandy panee or Old Tom, and smokes Manilla or Burmah cigars *a la Francaise.* Certainly the use of those eatables and drinkables is proscribed in the Hindoo Shastra, and an honest avowal of it will sooner or later expose him to public derision, and estrange him from the hearts of the orthodox Hindoos. A wise European, who has the real welfare of the people at heart, will never encourage such an objectionable line of conduct, because it is *per se* calculated to denationalise. To be more explicit, even at the risk of verbosity, it should be mentioned that Baboos resident in Calcutta not unjustly pride themselves on being the denizens of the great Metropolis of British India, which is unquestionably the focus of enlightenment, the centre of civilization and refinement, and the emporium of fashion in the East. People in the country glory and console themselves with the idea that in their adoption of social manners and customs they follow the example of the big Baboos of Calcutta. Although the fashions of Hindoo society in Calcutta do not change with the rapidity they do in Paris and London, monthly, fortnightly and weekly, yet they vary, perhaps, once in two or three years, and even then the change is partial and not radical. Slowly and gradually, the Hindoos of Bengal have abandoned their original and primitive dress, which consisted of thin slender garments, suited to the warm temperature of the climate at least for the greater part of the year, and adopted that of their conquerors. A simple *dhootee* and *dubjah*, with perhaps an *álkhálá* on the back and a folded *pugree* on the head, constituted the dress of a Bengali not long before the battle of Plassey. The court dress was, indeed, somewhat different, but then it was a servile imitation of that of a Rajpoot chief or a Mussulman king. When Rajahs Rajbullub, and Nubkissen, and Suddur-ud-din, a Mohamedan, attended the Government House in the time of Clive and Hastings, what was their court costume but an exact copy of the Mussulman dress? Even now, after the lapse of a century and a half, they use their primitive dress at home, *viz.*, a *dhootee* and an *uraney*. An Englishman would not easily recognise or identify a Bengalee at home and a Bengalee in his office dress, the difference being striking and marked. But the establishment of the British rule in India has introduced a very great change in the national costume and taste, irrespective of the intellectual revolution, which is still greater. Twenty years ago the gala dress of a Bengalee boy consisted of a simple Dacca *dhootee* and a Dacca *ecloye*, with a pair of tinsel-worked shoes; but now rich English, German and China satin, brocade and velvet with embossed flowers, and gold and silver fringes and outskirts, have come into fashion and general use. It is a common sight to see a boy dressed in a pantaloon and coat made of the above costly stuffs, with a laced velvet cap, driving about the streets of Calcutta during the festive days. Of course the more genteel and modest of the class, *sobered down* by age and experience, do not share in the juvenile taste for the gaudy and showy. As becomes their maturer years, they are satisfied with a decent broadcloth coat and pantaloon, with a white cloth or Çashmere shawl *pugree*, more in accordance with simple English taste. But both the young and the old must have patent Japan leather shoes from Cuthbertson and Harper, Monteith & Co., or the Bentinck Street Chinese shoemakers, the laced Mussulman shoes having gone entirely out of fashion. Nor is the taste of the Hindoo females in a primitive stage as far as costliness is concerned. Instead of Dacca *Taercha* or *Bale Booṭa* Sari, they must have either Benares gold embroidered or French embossed gossamer *Sari*, with gold lace borders and ends. It would not be out of place to notice here that it would be a very desirable improvement in the way of decency to introduce among the Hindoo females of Bengal a stouter fabric for their garment in place of the present thin, flimsy, loose *sari*, without any other covering over it. In this respect, their sisters of the North-Western and Central Provinces, as well as those of the South, are decidedly more decent and respectable. A few respectable Hindoo ladies have of late years begun to put an *unghia* or corset over their bodies, but still the under vestment is shamefully indelicate. Why ḍo not the Baboos of Bengal strive to introduce a salutary change in the dress of their mothers, wives, sisters and daughters, which private decency and public morality most urgently demand? These social reforms must go hand in hand with religious, moral and intellectual improvement. The one is as essential to the elevation and dignity of female character as the other is to the advancement of the nation in the scale of civilization.

The Lancashire and German weavers have ample cause to rejoice that their manufactured colored woollen fabrics have greatly superseded the Indian *Pashmina* goods—Cashmere shawls not excepted,—and European Cashmere, broadcloth, flannel, hosiery and haberdashery are now in great request. From the wealthiest Baboo to the commonest fruit seller, half hose or full stockings are very commonly used. This forms an essential part of the official gear of a *keranee* (writer) of the present day, though he is now seen without his national *pugree* or head dress.

A Bengalee Baboo is said to be a money-making man. By the most ingenious makeshifts he contrives to earn enough to enable him to make both ends meet, and lay by something for the evening of his life. He is generally a thrifty character, and does not much mind how the world goes when his own income is positive. He lacks enterprise, and is therefore most reluctant to engage in any haphazard commercial venture, though he has very laudable patterns amongst his own countrymen, who, by dint of energy, prudence, perseverance and probity, have risen from an obscure position in life to the foremost rank of successful Native merchants. He is destitute of pluck, and the risk of a commercial venture stares him in the face in all his highways and byways. In many cases he has inherited a colossal fortune, but that does not stir up in his breast an enterprising spirit. He seeks and courts service, and in nine cases out of ten succeeds. The sweets of service, and the prospect of promotion and pension, slowly steal into his soul, and he gladly bends his neck under the yoke of servitude. It is a lamentable fact that he is a stranger to that "proud submission of the heart which keeps alive in servitude itself the spirit of an exalted freedom." As a vanquished race, subordination is the inevitable lot of the Natives, but it is edifying to see how they hug its trammels with perfect complacency.

The English Government is to the people of Bengal a special boon, a god-send. Almost every respectable family of Bengalee Baboos, past or present, is more or less indebted to it for its status and distinction, position and influence, affluence and prosperity. The records of authentic history clearly demonstrate the fact that the Baboos of Bengal have been more benefited by their British rulers than ever they were under their own dynasty. Instances are not wanting to corroborate the fact. The love of money is natural in man, and few men are more powerfully and, in many cases, more dangerously influenced by it than the people of this country. "It is a thirst which is inflamed by the very copiousness of its draughts." Possession or accumulation does not sufficiently satisfy it.

Experience and observation amply attest the truth of the following current saying among the Hindoos of the Upper Provinces, *viz.*, "*Kamayta topeewallah, lotetah dhoteewallah,*" the meaning of which is, the English earn, the Bengalees plunder. To be more explicit, the English continue to extend their conquests, the Bengalee Baboos participate in the loaves and fishes of the Public Service. In a dejected spirit of mind, a Hindoosthanee is often heard to mourn; he addresses a Sahib in the most respectful manner imaginable, by using such flattering terms as "*Khodabund, garibparbar,*" but in nine cases out of ten the Sahib scornfully turns away his head; when, on the contrary, a Bengalee *gir gir karkay dho bath sanay diya, i. e.*, jabbers to him a few words, he patiently listens to him, and signifies his acquiescence in what he says by a nod. In his boorish simplicity, the Hindoosthanee concludes that the Bengalee Baboos are well versed in charms, or else how do they manage to tame a grim biped like a Sahib.

With a view to remove this erroneous impression, which until recently was so very common among the inhabitants of the Upper Provinces, and the existence of which is so prejudicial to the general encouragement of education throughout India, as well as to the impartial character and high dignity of the paramount power, the local Governments have been directed in future to select for public service all the educated Natives born and bred up under their respective Administrations in preference to the Bengalees. Thus the aspiration of a Bengalee Baboo, so far as Public Service is concerned, is now restricted within the limits of his own Province.

A Bengalee Baboo is an eager hunter after academic honors. The University confers on him the high degrees of B. A., M. A. and B. L., and he distinguishes himself as a speaking member of the British Indian Association or of the Calcutta Municipality. He also reads valedictory addresses to retiring Governors and other Government Magnificoes. He is created a Maharajah, a Rajah, a Rai Bahadoor, with perhaps the additional paraphernalia of C. S. I. or C. I. E. As a ripe man of vivid ambition and lofty aspiration, he necessarily hankers after and is all a-gog to dash through thick and thin for these new honors and decorations. He drives swiftly about in his barouche with his staff holder on the coach-box in broadcloth livery. Unfortunately no baronetcy blazons forth in Bengalee heraldry, like that bestowed on Sir Jamsetjee Jeejeebhoy. The cause is obvious. No millionaire Bengalee has to this day contributed so munificently to public charities as the Parsee baronet.

When that distinguished Hindoo reformer, Baboo Dwarkanath Tagore,—the most staunch coadjutor of Rajah Rammohun Roy,—visited England, it was reported that Her Majesty had most graciously offered to confer on him the title of a Rajah; and his liberality and public spirit fully entitled him to that high distinction, but he politely refused it on the ground that his position did not justify his accepting it. He felt that the shadow of a name without substance was but a mockery. When Rajah Radhakant Deb was elected President of the British Indian Association "he used to declare that he was more proud of that office than of his title of Rajah Bahadoor, inasmuch as it indicated the chiefship of a body which was a power in the State and was destined to achieve immense good for the country." At the time of the Prince of Wales' visit to Calcutta, it was said that a certain English-made Rajah was introduced by a Government Magnifico to the Maharajah of Cashmere; among other matters, the Cashmere Rajah out of curiosity asked the Bengal Rajah, "where was his Raj and what was the strength of his army?" The question at once puzzled him, and his answer was anything but satisfactory. Of all the Indian Viceroys, Lord Lytton was certainly the most liberal in bestowing these hollow titles on the Baboos of Bengal, under a mistaken notion of winning the love and confidence, which ought to constitute the solid basis of a good Government. A Rajahship,* without the necessary equipage and material and moral grandeur of royalty is but a gilt ornament that dazzles at first sight but possesses little intrinsic value. It is in fact a misnomer, a sham, a counterfeit. The love of honor or power constitutes one of the main principles of human nature. A Rajah, in the true sense of the word, is one who shares in the royalty of divine attributes. He should remember that a man is bound to look to something more than his mere wardrobe and title ; he must possess a goodness and a greatness which would benefit thousands and tens of thousands of his fellow-

* It is a disreputable fact, but it most assuredly *is* a fact, that when some years ago a teacher of the Government School of Art published a book in Bengallee on the ancient arts and manufactures of Hindoosthan, and sent a copy of it to one of these English-made Rajahs, he politely refused to take it—the price being one Rupee only—saying it was of no use to him though it was an instructive and suggestive manual. This refusal offers a sad comment on the liberality of my fellow countrymen towards the encouragement of learning. But turning from the dark to the bright side of the picture, I may perhaps be permitted to point with pardonable pride to the almost unparalleled munificence of the late Baboo Kally Prosono Singh of this City, in this respect. That distinguished patron of vernacular literature had, it is said, spent upwards of £50,000 on the compilation of Mohabharat, that grand Epic poem of the Hindoos, which says Talboys Wheeler, still continues to exercise an influence on the masses of the people "infinitely greater and more universal than the influence of the Bible upon modern Europe."

creatures by the exercise of real, disinterested virtue. Such a career alone can leave an imperishable and ennobling name behind, which will go down to posterity as a pattern of moral grandeur.* Politically considered these titles and decorations have their value, inasmuch as they have a tendency to promote the *entente cordiale* between the rulers and the ruled, and, next to the Public Debt, furnish, in an indirect way, an additional buttress to the stability of the British Indian empire.

In former times, when the English rule was in its inceptive stage, when external pageant—the outcome of vanity—was not much thought of, when the simple taste of the people was not tainted by luxury and corruption, an unnatural craving for titles exerted but a very feeble influence on the minds of the great. Instead of seeking "the bubble reputation" they vied with each other in the extent of their religious gifts and endowments, affording substantial aid to the learned of the land and to the poorer classes of the community. A spirit of disinterestedness and self-sacrifice never at variance with magnanimity was conspicuous in all their gifts. The immense extent of *Debatra* and *Brahmatra* land, *i. e.*, rent-free tenures throughout Bengal, even after the relentless operation of the Resumption Act, still bears testimony to their disinterested benevolence and the heartiness with which they entered into other men's interests. Of course they were incapable of comprehending the innumerable affinities and relations of life in all its varied phases, rising from the finite and transient to the infinite and the enduring, but whatever they gave, they

---

* Of all the English-made Rajahs of the present day, it is pleasing to recognise, in Moharajah Rajender Mullick of this City, some of the noble attributes of a Rajah. Modest and unassuming, he manifests to a great degree a generous disposition to relieve suffering humanity and to do good by stealth. Never did he struggle to thrust himself, by the nature of his work, upon public notice. Gifted with an intelligent mind, a refined taste, and considerable artistic ability, his moral greatness throws all other forms of greatness into the shade. He is not ambitious to make his name the theme, the gaze, the wonder of a dazzled community.

gave not with a stinted hand nor in an ostentatious way, but with a truly benevolent and disinterested heart, looking to the Most High for their guerdon. The sublime and elevated conception of organised charity never penetrated their minds. Religious gifts and endowments formed the great bulk of their contributions, but they also made permanent provision for the relief of the helpless and the destitute,* not on the recognised principles of English charity, *i. e.* the Hospital system, the Nurses' Institutions, Reformatories for unfortunates, parish relief, funds for the aged and infirm, provision of improved dwellings as well as for baths and wash-houses for the working-classes inaugurated by the magnificent gift by Mr. G. Peabody of £250,000, ragged schools and asylums for the deaf, dumb and blind, supported by voluntary contributions, and other organised methods for the relief of distress and destitution throughout the country. It is a sad reflection on the benevolent disposition of the Natives that they cannot boast of anything bearing a remote analogy to the above recognised forms of Charity. In India there is much individual charity of an impulsive and interested character, but the great element of success in English charity is combination and organisation, without which no work of public utility can be practically carried out.

* Of all the Hindoo millionaires whose life afforded the most ennobling example of a pious and disinterested man that of Lalla Baboo—the ancestor of the present Paikpárrá Rajah family, in the suburbs of Calcutta—was certainly one of the most remarkable. He possessed a princely fortune, a considerable portion of which he wisely set apart for the support of the poor and destitute. Unlike most of his wealthy countrymen, he renounced all the pleasures of the world, and in the evening of his life retired with only a shred of cloth into the holy city of Brindabun. As a practical illustration of self-denial he actually led the life of a religious mendicant, daily begging from door to door for a mouthful of bread. His religious endowments still continue to offer shelter and food to hundreds of poor people in and around Brindabun, which has been so graphically described by Colonel Tod. "Though the groves of Brinda" says he, "in which Kanaya (Krishna) disported with the Gopis, no longer resound to the echoes of his flute; though the waters of the Jumna are daily polluted with the blood of the sacred kine, still it is the holy land of the pilgrim, the sacred Jordan of his fancy, on whose banks he may sit and weep, as did the banished Israelite of old, the glories of Mathoora, his Jerusalem."

It is obvious that the peculiar social economy of the Natives presents an almost insuperable barrier to the harmonious amalgamation of the different classes artificially split into numerous subdivisions. In the neighbourhood of Poona, Mr. Elphinstone says, there are about 150 different castes, and in Bengal they are very numerous. They maintain their divisions, however obscurely derived, with great strictness.* The religious, social and moral duties of these classes, exhibit marked differences, which are opposed to the combination of united efforts in the cause of relieving suffering humanity. The idea of a national brotherhood and a system of universal philanthropy, such as Christianity has nobly inaugurated, is much too elevated for the narrow, contracted minds of the people. Independent of the numerous subdivisions of caste, unhappily there still exists an impassable gulf between the Hindoos and Mussulmans—at present the children of the same soil—which has hitherto kept up a state of unhallowed separatism, essentially at variance with a cordial coalition for the consummation of any comprehensive system of Public Charity designed to benefit both. Age has rooted in the minds of the two communities an implacable mutual hate, quite subversive of the best interests of humanity. Plausible arguments may be adduced in support of the existence of this race antagonism, but let both of them be assured that "by abusing this world they shall not earn a better." Let every act or feeling or motive of both races be merged in one harmonious whole, developing the perfection of human nature in a distinct and bright reality.

A Bengalee Baboo is fond of discussing European politics. The reading of history has given him a superficial insight into the rise and progress of nations. He does not

---

* Division always implies weakness and "estrangement intolerable isolation" impeding the expansion of genuine benevolent feelings in a comprehensive sense.

deny that he amplifies and emphasises the sentiments he has learnt in the school of English politics. The orations of Lall Mohun Ghose in England have proved that a native of India has mastered the art of thinking on his legs, which is the beginning and end of oratory. A few more men like him, steadily working in earnest at the fountain head of power, would certainly awaken public attention towards the present condition of our country. It was Lord William Bentinck who advised a body of Native Memorialists, anxious for the political emancipation of their country, "to continue to agitate until they gained their end." Constitutional representation to proper authority, his Lordship remarked, would as much command public attention as idle, factious declamation divert it.* He was emphatically the "People's William" in India, as Gladstone is the "People's William" in England. He was a statesman who directed his whole attention and energy to internal improvement, repudiating all schemes of aggression or conquest. His beneficence, immortalised in a noble monument—the Calcutta Medical College,—will be more gratefully acknowledged by the latest generation than the genius of a Hastings, a Wellesley, or a Dalhousie.

The complete emancipation of India, however, is a question of time. Baboo Lall Mohun Ghose's speeches in England have not been entirely fruitless, inasmuch as they have evoked and enlisted the sympathy of a few leaders of public opinion. He is manfully struggling to remove the bar of political disabilities, and to secure for his countrymen the benefit of representative institutions, for the recognition and appreciation of which they are now prepared. While they hope for the best, they must be prepared for the worst. They

* Very few persons remember the days when Chuckerbutty faction and grievance Thomson used to raise a hue and cry in the Fouzdairy Balakhánáh Debating Club, formed for the political emancipation of India before the people were fully prepared to appreciate the value of their rights and privileges.

must learn meanwhile to cherish, as among the essential elements of ultimate success, a firm, manly, independent and self-denying spirit.

A Bengalee Baboo is often voted a man of tall talk. Platitude is his forte. This is surely true to a certain extent; and until he descends from the elevated region of speculation to the matter of fact arena of practice, both his writings and harangues must necessarily prove abortive. He must learn to exchange his verbosity for action in the great battle of life. Every great politician or statesman must have a thorough practical training to enable him to overcome the opposition of different factions whose interests are jeopardised by his success, and to render his administration a blessing to the people. He must be prepared to grow and advance under adverse influences. The history of that consummate statesman, Sir Salar Jung, of that distinguished scholar and councillor, Sir T. Madeo Rao, of that astute minister, Maharajah Sir Dinkur Rao, furnishes the most convincing examples of superior adminstrative ability combined with practical wisdom. Lord Northbrook, in a recent speech at Birmingham, has made honorable mention of these three eminent statesmen, whose valuable services in their respective spheres have long since established their substantial claims to the the gratitude of their fellow countrymen. When Sir Salar Jung visited Europe, his very comprehensive and enlightened views elicited the admiration of several of the wisest statesmen of the age. His able and successful administration at Hyderabad, amidst the fierce opposition of factious parties, affords an admirable illustration of his superior practical wisdom. When, some thirty years ago, Maharajah Sir Dinkur Rao visited Calcutta, he was the wonder of all who heard him enunciate, in a telling speech at the Town Hall, his high, noble and practical views on civil Government. The speech was not made feverish by visions of indistinct good, as Mr.

Theodore Dickens said, but it was a clear exposition of the liberal sentiments of a wise statesman.

The Bengalees are not a warlike race. Their traditional habits and usages, their physique, their diet and dress, their natural tendency to slothfulness and effeminacy, their proverbial quietude, their general want of pluck and manly spirit, their ascetic composure, placing the chief joys of life in rest and competency,—an heirloom descended from their ancestors,—all indicate an unwarlike temperament. During the Mutiny of 1857,—an event which in atrocious acts of cruelty incomparably surpasses all other historical events ever recorded,—that kind hearted Governor General, Lord Canning, was advised to introduce Martial Law into Calcutta, but he negatived the proposal by emphatically declaring in the Council Chamber that the Bengalees are a mild, tame, inoffensive and loyal race of people, whose only weapon of defence is a simple penknife. A common Police constable with his baton is to them a grim master of authority. A red-coated Highlander is formidable enough to cope with and drive away an immense crowd of Bengalees even in the very heart of the City of Palaces, while in the villages all shops and houses are closed at the very sight of an European soldier in his uniform. In fact, Bengal can well be governed by a handful of Native Police constables, especially when the Arms' Act is in full force. Unlike the military races of Upper India, or the border tribes, the Bengalees will never, even under the influence of the most aggravated wrongs and injuries, retaliate or resort to such a desperate court of appeal as war and murder.

English is the adopted language of a Bengalee Baboo. It is an instructive study to take a cursory view of the rapid progress of English education throughout India from the day when David Hare had held out pecuniary inducements to Hindoo youths to attend his school, and Dr. Duff called in the aid of Rammohun Roy to found the infant General Assembly's Institution, now developed into the largest College in India. Fifty years ago, who dreamt or even hazarded a prediction that a Native lad of sixteen or seventeen years of age would venture to traverse the perilous ocean and compete for the Civil Service Examination in England, paying no heed whatever to the manifold disadvantages arising from social persecution, and the disruption of domestic relations of the tenderest nature. When Bacon said that knowledge is power, he certainly did not mean physical but intellectual power. It is the irresistible influence of this power that has inspirited an Indian youth to appear at the English "open competition" for the purpose of winning academic spurs and entering a closely fenced service; it is the quickening influence of this power, combined with an enterprising spirit, that has gradually enabled a mere handful of English adventurers to convert a small factory into one of the vastest empires in the East. The gigantic strides that English education has made in India within a short time, have been the wonder of the age, the foundation rock of her ultimate emancipation, socially, morally and intellectually. The prison wall round the mind which ages had reared and learning fortified has been completely demolished, and not only men but matronly zenana females have picked up a few crumbs of broken English words which they occasionally use in familiar conversation, for instance, Rail, Talygraf, Guvner, Juj Majister, High Cote, etc.

Some of the Bengalee Baboos read and write English with remarkable fluency, and the epistolary correspondence of most of them is commonly carried on in that language. When two or more educated Baboos meet together, or take their constitutional in the morning, they perhaps talk of some leading articles in the Anglo-Indian or English journals or periodicals, and eagerly communicate to each other "the flotsam and jetsam of advanced European thoughts, the ripest outcome in the Nineteenth century, or the aftermath in the Fortnightly," as if the vernacular dialect were not at all fitted for the communication of their ideas. It is a pity that the cultivation and improvement of a national literature—the embodiment of national thought and taste and the main-spring of national enlightenment—seldom or never engages their serious attention. But it is a great mistake to suppose that the large mass of the Indian population can be thoroughly instructed and reformed through the medium of a foreign language. The richness and copiousness of modern English, combining as it does conciseness with solidity and perspicuity, are admittedly very great; it is admirably adapted for the educated *few*, but it is not equally suited to the capacity and comprehension of the *many*. It is incumbent, therefore, on all well disposed Hindoos, who have the real welfare of their country at heart, to endeavour to fertilise their national literature by transplanting into it the advanced thoughts of modern Europe, and to enrich it with copiousness, such as would obviate its acknowledged deficiency and barrenness. Until this is done, it is as unreasonable to expect elegance and perfection in the national literature as it is to expect harvest in seed-time or the full vigor of manhood in the incipient state of childhood.

Assuredly the Bengalees are a race of *keranees* or writers, as Napoleon said the English were a nation of shop-keepers. Every morning and evening, almost all the main streets of Calcutta leading to the English quarter—bright prospect for the Tramway—are literally thronged with dense crowds of keranees in their white cloth uniform, busily making for their respective offices, either in shabby looking third class hackney carriages or on foot. A foreigner not used to such sights cannot fail almost unconsciously to come to a conclusion that the Bengalees are a nation of keranees.

Every Government, Railway or Merchant's office, is filled with these Baboos, either actually employed or serving on probation, biding their time in fond expectation of picking up a slice of official bread, buttered or unbuttered. Even graduates of the Calcutta University do not hesitate to serve as apprentices, because a collegiate course does not teach the rules of bureaucracy or official routine. Most of them are good copyists or clever accountants, while a few are correspondence clerks. As a rule, their pay is very small compared with what is given to English Clerks, for reasons which I need not dilate upon here.

Within the range of our experience, extending over fifty years, we remember only one Native gentleman—Baboo Shama Churn Dey, the present vice-chairman of the Calcutta Municipality—who, by his tried ability, intelligence and integrity has managed to climb to the top of keraneedom. In recognition of his high efficiency his salary has been raised to one thousand Rupees a month, in spite of many instances of supersession. I, in common with others, am fully persuaded that had he been a British-born Civilian, he would undoubtedly have drawn a much larger salary. But it is useless to repine at a misfortune which is inevitable.

Even the amusements of a Bengalee Baboo are more or less anglicised. Instead of the traditional *Jattras*, (representations) and *Cobees* (popular ballads) he has gradually imbibed a taste for theatrical performances, and native musical instruments are superseded by European flutes, concertinas and harmoniums, organs and piano-fortes. This is certainly a decided improvement on the old antiquated system, demonstrating the slow growth of a refined taste. Thus we see in almost every phase of life, at home or outside, the Bengalee Baboo is Europeanized. In his style of living, in his mode of dress, in his writings, in his public and private utterances, in his household arrangements and furniture, in his bearing and department, in his social intercourse, in his mental accomplishments, and in fact, in his passionate partiality for Western æsthetics, he is a modified Anglo-Indian. But it were devoutly to be wished that he possessed a larger admixture of the essential elements of European truthfulness of character, energy and manliness of spirit, straightforwardness in his dealings with society, nobility of sentiment, magnanimity combined with simplicity, disinterested love and sympathy, and above all,moral and spiritual elevation.

XVI.

THE KOBIRAJ OR NATIVE PHYSICIAN.

NOTWITHSTANDING the rapid progress of medical science throughout the country since the establishment of the Calcutta Medical College, it is an undeniable fact that the practice of Hindoo *Kobirajes* and Mussulman *hakims* still continues to find favour in the eyes of a large section of the Indian population. In Chemistry, Anatomy, Midwifery and Surgery, the decided superiority of the English over the Native system, is admitted by all. This is unquestionably an age of improvement; everything around us indicates the progressive development of arts and sciences, and a society that does not keep pace with the onward march of intellect is certainly much behind the age.

There was a time when upwards of sixteen original medical writers, some of whose works are still extant, flourished in India, and medicines prepared according to the formulas of the *Ayurveda*—the best standard medical work—were supposed to have produced wholesome results, affording no inconsiderable amount of relief to thousands afflicted with diseases of various kinds, and even of a most malignant character. Under the Hindoo dynasty, every encouragement was given to the cultivation and improvement of medical science. Next to the Brahmins, the Vidya class was respected, though sometimes they are unjustly twitted with what is called a hybrid origin. It is, however, foreign to our purpose to determine this point, which seems to be enveloped in obscurity. The common theory on which the Hindoo system of physic is based, has reference to the country, the season and the age of the patient, to which is superadded the course of regimen suited to his physical organisation. The scientific and philosophical theory is that there are certain defined elements in the human body on the natural equilibrium of which mainly depends the health of man. The disturbance of this normal equilibrium, either by the increase or decrease of the essential ingredients, deranges the system and requires the use of medicines generally obtained from several kinds of indigenous drugs, bark, root, wood, fruits, flowers, metals, &c.

From the existing medical works according to which medicines are prepared and cures effected, it is evident that the Hindoo system is not entirely destitute of science, but the light it is capable of diffusing is greatly dimmed by a combination of unfavourable circumstances brought about by the overthrow of the Hindoo dynasty, the decay of learning in every branch of human knowledge, and the consequent growth and progress of empiricism.

In his eleventh discourse before the Asiatic Society, that distinguished orientalist, Sir William Jones, has said "Physic appears in these regions to have been from time immemorial as we see it practised at this day by the Hindoos and Mussulmans, a mere empirical history of diseases and medicines." This is presumably a remark applicable to a society but little removed from a state of barbarism, but the existence of such scientific works as *Ayurveda*, *Nidan*, *Churruck-Swasru*, *Sarasungraha*, *Boidya*, *Sarvuswn*, &c., furnishes abundant proof that the Hindoo system of physic is not altogether founded on empiricism.

In 1838 the Honorable the East India Company appointed a Committee, consisting of Drs. Jackson, Rankin Bramby, Pearson, W. B. O'Shaughnessy and Mr. James Prinsep, to examine and report upon the state of the Honorable Company's Dispensaries, and the possibility of substituting native drugs for European medicines, the primary object being two-fold, namely cheapness and efficacy. Death, ill health and the casualties of the service dispersed the Committee long before the members could accomplish the task imposed on them, and subsequently the whole charge devolved upon Dr. W. B. O'Shaughnessy, who, after the unwearied labour of four years, assisted by some of the best Native physicians, produced a work entitled "The Bengal Dispensary" published under the authority of the Government of India, which still remains a valuable monument of his indomitable zeal and untiring devotion to medical science.

Great attention has also been given to the scientific analysis of the various indigenous drugs by Roxburgh, Wallick, Ainslie, White, Arson, Royle, Pereira, Lindlay, Richard, &c., &c. The result of their analytical examination, though not so exhaustive as the very great importance of the subject required, was nevertheless very favourable to the opinion that the native system was based on fixed scientific principles, and that many of the drugs possessed great curative properties. Unfortunately the improved principles and important discoveries of modern Europe have not been sufficiently brought to bear on the simultaneous development of the native system. They have, however, proved greatly beneficial in teaching the native *kobirajes* to adopt, to a certain extent, the European method and regime.

It is a remarkable fact that even now, when this science may be said to be in a retrogressive stage both for want of adequate culture as well as of sufficient encouragement, there are a few Hindoo *kobirajes* * in this City, and in other parts of the country, whose treatment in chronic cases of fever, dysentery, diarrhœa, phthisis, pulmonary consumption, asthma, &c., proves, in a great measure, successful. Hence

* The most popular and successful among them are, Gunga Prosad Sen, Chunder Coomar Roy, Gopee Bullub Roy, Prosono Chunder Sen, Brojendro Coomar Sen, Kally Dass Sen, &c. They profess to practise on the principles of *Ayurveda*, the best standard work on Hindoo Medical Science, and their mode of treatment is much appreciated by respectable Hindoos.

in almost every respectable Hindoo family there is a competent *kobiraj*, who is always consulted in cases of a serious nature. It is generally considered that on the subject of pulsation greater weight is attached to the opinion of a Hindoo *kobiraj* than to that of an English doctor. By the pulse, in the different parts of our physical organisation, the state of the body may be ascertained and suitable remedies applied. In cases of severe indisposition among the Hindoos, the friends of a patient have not only to contend against the struggle between life and death, but to closely watch the last expiring flicker of vitality that he may be removed in time to the banks of the sacred stream for insuring his entrance into heaven.

It has been urged by some native physicians that the Sanskrit work, *Ayurveda*, above-mentioned, treats of anatomy and of the doctrine of the circulation of the blood. If this be true, great credit is doubtless due to its author for having made in a comparatively dark age such considerable advances in an important branch of medical science, without which medicine and surgery are of little avail. Chemistry, which enables us to distinguish the real properties of different substances, was certainly not unknown to the Hindoo physicians, because their medicines indicate a scientific selection of several ingredients mixed together to produce a certain result. But it can by no means be asserted that the people ever attained to a thorough knowledge, either in the one or the other, which can bear comparison with the perfection of the modern European system. In almost every department of human knowledge steady progress is the grand characteristic of the age, but in this country unhappily a spirit of scientific investigation has very nearly been extinguished simply for want of adequate cultivation and support.

If empirics abound in enlightened Christendom, where chemical analysis, scientific researches in materia medica and pharmacy, and anatomical demonstration and surgical operations almost daily bring to light new discoveries and inventions, what can be expected in a country where medical science has long since been in a state of absolute stagnation. Ignorant and unprincipled quacks, quite unacquainted with the rules of the Hindoo medical shastras, abound all over the country, which has for some years past been severely suffering from malarious fever of a virulent type, carrying death and devastation wherever it prevails.* They literally sport with the health of their patients, and the natural consequence is, hundreds and thousands of human beings are mercilessly sacrificed to their ignorance and cupidity. Not one in a hundred of those who call themselves *kobirajes* is acquainted with the principles of physic as laid down in the standard medical works of the Hindoos. Some of them have a few nostrums of their own, the composition of which is unknown to every one but themselves.

A Bengalee *kobiraj* carries a miniature dispensary about him. He takes with him a small packet, containing different kinds of pills or powders, wrapped up in a piece of paper, in small doses which are commonly used twice a day with ginger, honey, betel, roots of doov-grass, &c. He seldom uses phials; liquids, when required, are made in a patient's own house. His medicines are chiefly made of drugs, but he has neither a proper classification of them, nor a complete system of botany. He uses, however, certain preparations of oil, which are sometimes beneficially administered in chronic

---

* The general climate of Bengal has for some years past become very unhealthy, and as fever is the most prevalent epidemic in the Lower Provinces, Dr. D. N. Gupto's Mixture has become a patent medicine, proving efficacious in the majority of cases, so that the doctor is said to have made a very large fortune by the sale of it within a few years. As far as success is concerned, Dr. D. N. Gupto has almost become the minimized Holloway of Bengal. Several other Native assistant surgeons have from time to time endeavoured to offer their anti-malarious mixture to the inhabitants of Lower Bengal, but they have signally failed in winning public confidence and favor. Attempts at counterfeit trade marks have also been tried, but on conviction before a Court of Justice the guilty have been punished.

cases. These preparations are rather expensive, selling from two to ten Rupees per pound. The popularity of some of these *kobirajes* stands very high in Native public estimation. Almost every wealthy family in the interior as well as in the Town has its own physician. The fee of a quack in the villages is one Rupee on the first day of his visit, and he continues to attend twice daily until the patient recovers. When completely recovered, the physician gets one or two Rupees more, a suit of clothes and some provisions.

The introduction of English medicines into the interior, though not scientifically administered in every case, has very considerably affected the trade of the native quacks. Their occupation, it may be said, is nearly gone, because the doctors of the Bengalee class, more systematically trained under the auspices of the Government Vernacular Colleges, have, in a manner, superseded them. In strong fevers, instead of compelling the patient to fast for twenty-one days or longer, and restricting his regimen to parched rice, the Bengalee class doctor first reduces him by evacuations,* and then gives him either fever mixture, or cinchona febrifuge, or qui-

* The late indisposition of the Marquis of Ripon gave rise to many alarming rumours as to the probable turn and termination of the disease—malarious fever—with which he was unhappily attacked during his travels to and from Bombay, and which, according to telegraphic messages, had considerably weakened his constitution, and diminished the wonted activity and vigor of his mind. The antiquated notion that violent paroxysm of fever in a European in this country causes the abnormal depletion of the system by constant evacuations has still a strong hold on the popular mind. Hence a pessimist view was generally taken of the speedy and complete recovery of so good and beneficent a Governor-General, whose rule, though only just begun, has been happily inaugurated by several circumstances of a peculiarly hopeful character, tending, in no small degree, to make the people happy and contented by anticipation. The termination of the disastrous and ruinous Afghan war, the few public utterances of his Lordship bearing on the future policy of the Government of India for the general well-being of the subjects, and the sure prospect of an abundant harvest, and the consequent appreciable reduction in the price of rice—the main staff of life in this country—by nearly fifty per cent., have all combined to evoke a sincere desire and fervent hope among the people for the long continuance of a rule so nobly begun and beneficently administered. May undisturbed peace and undiminished plenty and prosperity be the distinguishing features of such a liberal, generous and pure administration, and may it end fitly what it has begun so auspiciously. In speaking thus favorably of the Marquis of Ripon's Government, I merely echo the sentiments of my countrymen from one end of the vast British Indian empire to the other.

nine mixture as he thinks best. In place of warm applications—the quondam regimen of a kobiraj in strong fevers—he gives ice or cold water, thus relieving the patient from the effects of a merciless abstinence and excessive thirst. On the periodical return of the unhealthy season in Bengal, *i. e.*, in the months of September, October, November and December, when the atmosphere is surcharged with a large quantity of vapour, these doctors generally reap a harvest of gain from their practice. It should be mentioned, however, that their imperfect knowledge and want of sufficient experience, are too often attended with the most disastrous results.

XVII.

HINDOO FEMALES.

THE condition of a Hindoo female, partially described in the preceding pages, is usually deplorable. The changes and vicissitudes to which her chequered life is subject are manifold. From the day she is ushered into the world to her dissolution, she is surrounded by adventitious circumstances, which, from the peculiar constitution of the society in which her life is cast, contain a larger admixture of misery than of happiness. Weak and frail as she assuredly is made by nature, the conventional forms and social usages to which she is religiously enjoined to adhere alike tend to deprive her of temporal and spiritual happiness. Born under unfavorable circumstances chiefly by reason of her sex, her life is rendered doubly miserable by the galling chains of ignorance and superstition. "Accursed the day when a woman child was born to me," was the emphatic exclamation of a Rajpoot when a female birth was announced. "The same motive," says Colonel Tod, "which studded Europe with convents, in which youth and beauty were immured until liberated by death, first prompted the Rajpoot to infanticide: and, however revolting the policy, it is perhaps kindness compared to incarceration. There can be no doubt that monastic seclusion, practised by the Frisians in France, the Langobardi in Italy and the Visigoths in Spain, was brought from Central Asia, the cradle of the Goths.* It is in fact a modification of the same feeling, which

* "The Ghikers, a Scythic race, inhabiting the banks of the Indus, at an early period of history were given to infanticide". "It was a custom," says Ferishta, "as soon as a female child was born, to carry her to the market place, and there proclaim aloud, holding the child in one hand, and a knife in the other, that any one wanting a wife might have her; otherwise she was immolated. By this means they had more men than women, which occasioned the custom of several husbands to one wife. When any husband visited her, she set up a mark at the door, which being observed by the others, they withdrew till the signal was removed."

characterizes the Rajpoot and the ancient German warrior, —the dread of dishonor to the fair: the former raises the poniard to the breast of his wife rather than witness her captivity, and he gives opiate to the infant, whom, if he cannot portion and marry to her equal, he dare not see degraded." Descending from the lofty ideal of a chivalrous Rajpoot character to the more familiar portraiture of tame Hindoo life in Bengal, we find the same sad destiny is the portion of a female in both cases. "When a female is born no anxious inquiries await the mother—no greetings welcome the new comer, who appears an intruder on the scene, which often closes in the hour of its birth. But the very silence with which a female birth is accompanied forcibly expresses sorrow." In almost every stage of life, from infancy to old age, her existence presents a uniform picture of gloominess, uncertainty, despondency, and neglect. Freedom of thought and independence of action—the natural birthrights of a rational being—are denied her not by her Creator but by a selfish, narrow-minded and crafty priesthood. She is treated and disposed of as if she were entirely destitute of the feelings and ideas of a sentient being. She dare not emerge from the unhealthy seclusion of the closely confined *andarmahal*, or female department, where suspicions and jealousies, envy and malignity are not unfrequently brewing in the boiling caldron of domestic discord. Born within the precincts of an ill-ventilated zenana, and cooped up in the cage of an uncongenial cell, she is destined to breathe her last in that unwholesome retreat.

A European lady can have no idea of the enormous amount of misery and privation to which the life of a Hindoo female is subjected. In her case, the bitters far counterbalance the sweets of life. The natural helplessness of her condition, the abject wretchedness to which she is inevitably doomed, the utter prostration of her intellect, the ascendency of a dominant priesthood exacting unquestioning submission to its selfish doctrines, the unmerited neglect of an unsympathetic world, and the appalling hardships and austerities which she is condemned to endure in the event of the death of her lord, literally beggar description. All the graces and accomplishments with which she is blessed by nature, and which have a tendency to adorn and ennoble humanity, are in her case unreasonably denounced as unfeminine endowments and privileges, to assert which is a sacrilegious act.

If she is ever happy, she is happy in spite of the cruel ordinances of her lawgiver, and the still more cruel usages and institutions of her country. Manu, the greatest fountain of authority, has expressly inculcated the doctrine that no man other than a Brahmin should receive the blessings of knowledge, and much more severely was the rule enforced in the case of females, who were held to be naturally unfit for mental culture! It was worse than a blasphemy to attempt to educate a female; she was born in ignorance, she must die in ignorance. All the horrors of a premature and certain widowhood were pictured forth to her eyes, were she to make an effort to enlighten her mind.* How shamefully contracted were the views of the Hindoo lawgiver in respect of the progressive development of the human intellect! His prohibitory injunction was and is now more honored in the breach than in observance.

---

* The Hindoo lawgivers, whatever their shortcomings in other respects, showed a great insight into human nature when they looked more to women than men for the comparative stability of their doctrines. That the perpetual ignorance of the former promises a permanent harvest of gain to the hierarchy, is quite evident. If a correct return were available as to the number of pilgrims who periodically visit the different holy places throughout the country, it would doubtless establish the fact that upwards of two-thirds of such pilgrims are females. If it were not for their pertinacious adherence to their traditional faith, the Brahminical creed, at least in the great centres of education, would have long since fallen into desuetude. The blind unquestioning faith of the female devotees in their gods and goddesses is the great secret of the very high estimation in which they are still held. If we educate the females and gradually disabuse their minds of early prejudices, we not only lay the axe at the very root of idolatry, but pave the way for the ultimate recognition of the true religion.

From the moment a female child is brought into the world, a new source of anxiety arises in the minds of its parents, which becomes more and more intense as it advances in years. The thought of educating the child is not what troubles their heads, it is a thought which is at the furthest remove from their imagination; but the idea how to dispose of it in the world continually preys on their minds. The child, perfectly unconscious of the fate that awaits it, begins to handle the playthings set before it, and as nature in almost every case works intuitively, it soon learns to make a miniature kitchen with earthen pots and pans resembling that in the midst of which it has to spend the greater portion of its existence. It is a noteworthy fact that a Hindoo lady even when placed in affluent circumstances does not consider it beneath her dignity to occasionally take a part in the *cuisine*, or at least in making preparations for the same, though the family has professional cooks in its employ, the principal object being to feed her husband and children with extra delicacies prepared with her own hand. Instead of idle and unprofitable talk and scandalous gossipings, reflecting on the characters of others, such an occupation is deserving of commendation.*

When six or seven years of age, the mother endeavours to initiate the girl in the first course of simple *Bratas* or religious vows, which are destined, as has been already shewn, to exercise a vast influence on her mind. The germs of superstition being thus sown so early take a deep root. Meanwhile the anxiety of the mother for her marriage increases with her growth. Numerous proposals are received and rejected, till

* The late Baboo Rajbullub Roy Chowdhry, of Baripore, a very wealthy zemindar, south of Calcutta, used, it was said, to bring up the girls of his family, which was almost a small colony, in the art of cooking all sorts of native dishes, from the highly spiced *polowyá* to simple *dhall-bath* and vegetable curry; he also taught them to bring up water for culinary purposes from a tank inside of the house in silver *ghara* or pots. Though he possessed the most practical of all worldly advantages,—the power of a purse,—yet he did not hesitate to initiate the girls in the art of cooking, that they may be fully prepared to perform the duty in case of necessity. I can easily cite other instances of a similar nature, but I believe they are not necessary.

at length a selection is made according to the rules stated in a former sketch. In this manner, persons are married with as much indifference as cattle are yoked together, they are disposed of according to the judgment of their parents, without the parties, who are to live together till death, having the slightest opportunity of seeing each other, much less of studying each other's disposition.

If a female child possess, as is very rarely the case, finely chiselled features, embodying the ideal of a Hindoo beauty, the breast of the mother is freed for a time, but for a time only, from perturbation or internal agitation. It may be she is congratulated on the birth of so beautiful a child, and it is but natural that she should indulge in pleasant delusions about the future of her offspring. She looks forward to a match at once desirable and happy. Fed with such hopes, she cherishes many a fond idea of the wealth of joys in store for her daughter. But how often are our brightest hopes blasted by the ruthless hand of fortune.

If, on the contrary, the girl be deficient in beauty, the bosom of the mother is perpetually disturbed by gloomy forebodings, which no worldly advantage can effectually remove, no reasoning can sufficiently suppress. The reassuring admonition of congenial minds may sustain her spirits for a time, but whenever alone or disengaged from the toils of domestic duties, her mind almost involuntarily reverts to the future destiny of the girl. As day by day she grows older, and her features begin to assume a more distinctive form, the deformity, which was but faintly perceived at first, becomes more striking. The mother herself, perhaps, being a living illustration of how fruitless were the attempts of her parents to secure for her a desirable match, naturally feels a strong misgiving as to the good fortune of her child.

While the hearts of the parents are thus filled with disquieting thoughts, the girl is perfectly unconscious of the fate that awaits her. She laughs and sports about, regardless of what is written on her forehead by the *Bidhata poorooslı.* The performance of the religious vow in her infancy, having for its object the securing a good husband, might incidentally remind her of marriage, but the thought passes off in a moment like the streaks of a morning cloud. Hence it has been justly said that the happiest days in the life of a Hindoo female are those preceding her marriage. If in Bengal, under the paternal care of a Christian Government, she is not permitted to become a victim to the poppy at her dawn, or the flames at her riper years, like her Rajpoot sister in times of yore, she is ever and anon subject to the appalling hardships of a *bidhaba* life, or widowhood. Though too young to fully realise the thousand and one evils of such a wretched existence, yet the living examples she daily and hourly sees around her make, to use a native phrase, "her hands and feet enter into her belly."

To those who have studied the existing state of Hindoo society, it is a matter no less of wonder than of gratulation that the system of early marriage, the arbitrary manner in which it is consummated, and the utter absence of the voice and consent of the parties thus affianced, deriding the very idea of the slightest opportunity being given to study each other's disposition and habitude, should produce such a large amount of conjugal felicity, which is the fundamental object of this solemn compact. In every nation removed from barbarism, marriage is a recognised ordinance, alike sanctioned by the law of God and the law of man. It is a solemn covenant between a man and a woman to love each other through all the vicissitudes of life, till the union is dissolved by the death of either. We may go further and say that even then the tie of relationship does not become totally extinct, inasmuch as the party surviving has to provide for the nurture and education of children, should there be any. Such being the nature of a matrimonial engagement, it is next to impossible that a boy of fourteen wedded to a girl of nine should be capable of forming an adequate idea of the grave responsibility. The evil must work its own remedy with the general spread of education and the growth of a sound system of domestic and social ecomony, because the existing one is unhealthy and unnatural. It is useless to dilate on the evil consequences of early marriage, they are clearly apparent in the every-day life of a Hindoo.

Nature is so propitious to us in every respect that out of evil she brings good. When the female, destitute as she is of the blessings of knowledge, becomes the mother of several children, she is raised to the rank of a governess, or in other words, she becomes a *ghinni*, or head of the family. To all intents and purposes, she seems to understand her duties so thoroughly that almost instinctively she exercises a salutary control over a number of young girls, newly married, corrects all improprieties of conduct, and teaches them to cherish feelings of mutual kindness, love and affection.

In many cases, however, it must be acknowledged, the custom of several families—all branches of the same stem,—living together under one roof, is a fruitful source of evil, often embittering the sweet enjoyments of a peaceful conjugal life. Where there is no harmony among the several female members of a family, the slightest misunderstanding occasions bitterest quarrels, especially when there is no recognised *ghinni* or female head to check the same, or reconcile the parties by matronly advice. For instance, if one son in a family be well-to-do in the world, and another does not possess the same advantages, it is ten to one but that the wife of the former constantly advises him to mess separately, if not to remove to a different house, and as unequal combination is always disadvantageous to the weaker side, the latter has to put up with slights and indignities which are oftentimes unbearable, and terminate in a separation either in food or domicile, or both. It is a well established fact that a woman is the principal cause of a disruption between brothers and other members of a family. Though she is mild, soft, kind and flexible, yet she belies her nature when sordid self and mean avarice exert a dominant sway over her mind. Stinted in her culture and contracted in her views, Mammon is her god, and she looks to the welfare of her husband and her own children as the chief end of her existence. She is naturally loath to give a share of the affection of her husband to a rival; she also cannot brook the idea of frittering his earnings among his kindred. I have known of the most affectionate and devoted of brothers not being able to see each other's face under the all powerful influence of petticoat government. A European becomes a housekeeper as soon as he marries. The arrangement is an excellent one, no doubt, and as educated Hindoos are very much disposed to imitate English manners, the practice where feasible is gradually gaining ground, despite the prevalence of the old patriarchal system throughout the greater portion of the country. There is a common native saying, which runs thus: "as many brothers, so many abodes." It is to a certain extent a striking illustration of the existing state of things; harmony and peace can scarcely be found in a family where brothers are swayed, as they must be, by the irresistible influence of their wives.* To the credit of the patriarchal system, there still exist in every part of the country numerous families that scout the idea of a segregation.

* At the time of the *Churruck Poojah* or swinging festival, which takes place about the middle of April, the *Khàshàrees* or Braziers of Calcutta are accustomed to make *Sungs* or caricature-representations of different sorts of familiar scenes, illustrative of the prevailing manners of the present age. In many cases they hit off the mark so admirably that they cannot fail to make a deep impression on the popular mind. Among other representations they once exhibited a caricature of a son taking a wife on his shoulder, while dragging a mother by a rope round her neck, exemplifying thereby the respective estimation in which each is held.

Turning from the dark to the bright side of the picture, it is gratifying to observe that of late years, attention has been directed to, and laudable exertions are being made for, the education of Hindoo females. Nothing can compare in importance with the steady progress of this movement. After the movement had been begun by the Missionary Societies, the late Hon. Mr. Drinkwater Bethune gave an important impetus to this noble cause from the side of Government. These examples have since been followed up by other devoted friends of native improvement, and the Government has fully recognised the paramount importance of the object. This combination of efforts has already produced the most gratifying results. That there is a growing desire for learning among the females by the study of such elementary books, Bengallee and English, as have a tendency to improve their understanding, is a patent fact. Not only young girls, whose age permits them to attend schools, but grown up ladies, who are confined within the precincts of a zenana, are alike influenced by this commendable desire. Almost every respectable Hindoo family in Calcutta has a Christian governess, who besides giving primary and Bible instruction, teaches all sorts of needle-work—an art in which considerable progress has been made within the last few years.* This is an indication of the growth of a refined taste which is a great step towards the cause of national improvement. As we have said elsewhere, instead of spending their time in idle talk and unprofitable occupation, if not in unpleasant dissension, they now vie with each other in producing works of art and usefulness, and as a matter of course the annual distribution of rewards is a great incentive to exertion. It

* An annual fair or *mela* is held near Calcutta, at which the best specimens of needle-work executed by Hindoo females are exposed to public view, and prizes awarded by European and Native gentlemen. Great credit is due to Baboo Nobo Gopal Mitter, the editor of the National Paper, for this annual exhibition. Unfortunately the *mela* is languishing for want of sufficient public support.

is devoutly to be wished that this desire for learning and taste for works of art should gradually spread and be appreciated throughout the length and breadth of the land. In the interior, however, the mass of the people of all ranks and of both sexes are still as remote from the influence of this improvement as they were centuries ago.

It is a pity that Hindoo females are withdrawn from schools the moment they are married; this is an insuperable obstacle to the full development of their mental powers. The progress made by some of them in the zenana is really very creditable, and challenges the commendation of all who have the elevation of native female character at heart. They are not only assiduous in the cultivation of feminine graces and accomplishments, but their superior grasp of thought and language rank them among the literary women of their country. Some thirty years back the Hindoo females of Bengal were immersed in ignorance; they were represented as degraded beings incapable of improvement; not one in a thousand could read or write; but since proper steps have been taken to remove this national reproach, they have evinced an ardent desire to enrich their minds by a course of study which, though not profound, is well fitted to adorn female life. The English Church Mission, "The Scottish Ladies' Association," a department of the Church of Scotland Mission, the Free Church Mission, the American Mission, &c. are all doing an incalculable amount of good by their disinterested efforts to impart the blessings of knowledge to such zenana females as are precluded by being married from attending schools. The complete regeneration of India cannot be expected until the emancipation of the females is accomplished, practically proving to the world, as it has already done in a very limited degree, the palpable absurdity of Manu's interdictory edict, restraining them from cultivating their intellectual powers.

As a proof of the progress already made in the *higher* branches of female education, it is gratifying to state that two young ladies passed the First Arts' Examination of the Calcutta University at the end of last year. One of these was trained in the Bethune School, and the other in the Free Church Normal School. This examination represents a very considerable amount of acquirement, and is next to the B. A. Several other female candidates also passed the Entrance or Matriculation Examination at the same time. Similar progress has been reported from the Madras Presidency.

Authentic history furnishes abundant evidence of the prevalence of female education in the country to a considerable extent, until Mahomedan oppression not only proscribed Hindoo women from pursuing a literary career, but ultimately dragged them into a state of unhealthy seclusion for the preservation of their honor, which they valued more than their very life. In Rajpootana every respectable female was instructed to read and write. Of their intellectual endowments and knowledge of mankind, whoever has had opportunities of conversing with them could not fail to form a favorable impression.*

---

* "I have conversed for hours," says Colonel Tod, "with the Boondi queen-mother on the affairs of her government and welfare of her infant son, to whom I was left guardian by his dying father. She had adopted me as her brother: but the conversation was always in the presence of a third person in her confidence, and a curtain separated us. Her sentiments shewed invariably a correct and extensive knowledge, which was equally apparent in her letters, of which I had many. I could give many similar instances. The history of India is filled with anecdotes of able and valiant females. Ferishta in his history gives an animated picture of *Durgavati*, queen of Gurrah, defending the rights of her infant son against Akbar's ambition. Like another Boadicea, she headed her army, and fought a desperate battle with Asoph Khan, in which she was wounded and defeated; but scorning flight, or to survive the loss of independence, she, like the Roman of old in a similar predicament, slew herself on the field of battle."

The accomplished Maharatta lady—Roma Bai—who lately visited Calcutta, affords a remarkable example of an educated Hindoo woman. She is an excellent Sanskrit scholar, well read in *Sreemut Bhagabat*. Several Pundits were astonished at her wonderful acquirements.

XVIII.

POLYGAMY.

IN this, as well as in some other eastern countries, polygamy has from time out of mind been in existence. That it is subversive of moral order and of conjugal felicity, is admitted by all who have paid the slightest degree of attention to the very many evil consequences of this abnormal institution. It is a violation of a just and divine law, opposed to the nurture and education of children, and inconsistent with the due equality of the sexes. In every country where this obnoxious practice prevails, and is dignified with the hallowed name of a social and religious ordinance, as is done in India, woman occupies a degraded position, and society is rude and unexpansive in its character. The most heinous crimes are committed without remorse, and conscience is seared, as it were, with a red-hot iron. "Nature has designed woman to be the equal of man as a moral and intellectual being; and confined to the exercise of her own proper duties as a wife and mother, she is placed in a favourable position as relates to her own happiness and the happiness of her husband." Much of the civilization of Europe is due to the high position of the fair sex in the social scale. Their education, their capacity for rearing their children in orderly and virtuous habits, their elevated conceptions of a Supreme Being, their social and domestic manners, the purity of their lives, their natural tenderness and affection, their freedom, and the moral influence of their actions on society, give them a rank in no way inferior to that of the other sex. But in this country, it is painful to realise that they are not only denied the inestimable blessings of a good education but that their first lawgiver has condemned them to a state of abject servitude. "Women have no business" says Manu, "with the text of the Veda, this is the law fully settled: having, therefore, no evidence of law, and no knowledge of expiatory texts, sinful women must be as foul as falsehood itself; and this is a fixed rule. Through their passion for men, their mutable temper, their want of settled affection, and their perverse nature, (let them be guarded in this world ever so well,) they soon become alienated from their husbands." Manu allotted to such women "a love of their bed, of their seat, and of ornament, impure appetites, wrath, weak flexibility, desire of mischief and bad conduct. Day and night must women be held by their protectors in a state of dependence." Apart from their practically servile condition, the apparent complacence with which polygamy is tolerated, and the facility with which a plurality of wives can be obtained, are circumstances which poison the perennial source of conjugal felicity, reduce them to a state of moral and intellectual degradation, and sap the very foundation of virtue. "A barren wife," says Manu, "may be superseded by another in the eighth year; she whose children are all dead, in the tenth; she who brings forth only daughters, in the eleventh year; she who speaks unkindly, without delay." Bullal Sen, who, if I mistake not, had first established the system of *Koolinism* in Bengal, and prescribed certain rules in favor of polygamy, was singularly deficient in foresight and wisdom when he entirely overlooked the evil consequences inseparable from this monstrous matrimonial arrangement, so pregnant with mischief in whatever aspect we view it. Any artificial institution which is subversive of divine law will, in the main, prove highly unfavourable to the best interests of society. The marriage of a man with but one wife is an arrangement which should never be departed from. To dispose of the ministering angels of our existence, without the slightest regard to their future happiness, and yoke them to an unprincipled libertine, or a Koolin perhaps on the verge of his grave, is a system alike destructive of all social, benevolent and humane feelings. A Koolin has no regard, much less sympathy, for any one of his numerous wives, on the contrary he looks to them for gain and other worldly advantages. It is a notorious fact that Koolin wives after their marriage almost invariably live with their parents, thus virtually closing all avenues to the growth of affection between the husband and wife. The one is as estranged from the other as if there had been no bond of union between them. As the temptations to vicious indulgences are so very powerful and numerous in this wicked world of ours, the unscrupulous Koolin females of the sacerdotal class often sacrifice chastity at the altar of sensuality. The perpetration of the most horrible crimes is the necessary effect. The fault does not rest so much with the poor unfortunate females as with the diabolical system which openly tolerates and religiously upholds polygamy. That it is an unnatural state, even the most thoughtless will readily admit. In every case it is the source of perpetual disputes and misery. Domestic happiness can have no place in a family in which more than one wife lives. I have known many a person who under the impulse of passion had entered into this unnatural state deplore it as the greatest of all domestic afflictions. Even separate cook rooms, separate apartments, and separate *mehals*, and dining and sleeping alternately with two wives with the greatest punctuality, and giving the same set of ornaments to both, were not enough to ensure harmony, peace and tranquillity. Indeed it has become a proverb among the Hindoos, that "one wife would rather go with her husband to the gloomy regions of *yama* (Pluto) than see him sit with the other." As has already been described, a tender girl of five years of age is, as her *first* instruction before emerging from her nursery, initiated into the *Brata* or religious vow of *Sayjooty*, the primary object of which is the ruin and destruction of a *Sateen* or rival wife. The germs or jealousy against, and contempt for, a rival being thus sown so early, they take deep root and expand in time so as to become absolutely ineradicable.

When the presence of two wives in the same house is attended with so much disquietude, the evil arising from the practices of professional Koolins is much greater. They are married to a number of females whose prospect of connubial bliss is as remote as the poles are asunder. Instead of true love and genuine attachment, the legitimate conditions of matrimony, the natural apathy of the husband is often requited by the infidelity of his numerous wives; nor can it be otherwise, the visits of the husband being, like those of a meteor, few and far between. Being destitute of the finer susceptibilities of human nature, and looking upon matrimony as a matter of traffic, he regards his wives as so many automata whose happiness is not at all identified with his own. Influenced by a sordid love of gain, bred and brought up in the lap of ignorance and laziness, and pampered by effeminate habits, he leads a profligate life typical of utter demoralisation. He cares as little for the chastity of his wives as a child does for the nicety of his playthings. By rank, profession and habit he is a debauchee. His sense of female honor is totally blunted. The thought of nurturing and educating his numerous children never enters into his mind. He knows not how many sons and daughters he has, whether legitimate or illegitimate; he is not capable of recognising them, simply because he has seldom or never seen their faces. If he keep a register of the number of his wives, he keeps no record of the number of his children. When he wants money, he pounces on such a father-in-law as can satisfy him. If he keep one wife at home, it is not from warmth of affection that he does so, but merely for his own convenience and comfort; she is made to discharge all the menial offices of a domestic maid-servant. Though never placed in affluent circumstances, yet he is the lord of thirty, forty or fifty women. It has been very aptly remarked by an eminent writer who had paid much attention to the manners and customs of the Hindoos,—that "amongst the Turks, seraglios are confined to men of wealth, but here, a Hindoo Brahmin, possessing only a shred of cloth and a piece of thread, *(poita)* keeps more than a hundred mistresses." Indeed such a system of monstrous polygamy is without a parallel in the history of human depravity. Prostitution, adultery, and the horrible crime of the destruction of the foetus in the womb by means of deleterious drugs administered by old women, are the inevitable consequences of this unnatural state of things. It is an undeniable fact that the daughters of Koolin Brahmins, abandoned by their unprincipled husbands, are often led into the forbidden paths of life, partly through the impulse of passion amidst the seductions of a wicked world, and partly through their exceedingly miserable circumstances. The houses of ill fame in Calcutta and other large towns are filled with women of this infamous character, and the inhuman practice of *patefaláno* prevails to an alarming extent, notwithstanding the increased vigilance of the police. Some fifty years ago a number of respectable Hindoos felt so disgusted at the mischievous tendency of the Koolin system of marriage that they were on the eve of memorialising the Government to put down the practice by a legislative enactment, such as had been done in the prohibition of *sati* or female immolation, but they were assured that the authorities would not interfere in the domestic and social usages of the people.

It is gratifying to observe, however, that the growth of intelligence and the march of intellect has of late years greatly counteracted the influence of this monstrous evil. If the Rulers will not attempt to abolish a social system opposed to the feelings of natural affection by the denunciation of the severest temporal penalties, the good sense of the people who are victimised by it must be appealed to for its total suppression.

The following extract from Mr. Ward's excellent work on the Hindoos will give the reader an idea of the fearful extent to which Koolinism prevailed in Bengal some fifty or sixty years back, when English education could scarcely be said to have commenced the work of reformation or rather disintegration.

"Notwithstanding the predilection for *koolins* they are more corrupt in their manners than any of the Hindoos. I have heard of a Koolin Brahmin, who, after marrying sixty-five wives, carried off another man's wife, by personating her husband. Many of the Koolins have a numerous posterity. I select five examples, though they might easily be multiplied: Oodhoy Chunder, a Brahmin, late of Bágnápárá, had sixty-five wives, by whom he had forty-one sons, and twenty-five daughters. Ramkinkur, a Brahmin, late of Kooshda, had seventy-two wives, thirty-two sons, and twenty-seven daughters. Vishnooram, a Brahmin, late of Gundulpárá, had sixty wives, twenty-five sons and fifteen daughters. Gouree Churn, a Brahmin, late of Treebanee, had forty-five wives, thirty-two sons, and sixteen daughters. Ramakant, a Brahmin, late of Bhoosdaranee, had eighty-two wives, eighteen sons and twenty-six daughters; this man died about the year 1810, at the age of 85 years or more, and was married, for the last time, only three months before his death. Most of these marriages are sought after by the relations of the female, to keep up the honor of their families; and the children of these marriages invariably remain with their mothers, and are maintained by the relations of these females. In some cases, a Koolin father does not know his own children."

Not only the rules of caste, but *poverty* is also a great barrier to the marriage of Koolin women, a fact which has been very feelingly deplored in the following lines. Maidenly anxiety finds a natural vent in them :—

"Out spake the bride's sister,
As she came frae the byre,
O! gin I were but married,
It's a' that I desire;
But we poor folk maun live single,
And do the best we can,
I dinna care what I should want
If I could but get a man."
Another, and O! what will come o' me!
And O! what will I do?
That sic a braw lassie as I
Should die for a wooer, I trow."

When Bullal Sen first introduced this obnoxious system, which went under the euphonious title of the Order of Merit, he little anticipated that the very small seed of mischief he then planted would soon grow into a luxuriant tree, and produce an abundant crop of evils, poisoning the very source of domestic felicity. It requires no depth of thought to predict that the evil is destined to die a natural death, as all such social evils are fated to do, when ignorance and superstition are driven into their congenial darkness. Though many a Hindoo still lives in the sin of polygamy without any particular repentance, yet the irresistible progress of virtue, like that of truth, will ultimately teach him that it is an unsafe foundation on which to build the sober structure of domestic happiness.

The details of the following conversation between a husband, his old mother, and his two wives, placed at the disposal of the writer by a friend, may, he trusts, not be out of place:—

"What is this noise for," exclaims Radhamoney, a widow, (the name of the mother) coming out of the *thacoor ghur* in which she was worshipping; "this noise, this tumult, this quarrel, this wringing of the hands, these curses will surely drive away Luckhee from the house, it is enough to make the devil fly; you have lost every sense of shame, ***mago ma***, your clamour has deafened my ears, where shall I go? one is apt to leave her clothes behind. You have been served right; it was only the other day that Grish, (name of the son) lost 5,000 Rupees in a case at the Burra Adawlut (High Court.) If I be a *Sati* (chaste woman), I say, you two women (pointing to the two wives) will be beggared and reduced to the condition of *harrees* (those who carry night soil); in what unlucky hour did these two women enter the house. You are both *Rakhasees* (female cannibals.) Day by day, sorrow is eating into the vitals of my son, his golden body is being darkened every day; Oh! *Bidhata* (God) you have ordained this for me?" "Ullungo (name of the maid-servant) what is the cause of this uproar?" asks the mother. "*Ma*, what will I say," replies the maid-servant; "the cook *first* gave the *vath*, boiled rice to Comul," (name of the daughter of the first wife). "Is this all? nothing more?" continues the mother; "my Báchá (child) has had no food for seven days, being ill with fever. You all know this; the *kobeeraj* (physician) this morning has ordered some rice for her, whereupon the second wife, all this while roaring and bawling, cursing and swearing, stepped forward and said, it is past nine and my Hurree (her son's name, 12 years old) has not yet got a morsel, his belly has shrunk, and the school time is come; if late, his master will make him stand." Radhamoney, the old mother, or *ghini*, sent for the cook, and enquired if the rice were ready. "Yes, *ma*, Hurree Baboo came into the cook room half an hour ago, and I asked him to take his meal; *chotta ma* (second wife) prevented him, because I *first* gave the rice to Comul who was so long ill." "Where is Hurree now?" enquired the old lady. The maid-servant replied "*Chotta ma* gave him a few pice and told him to go to his school, though he could have eaten rice if he liked." "Let Grish return home," added the old lady, "and I will tell him to send me to Benares without delay; I am sick of your incessant broils; for giving Comul rice *first* you two *bous* fell into a quarrel, and cursed each other so fearfully that you, *burra bou* (first wife), ate the head of Hurree, and you, *chotta bou* (second wife), ate the head of Comul's husband."*

It was evening, and Grish, the son, returned home from office. Before he had time to take off his office dress, the old mother, impatient to tell him what had occurred during the day, and with tears in her eyes, thus addressed him: "You, my son, have brought the greatest curse on yourself by marrying two wives; to-day the whole family has been starving, and why? because Comul, suffering from fever for the last eight days, had got a little rice this morning, and she ate *first; chotta bou*, therefore, prevented her son from eating anything, and sent the little *bacha* to the school without rice. From what *pajee* (mean) families have you brought these two females? I can no longer remain in the house. Under the slightest pretext, like infamous wenches, they not only brawl but curse each other and the son and son-in-law into the bargain. Can Luckhee dwell in such a house? send me to Benares instantly, I can no longer live in such a hell of a place. Your wives have made it a regular hell." The son consoles the old mother, promising that everything would be done according to her wish, begging her at the same time to eat something, and adding that he does not mind whether his two wives eat or not. After going through the evening service, he slept outside that night, pondering what should be done for the future quiet of the family. Next day he removed the first wife to her father's house, because the second wife is always the *Zuburdust*, imagining that one hand can never make a

* Eating the head means wishing death. When two rival wives fall out they literally become frantic through anger and jealousy. With shaking hands and dishevelled locks they abuse and curse each other most violently.

clap. But he was sadly mistaken, the deserted wife, continually brooding over her misfortune, at length resolved to put an end to her existence, and accordingly one night took an overdose of opium, and bade a final adieu to the world.

The above story is founded on real life and should serve as a warning to those who under the impulse of passion blindly run into a state of polygamy, which is undoubtedly one of the greatest domestic evils among the natives.

XIX.

HINDOO WIDOWS.

THE system of early marriage, and the barbarous institution of condemning a Hindoo female to a life of perpetual widowhood after the death of her husband, are evils which cannot be too strongly deprecated. In this country, owing to the prevalence of early marriage and the manner in which it is consummated, a Hindoo does not become a housekeeper immediately after his marriage. The wife generally remains one or two years with her parents, occasionally going to her father-in-law's house for a few days only; her husband pays her a visit now and then, but not without the special invitation of his mother-in-law. The object of such an invitation is evidently to make the son-in-law behave well towards her daughter. For the attainment of this object, as I have described before, no means is left untried. Indeed it has become a proverb among the Hindoos that when a man fares sumptuously, it is said, he has been fed with all the fondness shown to a son-in-law. It has always struck me that if a Hindoo female were permitted to re-marry after the death of her first husband, the affection of a mother-in-law for a son-in-law would not have been so warm as it now is under the existing state of things, which admits of no alternative.

Living under the paternal roof for one or two years after her marriage, a Hindoo girl sometimes becomes a widow,*—

---

* Such a widow is called a *Korayraur*, or one who has never enjoyed the company of her husband. A stronger term of female reproach can scarcely be found in the Hindoo vocabulary. From the day this terrible bereavement occurs she is constrained by conventional rules, in such cases, to put off from her hand the *iron bangle*, but owing to her tender age she is tacitly permitted to continue to wear the gold bangle and a bordered *Saree* cloth. She is forbidden to use fish—her most favorite dish,—and she must partially fast on every *ekadossee*, or eleventh day of the increase or decrease of the moon. When she arrives at the age of twenty her life presents an unvaried picture of despair and wretchedness. She becomes a regular widow.

a state of life which is unspeakably miserable. When a young female of ten or eleven years of age loses her husband, with whom perhaps she had scarcely ever exchanged a single word, she is quite unconscious of the unmitigated misery she is fated to endure for the remainder of her long existence.* Deplorable as such a condition undoubtedly is, it becomes doubly miserable from the cold, uncongenial and unsympathetic atmosphere by which she is surrounded, and the uncared-for neglect with which she is treated ever afterwards. Except a mother, who can adequately conceive the thousand and one miseries which are in store for the daughter? It is a gloomy picture from the beginning to the end, and the gloom deepens as time rolls over her devoted head. Cursed be the name of the lawgiver who has made such a cruel ordinance, and cursed the society that has become a thrall to it! Opposed to the feelings of humanity and natural affection, the divine lawgiver of the Hindoos, Manu, expressly enjoins that "although the state of widowhood might be deemed onerous by the fair sex of the west, it would be considered little hardship in the east. Let her emaciate her body, by living voluntarily on pure flowers, roots and fruits, but let her not, when her lord is deceased, even pronounce the name

---

* It has been justly remarked, and I believe is in most cases borne out by facts, that a Hindoo widow generally lives to a very long age. Her simple and abstemious habits, her devotional spirit, her scanty meal once a day, her total abstinence from food of any kind on the eleventh day of the increase and decrease of the moon, besides other days of close fast, neutralising in a great measure the effects of every kind of irregularity from whatever cause arising, and the fearful amount of hardships she is accustomed to endure, all contribute to prolong her existence. Surely her life may be said to extend in the inverse ratio of her misery. It is a common expression used by a Hindoo widow, shewing her contempt of life, "will she ever die? *Yama*, Pluto, seems to have forgotten her?" If the statistics of the land are consulted, it will assuredly be found that Hindoo widows comparatively speaking enjoy a longer life than the adult male population, because the latter is subject to irregularities and other adverse contingencies of life which the former is almost entirely free from. It is not uncommon to see a Hindoo widow of eighty, ninety or a hundred years of age. In short, nature evidently seems to have exemplified in her the symbol of misery associated with longevity.

It is also a remarkable fact that idolatry and superstition chiefly owe their continued influence to the wide-spread ignorance of these female devotees. At a religious festival, nearly three-fourths of the assembly are composed of widows.

of another man. A virtuous wife ascends to heaven, if, after the decease of her lord, she devote herself to pious austerity; but a widow, who slights her deceased husband by *marrying again*, brings disgrace on herself here below and shall be excluded from the seat of her lord. Abstinence from the common pursuits of life, and entire self-denial, are rewarded by high renown in this world, and in the next the abode of her lord, and procure for her the title of *sadhvi* or the virtuous." From the above it is evident that widowhood has prevailed in this country from time out of mind. Its mischievous tendency is apparent in the degraded and corrupt state of female society. We can never thoroughly conquer nature; we can never restrain our passions so effectually as to render ourselves proof against temptation. The frailty of women is admittedly great, and the ease with which they may be seduced into the forbidden paths of life is too well-known to need being enlarged on. However sedulously a Hindoo mother may guard the virtue of her widowed daughter, and however forcibly she may inculcate the doctrine of purity of life and manners, it proves but a feeble barrier against the irresistible impulse of passion. Numerous instances are on record, proving the utter futility of human efforts to contend successfully against nature in this respect. A young widow may be sent to the holy cities of Benares and Brindabun, where she is not unfrequently removed with her mother or grandmother to spend the remainder of her days in a state of isolated seclusion and religious service, but this is a poor safe-guard for the preservation of constancy and virtue. Volumes after volumes have been written on the subject, denouncing in an unmistakable manner the monstrous perversity of the existing system, but the evil has taken such a deep root in the social economy of the people that the utmost exertions must be put forth before it can be wholly eradicated.

The evils of widowhood are not only confined to the endurance of accumulated hardships, and self-denials enough to rend asunder the tenderest chord of humanity, but they likewise extend to unlawful connections, and the perpetration of another crime, that of abortion, which is no less revolting in enormity than infanticide itself. Many respectable families, which are otherwise esteemed for their meritorious actions, have more or less sunk in honor from this indelible stigma; a few have even lost their caste and status in society from the above cause. In the primitive state of Hindoo society, when every female other than a wife was regarded either as a mother or sister according to age, irregular intercourse was almost unknown, but in these days of libertinism perfect purity of life is rarely known. Our divine lawgiver, in view to the interests of humanity and female honor, ought to have made proper provision by lending his authority and sanction to a system of widow remarriage within a reasonable period of life. Some such edict would have been alike honorable to our venerable sage, and beneficial to those who are morally and socially most deeply interested in it; but unfortunately his cruel dicta, running counter to the fundamental principles of virtue and morality, have necessarily engendered a rank crop of evils, undermining the very foundation of human happiness.

The benevolent exertions of that high priest of Nature, Pundit Isswara Chunder Vidyasagar, Baboo Keshub Chunder Sen, the Brahmo apostle, and other Hindoo reformers, to promote the cause of widow marriage in particular, and female emancipation in general, have not, it is sad to contemplate, been attended with the measure of success they deserve, simply because the state of Hindoo society is not yet ripe for the innovation. I am, however, sanguine in my expectation that at no very distant future the progress of enlightenment will ultimately bring about the consummation so devoutly to be wished for. It is for the advanced pioneers to endeavour to remove the incrustation which age and learning have formed and tradition and custom enshrined with jealous and sedulous care. Until this is done, a Hindoo widow must continue to mourn her lot amidst the denunciations of a heartless world. Sighs will never cease flowing from her heart so long as she finds herself deprived of the master charm of life. She is now cast amongst the dregs and tatters of humanity. Bereft of the *substance* of what endears life to a female, she is constrained to cleave to the *shadow*, which is destined to leave her when she leaves the light of life. Losing all hope of worldly enjoyments, she deposits the treasures of her heart in the sanctuary of religion, convinced that to sell the world for the life to come is profitable. It is terrible to contemplate the awful amount of physical and mental suffering with all its varied complications, to which she is doomed; her life is a steadfast battle against misery, her soul soars in a vacuum where all is unreal, empty and hollow, and all the sweet enjoyments of life fall flat on her taste. Her mental strife is never over. She is like a weary swimmer who throws himself back and floats, because he is too much exhausted to swim longer, yet will not sink and let the cold and merciless water close over his head. Her spirit has broken wildly loose from its normal attitude, and her mind is overwhelmed in a surging tide of misery. From the day she loses her husband, she has a new lease of life, and a miserable lease it must be. She will not cease to lament until her soul itself shall die. If she could say, joy was once her portion, it lighted on her as the bird rests on the tree in passing and takes wing, yet she would now say, her existence is so unlife-like that to her death is sweet. She is a poor fallen outcast of humanity. No one can enter into her feelings and views of things. She has no influence, no control over herself, she cannot turn over a new leaf within her own mind. Though society is almost a necessity of our existence, yet she lives wholly alone; a cheerless train of thoughts always haunts her mind, she feels a dismal void in her heart, she finds herself cut off at once and for ever from one most dear to her, no conversation, however pleasant, can bring her consolation or cheat her grief. The tide of settled melancholy threatens her reason. As an outcast, she is religiously forbidden to take a part in any of the social and domestic concerns of life, tending to relieve the ennui of a wearisome existence, and to enliven the mind for a while. She is a living example of an angel sent by heaven to minister to the comforts of man, turned by a cruel institution into a curse. Estranged from the affection of those who are, by the ties of consanguinity, nearest and dearest to her, she passes her days like a recluse, quite apart from the communion of society. She stares and gazes wildly at every festive celebration, while, as the poet sings,

> "The glad circle round them yield their souls
> To festive mirth and wit that knows no gall."

If she have longings irrepressible and cravings insatiable to lend her hand to any *shoova karma* (meritorious work), her widowed condition interposes an insurmountable barrier to her participation therein, as if everything would be desecrated when touched by her polluted hand.

As a sentient being, endowed with all the finer susceptibilities of human nature, is it possible that she should so far forget herself as not to feel the bitterest pangs of despondency at her hopelessly forlorn condition? Driven from the genial atmosphere of a social circle, she drags a loathsome existence in this selfish and unsympathetic world. Except she that gave her birth, who would deign to look upon her with love and affection? Instead of being regarded, as she assuredly should be, as the soul of simplicity, a living picture of sweet innocence, she is shunned as one whose very presence portends evil. If she possess unaffected modesty and a keen sense of honor and virtue, who is to recognise and appreciate those amiable qualities in a society which is preposterously estranged from all natural susceptibilities? If she have riches what would that avail her, a poor misguided victim of superstition! * Her charity, instead of being founded on the catholic principles of genuine liberality shewing a discriminate breadth of view, too often exhibits an unhappy tenacity of adhesion to exclusiveness in the performance of idolatrous ceremonies. If she is placed above the atmosphere of artificialness, it is her misfortune to be surrounded by a concatenation of conventional restrictions which render her life a visible embodiment of helpless misery and anguish, and if she ever appeals, she appeals to the Being who is the only friend of the hopeless and the poor. To attempt to reconcile a widow to her forlorn lot is to tell a patient burning with fever not to be thirsty. Her days are dismal, her nights are dreary.

It was the dread of widowhood, and the unmitigated life-long miseries inseparable from it, that led fifty wives at a time to ascend the funeral pyre of a Rajpoot husband, with all the composure of a philosophic mind. It redounds greatly to the credit of the British Government that its generous exertions have not only struck the death-knell of this inhuman practice, even in the remotest corner of the Empire, but, what is more commendable, endeavoured "to heal the wounds of a country bleeding at every pore from the fangs of superstition."

Not content with depriving her of the best enjoyments of life which society affords, and the laws of God sanction, by condemning her to a state of perpetual widowhood, the great lawgiver—the unflinching foe of freedom in females—has

---

* The worship of *Juggodhatri* (mother of the world), is performed by a widow for four years successively to forfend the calamity in the next birth.

further enjoined the strict observance of certain practices that add gall to her already overflowing cup of misery. As has been observed before, she is restricted to one scanty meal a day, always of the coarsest description, devoid of fish* which is generally more esteemed by an *ayistree* lady than any other article of food in her bill of fare. She must religiously fast on every *ekadossee*, twice a month, and on all other popular religious celebrations. She must bare her body of all sorts of ornaments, even the *iron* and the *gold* bangles, which once constituted the *summum bonum* of her life. As an appropriate substitute for the gold and pearl necklaces, she is enjoined to wear a *toolsee mala* (a basilwood chaplet), and count a *toolsee* wood bead roll for the final rest of her soul. She is prohibited from wearing any bordered clothes, a *thayti* being her proper garment; she is not permitted to daub her forehead with *sidoor*, (vermillion), once the pride of her life when her lord was alive; she is forbidden to use any bazar-made article of food, and to complete the catalogue of restrictions she sometimes shaves her head purposely that she may have an ugly appearance and thereby more effectually repel the inroads of a wicked, seductive world.

If she have any children to nurture, the happy circumstance affords a great relief to her wearisomely monotonous life. Day and night she watches them with great care, and looks forward to their progressive development with intense anxiety, forgetting in the plenitude of her solicitude her own forlorn condition. Should there be any mishap in their case, it causes an irreparable break-down in her spirit, which is for ever "sicklied over with the pale cast of thought."

* It should be mentioned here that, except the widows of Brahmins and Káyestus of Bengal, those of lower orders continue to use fish without any scruple. It is a remarkable fact that Hindoo *women* are more fond of fish than *men*. There are some men, especially among the *Boystubs*, followers of Krishna, who feel an abhorrence to eat fish at all by reason of its offensive smell, but there is not a single woman whose husband is alive that can live without it. When a girl becomes a widow, she can hardly take half the quantity of boiled rice she was accustomed to take before for want of this, to her, necessary article of food.

It is a painful fact that riches when not properly used have a tendency to corrupt the minds of human beings, and lead them from the path of virtue to that of vice. A wealthy widow who has the command of a long purse more readily falls a prey to the temptations of the world than one who, moving in an humbler sphere of life, has her mind almost wholly engrossed with domestic cares, and the thoughts of a future state of beatitude. "Verily," as Lord Lytton says, "in the domain of poverty there is God's word."

Considering the endless round of hardship and self abnegations to which she is inevitably doomed by a terrible stroke of fortune, "which scathes and scorches her soul," it is cheering to reflect that she so often shines brightest in adversity. Indeed she may be occasionally said "to die ten times a day," but her incredible powers of patient endurance, coupled with her high sense of female honor, are deserving of the highest admiration.

XX.

SICKNESS, DEATH, AND *SHRÁD*, OR FUNERAL CEREMONY.

AS I have said in the beginning that a Hindoo lives religiously and dies religiously, so his last days are attended with a degree of melancholy interest which is characteristic of the religion which he professes, as well as of the race to which he belongs. When a Hindoo becomes seriously ill, the first thing he does is to consult the Almanac as to the stellar mansion of the period, and engage the officiating priest to perform a series of religious atonements, called ***sastyána***, for the removal of the evil spirit, and the restoration of health. Mornings and evenings are dedicated to the service, and the mother or the wife of the patient, as the case may be, makes a vow to the gods, promising to present suitable offerings on his recovery, for which purpose a small sum of money is laid aside as a tangible proof of sincerity. If the patient should be a useful member of the family, enjoying a good income, greater solicitude is, as must naturally be expected, manifested for his sake than for that of an unproductive member; it being not uncommon that a whole family, consisting of eight or ten persons, male and female, depend for their sustenance on the earnings of a single individual,—the inevitable result of a joint Hindoo family. It is customary among the Hindoos, as it is among other civilized nations, that when a person is ill, his friends and relatives come to see and console him. The sick man generally remains in the inner apartment of the house, where the females—the ministering angels of life—watch him and administer to his comfort. When visitors enter the room, they go away for a time, but it must be mentioned that they are not wanting in attention, kind-heartedness and careful nursing. Days and nights of watching pass over their heads without a murmur, prayers are continually offered to the guardian deity for a favorable turn in the fortune of the family, and available supernatural agency is secretly employed for the attainment of the end. The following conversation will give some idea of the melancholy scene :—

Rámkánto (a neighbour), enters the room, and gently accosts Mohun (the son of the patient.)

Rámkánto, sitting, asks How is your father? I see he is very much pulled down ; the times are very bad, I hear of sickness on all sides, when did he get ill? Have you seen the almanac? Have you arranged for *sastyána* (religious atonement)? Don't you despair. He will get well through the blessing of God; who attends him?

Brojobundhoo (doctor) replies Mohun.

Rámkánto. Yes, he is a good doctor, but you must have a good *Khobiraj* also (native physician) who understands the *naree* (pulse) well; these English doctors do not much care about the pulse.

Mohun–Well, sir, I have engaged Gopeebullub(native physician) to feel the pulse and watch the progress of the disease.

Rámkánto—That is good, Gopeebullub is a very clever physician, though not old, he understands pulsation and other symptoms thoroughly. When does the fever come on? See, how he remains to-day; should the pulse sink after fever, send for an English doctor to-morrow, either Dr. Charles or Dr. Coates, both are very good doctors.

Mohun—My uncle gave the same advice.

Rámkánto, (taking Mohun aside) Baba, what will I say? To tell you the truth, I have no very great hopes of his recovery, the case is serious, if through the blessing of God he gets well, it would be a *second* birth; your father has been a great friend of mine, you all know very well, he is a staunch Hindoo; in these days of depravity, when the customs of the *Mlechas* (Christians) threaten to obliterate all traces of distinction, and merge everything in one homogeneous element after the English fashion, very few men are to be found like your father, ready to sacrifice his life for the purity of his religion; if his end do not accord with his faith, his future state *(parakáll)* is jeopardised; you, young men may laugh at us, old fools, thinking we have no sense; a few pages of English do not make a man learned; English shastra does not make us wise unto salvation; one's own religion is the best panacea for the good of his *parakáll* or future state. If you lose your father, you will never get a father again, he has nourished you with care and affection up to this day; as a dutiful son you are bound to serve him in this his last stage; you must be prepared to take him to the river side when need be, and that is not far distant; if you neglect, you commit a very great sin, quite unpardonable. What do fathers and mothers wish children for? It is only for the good of the *parakáll*, and to take them to Gunga (Ganges) in proper time. Let your father pass three nights on the river side. I return this afternoon; take care, watch him closely and let Gopeebullub see him constantly.

Giving these instructions, Rámkánto goes away. After three or four hours, the fever returns, the patient becomes delirious and talks nonsense, and the wife becoming very uneasy calls the son in a very depressed tone, and tells him to send for the English doctor. The son obeying the order sends for the English doctor at once.

After an hour or so, in comes Dr. Charles accompanied by Baboo Brojobundhoo. Entering the sick man's room, Dr. Charles examines the patient carefully, asks Brojobundhoo what medicines he has been giving him, (the women all the while peeping through the window, unable to understand what the doctors are talking about), and being satisfied on this point, comes out and tells the son that his father is dangerously ill, and that his friend's prescriptions are all right; he, Dr. Charles, could not do better.

Here enters Rámkánto with two other friends. Before going inside he thus speaks to the son: I hear Dr. Charles was here, what did he say? How was the fever to-day.

Mohun answers, Dr. Charles said father is very ill, the paroxysm to-day was somewhat more violent than that of other days.

Rámkánto—That's bad; day by day the fever eats into the vitals of his system. (Here the native physician comes). Well, *Khobiraj Mohashoy*, please go and see how the patient is doing? Gopeebullub (native physician) goes inside, examines the sick man with great care, satisfies the eager enquiries of the women by assuring them that there is no fear, and returns outside.

Rámkánto to Gopeebullub—How did you find him? Is the pulse in its right place? Do you apprehend any immediate danger? Dr. Charles was here, you have heard what he has said, whatever the youngsters may say, I have greater confidence in you than in the English doctors; take good care and tell us the exact time when to remove the patient to the river side, that is our last sacred office; should anything happen at home, which God forbid, we shall never be able to show our faces through shame. What with such a big son, and so many friends and relations, it would be a crying shame if the patient die at home? Destiny will have its course but your *hathjuss* (skill) will go a great way.

Gopeebullub—Everything depends on the will of God, what can we mortals do? Whatever fate has ordained must come to pass, we are mere instruments in the hands of God; the patient is gradually sinking, the pulse neither steady nor in its right place, we must be prepared for the worst, a *strong* pulse in a *weak* body is an ominous sign, there is no fear to-night, I can guarantee that.

Rámkánto—Well, it appears his end is nigh, he is no more destined to have rice and water.* Then, pointing to Mohun, Rámkánto says, to-morrow morning his *Boyetarni* rite† must be performed; make the necessary preparations at once, and send a man to procure a cot (charpoy), also see that nothing may be wanting to hurry him to the riverside.

Mohun—I must do what you bid me do, hitherto I remained behind a mountain, now I shall be without protection.

Next morning, the rite of *Boyetarni* being performed, preparations are made to carry the sick man to the river side: all the nearest relations and friends assemble, and the patient, then in the full possession of his senses, is brought outside and laid on the *chárpoy;* his forehead is daubed with the mud of the Ganges, and a *toolsee* plant is placed about his head. He is told to repeat the name of his guardian deity, and one man going up to him says, let's go to visit the mother Gunga, at which he nods; this serves as a signal for lifting the *charpoy*, and putting it on the shoulders of four strong persons of equal size. The heart-rending scene that ensues hereupon among the females cannot be adequately described. Their falling on the ground, their loud and affecting cries, the tearing of their dishevelled locks, the wringing of their breast, the contortions of their bodies, all produce a mournful scene of anguish and despair which my feeble pen can hardly pourtray.

The sick man is thus carried, perhaps a distance of two or three miles, in a state of consciousness‡ exposed to all

* This means that he must soon die.

† *Boyetarni* is a river which must be crossed before one gets to heaven; the rite consists in distributing a certain amount of *cowries* among the Brahmins for guiding the soul through the Death Valley to the other side.

‡ A Hindoo, especially a grown up man, if he die at home is branded as an unrighteous person; many a one otherwise esteemed righteous in his lifetime is denounced as a sinful being should he not expire on the banks of the holy stream. In the *rári*, or inland provinces, through which the Ganges does not flow, people are constrained to breathe their last on the banks of a neighbouing tank and are consequently precluded, from their geographical position, from securing the benefit of this *cheap* mode of salvation. As a partial atonement for this natural disadvantage, they bring the navel of the dead and throw it into the holy stream, which, in their supposition, is tantamount to the purification of the soul.

the dangers of inclement weather, fully aware of his approaching end, the carriers exchanging their shoulders every now and then, and shouting out every five minutes, "Hurry, Hurrybole, Gunga Narain, Brahma, Shiva Ráma," until they reach their destination, which, in Calcutta, is Nimtollah Ghaut, on the banks of the Hooghly.* When the *chárpoy* on which the sick man is borne is placed on the ground, some one calls out to the patient to see the sacred stream, which he does in a state of mind that can be better imagined than described. On opening his eyes he beholds a dark, gloomy scene, the ghastliness of which is enough to strike horror into the heart of the most callous and indifferent. Here a dying man suffering from the convulsive agony of acute pain, is, perhaps, gasping for breath, there a fellow mortal is taken in a hurry to the very edge of the holy water to breathe out the last flicker of life; to deepen the gloom perhaps a corpse borne on a Hindoo hearse is just brought to the Ghaut amidst the vociferous cries of "Hurry, Hurrybole," which is a significant death-warrant.

> "'Tis too horrible;
> The weariest and most loathed earthly life
> Which age, ache, penury, and imprisonment
> Can lay on nature, is a paradise
> To what we fear of death?"

---

* A few years back the Calcutta Municipality proposed to have the burning Ghaut removed to Dháppá, a notoriously unhealthy marshy swamp, some six miles east of Calcutta, bordering on the Soonderbunds, because the present site was considered a nuisance to the city. As must naturally be expected, great sensation was produced among the Hindoo population, and memorials were submitted to the Government of Bengal, signed by the most influential portion of the Hindoo community. In spite of solicitation and remonstrance, the Municipality were determined to carry out their plan, but the *mighty* Ramgopal Ghose, as the late Mr. James Hume, the Editor of the "*Eastern Star*," styled him, interposed and exerted his best, at great personal sacrifice, to nullify the proposal. The Hindoos called a meeting, and Ramgopal, moved by the entreaties of his countrymen, made an admirable speech at the Town Hall, on which occasion no less than fifty thousand people assembled on the *maidan* facing the Town Hall. In the speech he set forth, in a graphic manner, the suitableness of the present site, and the distress and hardship of the people, as well as the shock to religious feeling which the removal would involve. He eventually succeeded in prevailing on the authorities to withdraw the proposal. When he came out of the Town

Can imagination conceive a more dismal, ghastly scene? But religion has crowned the practice with the weight of national sanction, and thus deadened the finer sensibilities of our nature. Sad as this picture is, the most staunch advocate of liberalism can hardly expect to escape such a fate. To a person accustomed to such scenes, death, and its concomitant agony, loses half its terrors. How many Hindoos are annually hurried to their eternal home by reason of this superstitious, inhuman practice? Instances are not wanting to corroborate the truth of this painful fact. Persons entrusted with the care and nursing of a dying man at the burning Ghaut soon get tired of their charge, and rather than administer to his comfort, are known to resort to artificial means, whereby death is actually accelerated. They unscrupulously pour the unwholesome, muddy water of the river down his already choked throat, and in some cases suffocate him to death. "These are not the ebullient flashes from the glowing caldron of a kindled imagination," but undeniable facts founded on the realities of life.

The process of Hindoo *antarjal* or immersion is another name for suffocation. Life is so tenacious, especially in what the Hindoos call *old bones*, or aged persons, that I have seen some persons brought back home after having undergone this murderous process nine or ten times in as many days. The patient, perhaps an uncared-for widow cast adrift in the world, retaining the faculty of consciousness unimpaired, is willing to die rather than continue to drag on a loathsome existence, but nature would not readily yield the vital spark. In spite of repeated murderous processes, the apparently dying flicker of life would not become extinct. In the case of an aged man, the return home after *immersion* is infamously scandalous, but in that of an aged widow the disgrace is more

---

Hall, he was most enthusiastically cheered by thousands of people, Brahmins and Soodras, and loud cries of "may he live long" were heard on all sides.

poignant than death itself. I have known of an instance in which an old widow was brought back after fifteen *immersions*, but being overpowered by a sense of shame she drowned herself in the river after having lived a disgraceful life for more than a year. As I have observed elsewhere, no expression is more frequent in the mouth of an aged widow than the following: "Shall I ever die?" Scarcely any effort has ever been made to suppress or even to ameliorate such a barbarous practice, simply because religion has consecrated it with its holy sanction.

But to return to the thread of my narrative, the sick man dies after a stay of four days at the Ghaut, suffering perhaps the most excruciating pangs and agony generally attendant on a deathbed. The names of his gods are repeatedly whispered in his ears, and the consolations of religion are offered him with an unsparing hand, in order to mitigate his sufferings, and if possible to brighten his last hours. The corpse is removed from the resting place to the burning Ghaut, a distance of a few hundred yards, and preparations for a funeral pile are speedily made. The body is then covered with a piece of new cloth and laid upon the pyre, the upper and lower part of which is composed of firewood, faggots, and a little sandalwood and ghee to neutrathe effects of effluvia. The *Marooyapora* Brahmin,* (an outcast) reads the formula, and the son or the nearest of kin sets fire to the pile; the body is consumed to ashes, but the navel remaining unburnt is taken out and thrown into the river. Thus ends the ceremony of cremation; the son

---

* Some forty years back these Brahmins and their whole crew of *murdurfarashassys* were a regular set of ragamuffins whose sole occupation was to fleece their victims in the most extortionate manner imaginable; the Brahmin would not read the formula, nor his myrmidons put up the funeral pile, without having received nearly four times the amount of the present cost. Great credit is due to Baboo Chunder Mohun Chatterjee, the late Registrar, for his strenuous exertions in making the Police frame a set of rules for regulating the funeral expenses at the burning Ghaut. It is a public boon which cannot be too highly appreciated.

putting a few jars of holy water on the pile, bathes in the stream, and returns home with his friends, changing his old garment for new white clothes, called *uttary*, on one end of which is fastened an iron key to keep off evil spirits. It is worthy of remark here, that providence is so propitious to us in every respect that in a few hours the son becomes reconciled to his unhappily altered circumstances caused by the loss of his father; instead of bemoaning his loss in a despondent frame of mind, he is soon awakened to a sense of his new responsibility.

On reaching the gate of the house, all persons touch fire, and putting *neem* leaves and a few grains of *kalie* (a kind of pulse) into the mouth, cry out as before "Hurrybole, Hurrybole" and enter the house. The lamentation of the females inside the house, which was suppressed for a while through sheer exhaustion, is instantly renewed at the sound of "Hurrybole," as if fresh fuel were added to the flame, and every voice is drowned in the overwhelming surge of grief. Their melancholy strain, their pointed, pathetic allusion to the bereavement, the cadence of their plaintive voices, the utter dejection of their spirit, their loud, doleful cries reverberating from one side of the house to the other, the beating of their breasts, and the tearing of their hair, are too affecting not to make the most obdurate shed tears of sorrow.

The son, from the hour of his father's death to the conclusion of the funeral ceremony, is religiously forbidden to shave, wear shoes, shirts, or any garment other than the piece of white cloth, his food being confined to a single meal consisting only of *atab* rice, *khasury dhall* (a sort of inferior pulse) milk, ghee, sugar and a few fruits, which must be cooked either by his mother or his wife; at night he takes a little milk, sugar and fruits. This course of *regime* lasts ten days in the case of a Brahmin, and thirty-one days in that of a *Soodra.** Here the advantages of the privileged class are twofold; (1), he has to observe the rigid discipline for ten days only; (2), he has ample excuse for small expenditure at the funeral ceremony on the score of the shortness of time. This austere mode of living for a month in the case of a *Kayast*, by far the most aristocratic and influential portion of the Hindoo population, serves as a tribute of respect and gratitude to the memory of a departed father. As the country is now in a transition state, a young educated Hindoo does not strictly abide by the above rule, but breaks it privately in his mode of living, of which the inmates of the family only are cognisant. He repudiates publicly what he does privately. Thus the outer man and the inner man are not exactly one and the same being, he dares not avow without what he does within, in short, he plays the hypocrite. But an orthodox Hindoo observes the rule in all its integrity, he is more consistent if not more rational, he does not play a double game, but conforms to the rules of his creed with scrupulous exactness.

Fifteen or sixteen days after the demise of his father, the son, if young, is assisted by his friends in drawing an estimate of the probable cost of the approaching *Shrád* or funeral ceremony. In the generality of cases, an estimate is made out according to the length of the purse of the party; a few exceed it under a wrong impression that a debt is warranted by the special gravity of the occasion, which is one of great merit in popular estimation.†

---

* In the case of a daughter (married) the mourning lasts for three days. On the morning of the fourth day she is enjoined to cut her nails, and perform the funeral ceremony of a departed father or mother. An entertainment is to be given to the Brahmins and friends. This is always done on a comparatively small scale, and in most cases the husband is made to bear all the expenses of the ceremony and the entertainment.

† Apart from erroneous popular notions, which in this age of depravity are corrupted by vanity, the Hindoo Shastra, be it mentioned to its credit, abounds in explicit injunctions on the subject of a funeral ceremony in various ways accord-

The Sobha Bazar Rajah family, the Dey family of Simla, the Mullick and Tagore families of Patooriagháttá, all of Calcutta, were said to have spent upwards of £20,000 or two lacks of Rupees each on a funeral ceremony. They not only gave rich presents to almost all the learned Brahmins of Bengal, in money and kind, fed vast crowds of men of all classes, but likewise distributed immense sums among beggars and poor people,* who for the sake of one Rupee, walked a distance of perhaps thirty miles, bringing with them their little children in order to increase their numerical strength. Some really destitute women, far advanced in a state of pregnancy, were known to have been delivered in the midst of this densely crowded multitude. Although, now-a-days, the authorities do not sanction such a tumultuous gathering, or tolerate such a nuisance oftentimes attended with fatal accidents, no *Shrad* of any note at all takes place without the assemblage of a certain number of beggars and paupers, who receive from two to four annas each.

After the twentieth day, the son, accompanied by a Brahmin and a servant who carries a small carpet for the Baboo to sit on, walks barefooted to the house of each and every one of his relations, friends and neighbours, to announce that the *Shrad* is to take place on such a day, *i. e.*, on the

---

ing to the peculiar circumstances of parties. From an expenditure of lacks and lacks of Rupees to a mere trifle, it can be performed with the ultimate prospect of equal merit. It is stated in the holy Shastra that the god Ramchundra considered himself purified (for a Hindoo under mourning is held unclean until the funeral ceremony is performed) by offering to the manes of his ancestors simple balls of sand, called *pindas*, on the bank of the holy stream. In these days a poor man would be held sanctified or absolved from this religious responsibility by making a *tilakánchán Shrád*, or offering a small quantity of rice, *teelseed* and a few fruits, and feeding only one Brahmin, all which would not cost more than four Rupees.

* At the Shrád of Raja Nubkissen, Nemy Churn Mullick and Ramdoolal Dey, very near 100,000 beggars were said to have assembled together; this mode of charity is much discountenanced now and better systems are adopted for the ostensible gratification of generous propensities. The District Charitable Society should have a preference in every case. Instead of making a great noise by sound of trumpet and raising an ephemeral name from vainglorious motives, it is far wiser that a permanent provision should be made for the relief of suffering humanity.

thirty-first day after death, and to request that they should honour him with their presence and see that the ceremony is properly performed, adding such other complimentary epithets as the occasion suggests. This ceremonious visit is called *lowkata*, and those who are visited return the compliment in time. The practice is deserving of commendation, inasmuch as it manifests a grateful remembrance for the memory of one to whom he is indebted for his being.

Precisely on the thirtieth day, the son and other near relatives shave, cut their nails, and put on new clothes again, giving the old clothes to the barber. Meantime invitations are sent round to the Brahmins as well as to the Soodras, requesting the favor of their presence at the *Sabhá* or assembly on the morning of the *Shrád*, and at the feast on the following day or days. On the thirty-first day, early in the morning, the son, accompanied by the officiating priest, goes to the river side, bathes and performs certain preliminary rites. Here the *rayowbhats* and *tastirams* (religious mendicants), who watch these things just as closely as a vulture watches a carcase, give him a gentle hint about their rights, and follow him to the house, waiting outside for their share of the articles offered to the manes of the deceased. These men were so troublesome or boisterous in former days, when the Police were not half so vigilant as they now are, that for two days successively they would continue to shout and roar and proclaim to the passers by that the deceased would never be able to go into *Boykanta* or paradise, and that his soul would burn in hell fire until their demands were satisfied. Partly from shame, but more from a desire to avoid such a boisterous, unseemly scene, the son is forced to succumb and satisfy them in the best way he can.

As the style of living among the Hindoos has of late become rather expensive, and the potent influence of vanity —purely the result of an artificial state of society—exerts its pressure even on this mournful occasion, the son, if he be well to do in the world, spends from five to six thousand Rupees on a *Shrad;* the richer, more. He has to provide for the apparently solemn purpose the following silver utensils, *viz.:—Ghara, Gharoo, Thalla, Batta, Battee, Raykab,* glass, besides couch, bedding, shawls, broadcloth, a large lot of brass utensils and hard silver in cash, all which go to pay the Brahmins and Pundits, who had been invited. The waning ascendency of this privileged class is strikingly manifest on an occasion of this nature. For one or two rupees they will clamour and scramble, and unblushingly indulge in all manner of fulsome adulation of the party that invited them. *

The Pundits of the country, however learned they may be in classical lore and logical acumen, are very much wanting in the rules of polished life. The manner in which they display their profound learning is alike puerile and ludicrous. History does not furnish us with sufficient data regarding their conduct in ancient days. As far as research or investigation has elucidated the point, it is reasonable to conclude that the ascendency of the Brahmins was built on the ignorance of the people, and there is a very strong probability that there was a secret coalition between the priests and the rulers for the purpose of keeping the great mass of the nation in a state of perpetual darkness and subjection, the latter being oftentimes content with the barter of "solid pudding against empty praise." But the progress of enlightenment is so irresistible that the strongest bulwark of secret compact for the conservation of unnatural Brahminical authority is liable, as it should be, to crumble into dust. It would be a great injustice to deny that among these Brahmins there were some justly distinguished for their profound erudition and saintly lives; they displayed

* The appearance of Brahmins on such occasions has the ludicrous admixture of the learned and the ragged, exhibiting the insolence of high caste and the low cringe of poverty.

a piety, a zeal, a constant and passionate devotion to their faith, which contrast strangely enough with the profligacy and worldliness of the present ecclesiastics.

The Pundits of the present day, when they assemble at a *Shrad*—and that is considered a fit arena for discussion—are generally seen to engage in a controversy, the bone of contention being a debatable point in grammar, logic, metaphysics or theology. They love to indulge in sentimental transcendentalism, as if utterly unconscious of the matter-of-fact tendency of the age we live in. A strong desire of displaying their deep learning and high classical acquirements in Sanskrit, not sometimes unmixed with a contemptible degree of affectation, insensibly leads them to violate the fundamental laws of decorum. When two or more Pundits wrangle, the warmth of debate gradually draws them nearer and closer to each other, until from sober, solid argumentation, they descend to the *argumentum ad ignorantiam*, if not, to the *argumentum adbaculum.* Their taking a pinch of snuff, the quick moving of their hands, the almost involuntary unrobing of their garment, which consists of a single *dhooty* and *dubja* often put round the neck, the vehement tone in which they conduct a discussion, the utter want of attention to each other's arguments, and their constant divergence from the main point whence they started, throw a serio-comic air over the scene which a Dave Carson only could imitate. They do not know what candour is, they are immovable in their own opinion, and scarcely anything could conquer their dogged persistence in their own argument, however fallacious it may be. They are as prodigal in the quotation of specious texts in support of their own particular thesis as they are obstinately deaf to the sound logical view of an opponent. Brahminical learning is certainly uttered in "great swarths" which, like polished pebbles, are sometimes mistaken for diamonds. The way in which the disputants give flavour to their arguments is quite a study in the art of dropping meanings. The destruction of the old husks, and the transparent sophistries, of the disputatious Brahmins, is one of the great marvels achieved by the rapid diffusion of Western knowledge.

When engaged in an animated discussion, these Pundits will not desist or halt until they are separated by their other learned friends of the faculty. Some of them are very learned in the Shastra, especially in *Smrittee*, on which a dispute often hangs, but they have very little pretension to the calm and dispassionate discussion of a subject. Cogency of argument is almost invariably lost in the vehemence of declamation and in the utterance of unmeaning patter. Their arguments are not like Lord Beaconsfield's speeches,—a little labored and labyrinthine at first, but soon working themselves clear and becoming amusing and sagacious. Let it not be understood from this that the language (Sanskrit) in which they speak is destitute of sound logic, as Mr. James Mill would have his readers believe; it is certainly deficient in science and the correct principles of natural philosophy as developed by modern discoveries, but the elegance of its diction, the beautiful poetical imagery in which it abounds, the sound moral doctrines which it inculcates, the force of argument by which it is distinguished, and the elevated ideas which its original system of theology unfolds, afford no good reason why it should not be stamped with the dignity and importance of a classical language, and why "the deep students of it should not enjoy some of the honors and estimation conferred by the world on those who have established a name for an erudite acquaintance with Latin and Greek." If the respective merits of all the classical languages are properly estimated, it is not too much to say that the Sanskrit language will in no way suffer by the comparison, though as history abundantly testifies it labored under all the adverse circumstances of mighty political changes and convulsions, no less than the intolerant bigotry of many of the Moslem conquerors, whose unsparing devastations have destroyed some of the best specimens of Sankrit composition. "When our princes were in exile," says a celebrated Hindoo writer, "driven from hold to hold and compelled to dwell in the clefts of the mountains, often doubtful whether they would not be forced to abandon the very meal preparing for them, was that a time to think of historical records," and we should say, of literary excellence? The deep and laborious researches of Sir William Jones, Colebrooke, Macnaghten, Wilson, Wilkins, and a host of other distinguished German and French savants, have, in a great measure, brought to light the hidden treasures of the Sanskrit language.

From eight o'clock in the morning to 2 o'clock in the evening, the house of a *Shrad* is crammed to suffocation. A spacious awning covers the open space of the court-yard, preventing the free access of air; carpets and satterangees are spread on the ground for the *Kayastas* and other castes to sit on, while the Brahmins and Pundits by way of precedence take their seats on the raised *Thacoordallan*, or place of worship. The couch-cot with bedding, and the *dan* consisting of silver and brass utensils enumerated before, with a silver salver filled with Rupees, are arranged in a straight line opposite the audience, leaving a little open space for *kittanees*, or bands of songsters or songstresses and musicians, which form the necessary accompaniment of a *Shrad* for the purpose of imparting solemnity to the scene. Three or four door-keepers guard the entrance, so that no intruders may enter and create a disturbance. The guests begin to come in at eight, and are courteously asked to take their appropriate seats (Brahmins among Brahmins, and Kayastas among Kayastas,) the servants in waiting serve them with *hookah* and tobacco,* those given to the Brahmins having a thread or string fastened at the top for the sake of distinction. The Kayastas and other guests are seen constantly going in and coming out, but the generality of the Brahmins stick to their places until the funeral ceremony is completed. The current topics of the day form the subject of conversation while the *hookah* goes round the assembly with great precision and punctuality. The female relatives are brought in covered *palkees*, as has been described before, by a separate entrance, shut out from the gaze of the males. But as this is a mourning scene their naturally convivial spirit gives way to condolence and sympathy. Excessive grief does not allow the mother or the wife of the deceased to take an active part in the melancholy proceedings of the day; they generally stay aloof in a separate room, and are perhaps heard to mourn or cry. The very sight of the mourning offerings, instead of affording any consolation, almost involuntarily enkindles the flame of sorrow, and produces a train of thoughts in keeping with the commemoration of the sad event. Sisters of a congenial spirit try to soothe them by precepts and examples, but their admonition and condolence prove in the main unavailing. The appearance of a new face revives the sad emotions of the heart. Nothing can dispel from the minds of a disconsolate mother or wife the gloomy thoughts of her bereavement, and the still more gloomy idea of a perpetual widowhood. The clang of *khole* and *kharatal* (musical instruments), which is fitted, as it were, from its very dissonance,

---

* The Hindoos are so much accustomed to smoking that it has almost become a necessary of life. At a reception it is the first thing required. The practice is regulated by rules of etiquette, so that a younger brother is not permitted to smoke in the presence of his elder brother or his uncle. Even among the reformed Hindoos, I have seen two brothers eat aud drink together at the same table in European style, but when the dinner is over the youuger brother would on no account smoke in the presence of his elder brother, if he do, he would be instantly voted a *bayádub*, or one wanting in the rules of good breeding. The observance of this etiquette, however, is confined only to the high caste people; among the lower orders, a son smokes before a father with the same freedom as if he were taking his ordinary meal.

to drive away the ghost and kill the living, falls doubly grating on her ears, while the fond endearments of *Jasoda*, the mother of Krishna, rehearsed by the songsters in the outer court-yard, but aggravate her grief the more. Weak and tenderhearted by nature, she gradually sinks under the overwhelming load of despondency, and raising her hand to her forehead mournfully exclaims, "has Fate reserved all this for me?" In such cases, there is appropriateness in silence.

About ten o'clock the son begins to perform the rite of the funeral obsequies, taking previously the permission of the Brahmins and the assembled guests to do so. The officiating priest reads the formulas, he repeating them. It must be noticed here that tenacious as the Hindoos are in respect of the distinction of caste, they do not scruple to invite lower orders on such an occasion, but they would not mix with them at the time of eating. The *Dulloputty* or head of the party, makes his appearance about this time; when he enters the house, all other guests then present, except the Brahmins, as a token of respect for his position, rise on their legs, and do not resume their seats until he sits down, For this distinction or honour a *Dullopatty* has to spend an immense sum of money, to which allusion has already been made. His appearance serves as a signal for the performance of the rite, called *mala chandan*, or the distribution of garlands and sandal paste among the assembled multitude. As a matter of course, the Brahmins by way of pre-eminence receive the first garland, and after them the *Dullopatty* obtains the same honour, and then the *Koolins** and other guests

* The following anecdote illustrating the very great honor shewn to first-class Koolins, will, I trust, not be considered out of place.

When the late Rajah Rajkissen Bahadoor of Calcutta had to perform the *Shrád* or funeral ceremony of his illustrious father, the late Moha Rajah Nubkissen (the ceremony was said to have cost about five lacks of Rupees or £50,000,) he had to invite almost all the celebrated Koolins of Bengal at considerable expense. On the day of the *Shrád* those who were invited assembled at his mansion in Sobha Bazar, when all eyes were dazzled at the unparalleled magnificence of the scene, displaying a gorgeous array of gold, silver and brass according to rank. Where there is no *Dullopatty*, the garland is put round the neck of a boy, at which no one can take any offence, and afterwards they are distributed indiscriminately.

Meantime the son is engaged in the performance of the ceremony, while the bands of songsters quarrel with one another for the privilege of entertaining the audience with their songs, which renders confusion worse confounded. Female songsters of questionable virtue are now more in favor than their male rivals, which is an unerring proof of the degeneracy of the age. Only one band is formally engaged, but thirty bands may come of their own accord, quite uninvited. The disappointed ones generally get from two to four Rupees each, but the party retained gets much more, the rich guests coming in making them presents, besides what they obtain from the family retaining them.

About one in the afternoon, the ceremony is brought to a close, and the assembled multitudes begin to disperse. Those who have to attend their offices return earlier, but not without offering the compliments suited to the gravity of the occasion. Some of the Brahmins remain behind to receive their customary *bidhay* or gift. According to their reputation for learning they obtain their rewards. The first in the list gets, in ordinary cases, about five Rupees in

---

utensils for presents to Brahmins, exclusive of large sums of money, Cashmere shawls, broadcloth, &c. After the performance of the ceremony, as is usual on such occasions, the distribution of garlands and sandal paste had to be gone through; the whole of the splendid assemblage had been watching with intense anxiety as to who should get the *first* garland—the highest respect shewn, according to precedence of rank, to the *first* Koolin present. This is a very knotty point in a large assemblage to which all orders of Koolins had been brought together. The honor was eagerly contested and coveted by many, but at length a voice from a corner loudy proclaimed to the following effect: "Put the garland on my *gode*," (elephantiasis) laying bare and stretching his right leg at the same time and thus suiting the action to his words. The attention of the assembled multitude was immediately directed in that direction, and to the amazement of all, the garland had to be put round the neck of the very man who shouted from a corner, because by a general consensus he was pronouced to be the *first* Koolin then present. But such artificial and demoralising distinctions, built on the baseless fabric of quicksand, having no foundation in solid, sterling merit, are fast falling, as they should, into disrepute.

cash, and one brass pot valued, at four or five Rupees, the second and third in proportion, and the rest, say, from one to two Rupees each, in addition to a brass utensil. The silver utensils of which the *soroshes* are made are afterwards cut and allotted to the Brahmins according to their worth or status in the republic of letters. The *Gooroo* or spiritual guide, and the *Purrohit* or officiating priest, being the most interested parties, generally carry off the lion's share. So great is their cupidity that the one disputes the right of the other as to the amount of reward they are respectively entitled to. As a matter of course, the *Gooroo*, from his spiritual ascendency, manages to carry off the highest prize. The distribution of rewards among the Brahmins and Pundits of different degrees of scholarly attainments, is a rather thankless task. In common with other human beings, they are seldom satisfied, especially when the question is one of Rupees. Each sets a higher value on his own descent and learning, undervaluing the worth of his compeers. The voice of the President, who has many a knotty question to solve, decides their fate, but it is seldom that a classification of this nature results in producing general satisfaction. As these Pundits, or rather professors, called *Adhaypucks*, do not eat in the house of *Soodras*, in addition to their reward in money and kind, they, each of them, receive a small quantity of sweetmeats and sugar, say about two pounds in all in lieu of *achmany jalpan* or fried and prepared food. On a *Shrad* day in the afternoon one can see numbers of such Brahmins walk through the native part of the city, with an earthen plate of sweetmeats in one hand and a brass pot in the other, the fruits of their day's labor. Such gains being quite precarious, and the prospect looming before them quite discouraging, the annual sum total they derive from this source is quite inadequate to their support, and that of the *chottoospattee* or school they keep. Hence many such institutions for the cultivation of Sanskrit have been abandoned for want of sufficient encouragement, and as a necessary consequence the sons and grandsons of these Brahmins have taken to secular occupations, quite incompatible with the spirit of the Shastra. In the halcyon days of Hindoo sovereignty, when Brahminical learning was in the ascendant and rich religious endowments were freely made for the support of the hierarchy,* as well from the influence of vanity as from the compunctions of a death-bed repentance, such *chottoos-pattees* annually sent forth many a brilliant scholar,—the pride of his professor and the ornament of his country. But the advancement of English education—the only passport to honor and emoluments—has necessarily laid, as it were, an embargo on the extensive culture of Brahminical erudition. The University curriculum, however, under the present Government, embraces a system well calculated to remove the reproach.

The day following the funeral ceremony is spent in giving an entertainment to the Brahmins, without which a Hindoo cannot regain his former purity. About twelve, they begin to assemble, and when the number reaches two or three hundred, *Koosasan* or grass seats in long straight rows are arranged for them in the spacious court-yard, and as Hindoos use nothing but green plantain leaves for plates on such grand occasions, each guest is provided with a cut piece on which are placed the fruits of the season, ghee-fried *loochees* and *kachoories*, and several sorts of sweetmeats in earthen plates for which there are no English names. In spite of the utmost vigilance of door-keepers and others, intruders in rather decent dress enter the premises and sit down to eat with the respectable Brahmins, but should such

* Manu commands, "Should the king be near his end, through some incurable disease, he must bestow on the priests all his riches accumulated from legal fines."

a character be found out, steps are instantly taken to oust him. On a grand occasion, some such unpleasant cases are sure to occur. There are loafers among Hindoos as there are among Europeans. These men, whom misfortune or crime has reduced to the last state of poverty, are prepared to put up with any amount of insult so long as they have their fill. When a Hindoo makes a calculation about the expenses of an entertainment at a *Shrad* or marriage (both grand occasions), he is constrained to double or treble his quantum of supply that he may be enabled to meet such a contingency without any inconvenience. The practice referred to is a most disreputable one, and beseems a people not far above the level of a Nomad tribe. Even some of the Brahmins* who are invited do not scruple to take a portion home, regardless of the contaminated touch of a person of the lowest order, simply because the temptation is too strong to be resisted. Before departure, each and every one of the Brahmins obtains one or two annas as *dakhinah*, a concession which is not accorded to any other caste.

The next day, a similar entertainment is given to the Káyastas and other classes, which is accompanied by the same noise, confusion and tumult that characterised the entertainment given on the previous day. The sober and quiet enjoyments of life which have a tendency to enliven the mind can seldom be expected in a Hindoo house of *Shrad*, where all is *golemal*, confusion and disorder. When a dinner is announced, a regular scramble takes place, the rude and the uninvited occupy the *first* seats to the exclusion of the genteel and respectable, and when the eatables are

* To preserve order and avoid such unseemly practices, a wealthy Baboo—the late Doorgaram Cor—when he invited a number of Brahmins allotted to each two separate rations, one on the plantain leaf for eating on the spot, and another in an earthen *handy* or pot for carrying home for the absent members of the family. Even this excellent arrangement failed to satisfy the greedy cravings of the voracious Brahmins. As a *dernier ressort*, he at last substituted *cash* for *eatables*, which was certainly a queer mode of satisfying the *inner* man.

beginning to be served, the indecent cries of "bring *loochee*, bring *kachoorie*, bring *tarkari*," and so on, are heard every now and again, much to the disturbance of the polite and the discreet.

The day following is called the *neeumbhanga*, or the day on which the son is allowed to break the rules of mourning after one month. In the morning the band of songsters previously retained come and treat the family to songs of Krishna, taking care to select pieces which are most pathetic and heart-rending, befitting the mournful occasion of a very heavy domestic bereavemeht. The singing continues till twelve or one o'clock, and some people seem to be so deeply affected that they actually shed tears, and forget for a while their worldly cares and anxieties. When the songs are finished, the son and his nearest relatives, rubbing their bodies with oil and turmeric, remove the *brisakát* on their shoulders from the house to a place near it. A hole is made, and the *brisakat* (a painted log of wood about six feet high) with an ox on the top, &c., is put into it; after this they. all bathe and return home. The songsters are dismissed with presents of money, clothes and food.

The son then sits down to a dinner with his nearest blood relation, and this is the *first* day that he leaves his *habishee* diet after a month's mourning, and takes to the use of fish and other Hindoo dishes. He is also allowed to change his mourning dress and put on shoes, after having made a present of a pair to a Brahmin; he, moreover, sleeps with his wife from this day as before, in fact he reverts to his former mode of living in every respect.

As the entertainment this time consists of *vojan*, made up of rice and curries, and not *jalpan*, made up of *loochees* and sweetmeats, comparatively a smaller number of guests assemble on the occasion* and that of loafers and intruders ex-

* There is a vast difference between a *vojun* and a *jalpán* dinner. If there be a thousand guests at the latter, at the most there would be only three hundred at the former, as none but the nearest relatives and friends will con-

hibits a very diminished proportion. Even on such occasions, one can always tell from a distance that there is a feast at such a house from the noise it is invariably attended with.

Having described above the details connected with the funeral ceremony, I will now endeavour to give an account of one or two of the most celebrated *Shrads* that took place in Bengal after the battle of Plassey, premising that every thing which shall be said on the subject is derived chiefly from hearsay, as no authentic historical records have come down to us. The first and most celebrated *Shrad* was that performed by Dewan Gunga Gobind Set, on the occasion of his mother's death. It was performed on so large a scale that he caused reservoirs to be made which were filled with ghee and oil, immense heaps of rice, flour and *dhall* were piled on the ground. Several large rooms were quite filled with sweetmeats of all sorts. Mountains of earthen pots and firewood were stacked on the Maidan. Hundreds of Brahmin cooks and confectioners were constantly at work to provide victuals for the enormous concourse of people. Silver and brass utensils of all kinds were arranged in pyramids. Hundreds of couches with bedding were placed before the *Sabha*, (assembly). Elephants richly caparisoned with silver trappings formed presents to Brahmins. Tens of thousands of silver coins bearing the stamp of *Shah Allum* were placed on massive silver

---

descend to take rice *(vath)*, which is almost akin to one and the same clanship, whereas in a *jalpán*, not only the members of the same caste but even those of the inferior order are tacitly permitted to partake of the same entertainment without tarnishing the honor of the aristocratic classes.

The following anecdote will, I hope, prove interesting :—

At the marriage procession of a washerman, confessedly very low in the category of caste, two *Káyastas* (writer caste) joined it on the road in the hope of getting a hearty *Jalpán* dinner; but lo! when, after the nuptial rites were over, rice and curries were brought out for the guests, the two *Káyastas*, who sat down with the rest of the company, tried to escape unnoticed, because if they ate rice at a washerman's they were sure to lose their caste, but the host would not let them go away without dinner. They at last spoke the truth, asked forgiveness and were then allowed to leave the house. To such disappointments unfortunate intruders are sometimes subjected.

plates. And to crown the whole, thousands of learned Pundits from all parts of the country congregated together to impart a religious solemnity to the spectacle. All these preparations lent a grandeur to the scene, which was in the highest degree imposing. Countless myriads of beggars from the most distant parts of the Province assembled together, and they were not only fed for weeks at the expense of the Dewan, but were dismissed with presents of money, clothes and food, with the most enthusiastic hosannas on their lips. For more than two months the distribution of alms and presents lasted, and what was the most praiseworthy feature in the affair was the Job-like patience of the Dewan, whose charity flowed like the rushing flood-tide of the holy Ganges on the banks of which he presented offerings to the manes of his ancestors. Some of the *Adhapucks* or Professors obtained as much as one thousand Rupees each in cash and gold and silver articles, or rather fragments of the same, to a considerable value. Besides these magnificent honorariums the whole of their travelling and lodging expenses were defrayed by the Dewan, who was reputed to be so rich that like Croesus of old he did not know how much he was worth; hence there is still a current saying amongst the Bengalees, which runs thus: "If ever money were wanted, Gouri Set will pay." Gouri Set was the son of Gunga Gobind Set. The expenses of the *Shrad* have been variously estimated at between ten and twelve lacks of Rupees. The result of this truly extravagant expenditure was wide-spread fame, and the name of the donor is still cherished with grateful remembrance. But as all human greatness is evanescent, the fame of the family for charity once unparalleled in the annals of Bengal has long since dwindled into insignificance.

The next *Shrad* of importance was that of Maharajah Nabkissen Bahadoor of Shobhabazar, Calcutta. His son Raja Rajkissen performed the *Shrad*, which, to this day, stands unrivalled in this city. Four sets of gold and sixty-four sets of silver utensils described before, amounting in value to near a lakh of Rupees, were given on the occasion. Such paraphernalia go by the name of *dansagor* or "gift like the sea." Besides these presents in money to Brahmins upwards of two lakhs of Rupees were given to the poor.

If these immense sums of money had been invested for the permanent support of a Charitable Institution, it would have done incalculable good to society. But then there was no regularly organised system of Public Charity, nor had the people any idea of it. Such immense sums were spent mostly for religious purposes according to the prevailing notions of the age. Tanks, reservoirs, flights of steps on the banks of the river,* fine rows of trees, every three miles stone buildings or choultries for travellers, affording a grateful shelter throughout the country, were among the works of public utility constructed by the charitably disposed.

---

* In the sacred city of Benares vast sums of money have been sunk in building Ghauts with magnificent flights of steps stretching from the bank to the very edge of the water at ebb-tide, affording great convenience to the people both for religious and domestic purposes, but the strong current of the stream in the months of August, September and October, has played a sad havoc with the masonry works. Scarcely a single Ghaut exists in a complete state of preservation.

XXI.

SUTTEE, OR THE IMMOLATION OF HINDOO WIDOWS.

FIFTY years ago, when the British Government was endeavouring to consolidate its power in the East, and when the religious prejudices of the Natives were alike tolerated and respected, there arose a great man in Bengal who was destined by Providence to work a mighty revolution in their social, moral and intellectual condition. That great man was Rammohun Roy, the pioneer of Hindoo enlightenment. Having early enriched his mind with European and Eastern erudition, he soon rose, by his energy, to a degree of eminence and usefulness which afterwards marked his career as a distinguished reformer and a benevolent philanthropist. He was emphatically an oasis in this sterile land—a solitary example of a highly cultivated mind among many millions of men grovelling in ignorance. To his indefatigable exertions we are indebted for the abolition of the inhuman practice of Suttee, the very name of which evokes a natural shrinking from the diabolical deed, which appallingly and suddenly expunged a tender life from the earth, and severed the dearest tie of humanity. It was the severest reflection on the satanic character of a religion that ignores the first principle of divine law. Women are of an impressionable nature, their enthusiasm is easily fanned into intensity, and superstition and priestcraft took advantage of it.

Not content with sending a sick man to the riverside to be suffocated and burnt to ashes, a narrow-minded hierarchy lent its sanction to the destruction of a living creature, by burning the Hindoo widow with the dead body of her husband, the fire being kindled perhaps by the hand of one whom she had nurtured and suckled in infancy. It is awful to contemplate how the finest sensibilities of our nature are sometimes blunted by a false faith.

My apology for dwelling on this painful subject now that the primary cause of complaint has long since been removed by a wise Legislature, is no other than that I had been an eye-witness of a melancholy scene of this nature, the dreadful atrocity of which it is impossible even at this distance of time to call to mind without horror and dismay. As the tale I am going to relate is founded in real life its truthfulness can be thoroughly relied upon.

When I was a little boy reading in a *Patsálá* at home, my attention was one morning roused by hearing from my mother that my aunt was "going a Suttee." The word was then scarcely intelligible to me. I pondered and thought over and over again in my mind what could the word 'Suttee' mean. Being unable to solve the problem, I asked my mother for an explanation; she, with tears in her eyes, told me that my aunt (living in the next house) "was going to eat fire." Instantly I felt a strong curiosity to see the thing with my own eyes, still laboring under a misconception as to what the reality could be. I had then no distinct notion that life would be at once annihilated. I never thought for a moment that I was going to lose my dear aunt for ever. My mind was quite unsettled, and I felt an irresistible desire to look into the thing more minutely. I ran down to my aunt's room and what should I see there, but a group of sombre complexioned women with my aunt in the middle. I have yet after fifty years, a vivid recollection of what I then saw in the room. My aunt was dressed in a red silk *sari* with all the ornaments on her person, her forehead daubed with a very thick coat of *sidoor* or vermillion, her feet painted red with *alta*, she was chewing a mouthful of betel, and a bright lamp was burning before her. She was evidently wrapt in an ecstacy of devotion, earnest in all she did, quite calm and composed as if nothing important was to happen. In short, she was then at her matins, anxiously watching the hour when this mortal coil should be put off. My uncle was lying a corpse in the adjoining room. It appeared to me that all the women assembled were admiring the virtues and fortitude of my aunt. Some licking the betel out of her mouth, some touching her forehead in order to have a little of the *sidoor* or vermillion, while not a few falling before her feet, expressed a fond hope that they might possess a small particle of her virtue. Amidst all these surroundings, what surprised me most was my aunt's stretching out one of her hands at the bidding of an old Brahmin woman and holding a finger right over the wick of the burning lamp for a few seconds until it was scorched and forcibly withdrawn by the old lady who bade her do so, in order to have a foretaste of the unshaken firmness of her mind. The perfect composure with which she underwent this fiery ordeal fully convinced all that she was a real Suttee, fit to abide with her husband in *Boykonto*, paradise. Nobody could notice any change in her countenance or resolution after she had gone through this painful trial.

It was about eleven o'clock when preparations were made for the removal of the corpse of my uncle to the Ghaut. It was a small mourning procession, nearly thirty persons, all of respectable families, volunteered to carry the dead body alternately on their shoulders. The body was laid on a *charpoy*, my aunt followed it, not in a closed but an open Palkee. She was unveiled and regardless of the consequences of a public exposure; she was, in a manner, dead to the external world. The delicate sense of shame so characteristic of Hindoo females was entirely suppressed in her bosom. In truth, she was evidently longing for the hour when her spirit and that of her husband should meet together and dwell in heaven. She had a *toolsee mala* (string of basil beads) in her right hand which she was telling, and she seemed to enjoy the shouts of "Hurree, Hurree bole" with perfect serenity of mind. How can we account for the strange phenomenon wherein a sentient being in a state of full consciousness was ready to surrender at the feet of "Hurree" the last vital spark of life for ever, without a murmur, a sigh, or a tear? A deep, sincere religious faith, which serves as a sheet-anchor to the soul amidst the storms of life, can only unriddle the enigma and disarm death of its terrors. We reached Nimtollah Ghaut about twelve, and after staying ten or fifteen minutes, sprinkling the holy water on the dead body, and all proceeded slowly to Kooltollah Ghaut, about three miles north of Nimtollah. On arriving at the destination which was the dreary abode of Hindoo undertakers, solitary and lonesome, the Police Darogah, (who was also a Hindoo) came to the spot and closely examined my aunt, in various ways attempting if possible, to induce her to change her mind, but she, like "Joan of Arc," was resolute and determined, she gave an unequivocal reply, to the purport that "such was her predestination, and that Hurree had summoned her and her husband into the Boykonto." The Darogah, amazed at the firmness of her mind, staid at the Ghaut to watch the proceedings, while preparations were being made for a funeral pile, which consisted of dry firewood, faggots, pitch with a lot of sandalwood, ghee, &c. in it to impart a fragrant odour to the air. Half a dozen Bamboos or sticks were procured also, the use of which we afterwards understood and saw. We little boys were ordered to stand aloof. The Brahmin undertaker came and read a few *mantras* or incantations. The dead body wrapped in new clothes being placed on the pyre, my aunt was desired to turn seven times round it, which she did while strewing a lot of flowers, cowries (shells) and parched rice on the ground. It struck me at the time that at every successive circumambulation, her strength and presence of mind failed, whereupon the Darogah stepped forward once more and endeavoured even at the last moment to deter her from her fatal determination, but she, at the very threshold of ghastly death, in the last hour of expiring life, the fatal torch of *Yama* (Pluto) before her, calmly ascended the funeral pile and lying by the side of her husband with one hand under his head and another on his breast, was heard to call, in voice half suppressed, on "Hurree, Hurree,"—a sign of firm belief in the reality of eternal beatitude. When she had thus laid herself on the funeral pyre, she was instantly covered or rather choked with dry wood, while some stout men held and pressed down the pyre which was by this time burning fiercely on all sides, with the Bamboos. A great shout of exultation then arose from the surrounding spectators, till both the dead and living bodies were converted into a handful of dust and ashes. When the tragic scene was brought to a close and the excitement of the moment subsided, men and women wept and sobbed, while cries and groans of sympathy filled the air.

If all religions be not regarded as "splendid failures,' that outlook into the future, which sustains us amid the manifold griefs and agonies of a troublous life, holds out the sure hope of a blessed existence hereafter. My aunt, Bhuggobutty Dassee, though a victim of superstition, had nevertheless a firm, unalterable faith in the merciful dispensations of Hurree which prompted her to renounce her life for the salvation of her own and her husband's souls, giving no heed whatever to the importunity of her friends or the admonition of the world. The sincerity of her religious conviction immeasurably outweighed every other worldly consideration, and no fear or temptation could deter her from her resolute purpose, despite its singularly shocking character. It was the depth of a similar religious conviction and earnestness of purpose that led Joan of Arc to suffer martyrdom on a funeral pile. When asked by the executioner if she believed in the reality of her mission, "Yes," she firmly replied, while the flames were ascending around her. "My voices were of God. All that I have done was by the command of God. No, my voices did not deceive me. My revelations were of God." "Nothing more was heard from her but invocations to God, interrupted by her long drawn agony. So dense were the clouds of smoke that at one time, she could not be seen. A sudden gust of wind turned the current of the whirlwind and Jeanne was seen for a few moments. She gave one terrific cry, pronounced the name of Jesus, bowed her head, and the spirit returned to God who gave it. Thus perished Jeanne, the maid of Orleans," and thus perished Bhuggobutty Dassee, my aunt.

About the year 1813, Rammohun Roy published a pamphlet in which he very clearly exposed the barbarous character of the rite of burning widows alive. He was unfortunately backed by few friends. The orthodox party was then very strong, and included the most influential and wealthy portion of the Hindoo community. Maharajah Tejchunder Bahadoor of Burdwan, Rajahs Gopeemohun and Radhakanto Bahadoors, Promothnath Dey, Boystubchunder Mullick, Rammohun Mullick and, in fact, the entire aristocracy of Calcutta were enlisted on the side of opposition. The "Sumachar Chandrika," the recognised organ of the *Dhurmo Shabha*, edited by Bhowbany Churn Bonerjea, vilified Rammohun Roy, as an outcast and infidel and persecuted those who were bold enough to avow their sentiments in favour of the abolition of this inhuman practice. Rammohun Roy almost single-handed encountered this formidable opposition, he fought for a just and righteous but not a popular cause, regardless alike of the consequences of social persecution and the threats and scoffs of his orthodox countrymen. Patiently but steadily and consistently he worked his way, until at last his appeal finding a responsive echo in a Christian heart, that noble minded Governor General—Lord William Bentinck—gradually put a stop to the practice. That eminent statesman had many a conference with Rammohun Roy on the propriety or otherwise of abolishing this shocking practice. The anti-abolitionists presented a memorial to Government, urging therein its unjustifiable interference with the religious usages of the country. That wise Governor General, who was very anxious to preserve in full integrity the solemn pledge of government about a neutral policy in matters of religion, consulted the distinguished Orientalist, Mr. H. H. Wilson, on the subject, and finally came to the resolution of abolishing this inhuman institution throughout the British dominion in the East. But before giving effect to the resolution, he recorded in a Minute that the authoritative abolition of the practice would be an outrageous violation of the engagement of the Supreme Government. Accordingly his Lordship observed: "I must acknowledge that a similar opinion, as to the probable excitation of a deep distrust of our future intentions, was mentioned to me in conversation by that enlightend Native, Rammohun Roy, a warm advocate for the abolition of Suttees, and of all other superstitions and corruptions engrafted on the Hindu religion, which he considers originally to have been a pure deism. It was his opinion that the practice might be suppressed quietly and unobservedly by increasing the difficulties, and by the indirect agency of the Police. He apprehended that any public enactment would give rise to general apprehension, that the reasoning would be, while the English were contending for power, they deemed it politic to allow universal toleration and to respect our religion; but having obtained the supremacy, their first act is a violation of their professions and the next will probably be, like Mahomedan conquerors to force upon us their own religion."

The argument urged by Government was as reasonable as its conduct was compatible with its known policy. But it must be mentioned to the credit of an enlightened Government that its generous exertions have effectually healed one of the most shocking wounds inflicted by inhuman superstition upon our unhappy country

XXII.

THE ADMIRED STORY OF THE SABITRI BRATA, OR THE WONDERFUL TRIUMPH OF EXALTED CHASTITY.

IN the halcyon days of the Hindoo *Raj*, when religion was regarded as the mortar of society, and righteousness the cement of domestic happiness, when Judhistra the Just inculcated, by precept and example, the inflexible rules of moral rectitude, there reigned in the country of Madra a very pious, truthful, wise and benevolent king named *Aswapati*. For a long time he had no child, which made him extremely unhappy. Seeing that the evening of his life was drawing nearer every day and there was no sign of the approach of the wished-for consummation, he undertook to perform a grand religious ceremony with the object of obtaining a son and heir, and daily made ten thousand offerings to please the goddess, Sabitri, from whom the boon was expected.

Thus passed away several long and painful years, at the end of which it came to pass that the goddess, Sabitri, one day suddenly appeared before him in the shape of a beautiful woman, and told him that she was ready to grant him any boon he might ask for, because she was well pleased with him for his austere asceticism, for the purity and sincerity of his heart, for the strict observance of his vow, and for his firm, unshaken faith in her. As was to be expected, he prayed for a good number of sons, affirming that without offspring the life of man upon earth is but a wilderness, obscuring the transitory sunshine of bliss into a chaotic mass of settled gloom.

The goddess said that foreknowing this to be his cherished desire, she had gone to the Creator (Brahmá) to consult him as to the best means for its realization, and through his mercy he would soon be blessed with a female child, in every way worthy of such a pious and virtuous father. Her beauty would shed a lustre around her name and the fame of her rare gifts of nature spread far and wide. She would be the cynosure of all princely eyes, and her charms radiate in all directions. So saying, the goddess disappeared and the king returned to his own capital.

In a short time, the eldest queen became pregnant and in due course of time, gave birth to a daughter of matchless beauty. The king and his Brahmin friends called her Sabitri, after the name of the goddess who granted the boon. Day by day, the princess grew fairer and fairer, and soon passed from the incipient stage of smiling childhood to that of blooming youth. Every one that saw her chiselled features and prepossessing appearance believed that some angelic beauty,—the embodiment of loveliness itself—had descended upon earth in the shape of a lovely damsel. Indeed she was so surpassingly beautiful that no prince, how great or eminent he might be, dared seek her hand in marriage lest his suit should be spurned.

The king, Aswapati, thought of marrying his only daughter, then in the fullness and freshness of youth, to some one worthy of the honor. For some time no royal suitors ventured to solicit her hand for the reasons stated above. At length, Sabitri sought and obtained her father's permission to secure for herself a suitable match. In complying with her request, the father moreover allowed her to take in her travels some of the wisest ministers of the state, whose experience and counsel would be available to her in so momentous an affair. Mounted on a golden chariot and accompanied by a number of gray headed ministers, she left the capital with the benedictions of the hereditary priests, and journeyed far and wide through many a strange country, visiting on her way some of the most delightful hermitages of the venerable old *Rishis*, who were absorbed in meditation.

Sometime after, while the king was attending to the duties of the State and conversing with that renowned sage, Nárada, Sabitri with the ministers returned home from her peregrination. The princess, seeing her father talking with the great Rishi, Nárada, bowed her head down in token of due homage to the venerable Rishi and her respected father. The bustle consequent on the first interview after a long absence being over, Nárada asked the king: "O monarch, where did your daughter go? Whence is she now coming? It is high time that you should give her in marriage to some noble prince worthy of her hand." The king replied, "O revered Rishi, I sent her abroad with some of my wisest ministers in quest of some noble prince, who, to a beautiful person should add all the rarest gifts of wisdom, courage, piety and virtue; now hear from her own mouth, how far she has succeeded in her sacred mission." So saying, the king desired Sabitri to tell them whom she had chosen for her husband. Sabitri, in obedience to her esteemed father's behest, thus spoke in a tone becoming her age and sex. "Father, a pious king named Dyumutsen once ruled the kingdom of Sala. A few days after his accession he lost both his eyes and became totally blind. At that time, his only child was in his infancy, quite incapable of conducting the affairs of the kingdom. His treacherous enemies, taking advantage of his blindness and the infancy of his child, invaded his kingdom and wrested it from his hands. The dethroned king and his beloved queen with their infant child betook themselves to a quiet life of contemplation in an adjacent wood, renouncing all the pleasures of a wicked, ungrateful world. For some years they passed their days in the sequestered wood amidst the abodes of many revered sages, who took a special delight in imbuing the nascent mind of the boy with the germs of moral and religious instruction, promising a full development in maturer years. He was in every way my equal, and him have I chosen as my worthy husband. His name is Satyavana."

Hearing this, the hoary headed Rishi, Narada, thus addressed the monarch. "O monarch, I am grieved to say that your daughter has been unfortunate in her choice, in having thoughtlessly selected the virtuous Satyavana as her husband." The king feelingly enquired: "O great Rishi, are the noble qualities of valour, prudence, forgiveness, piety, devotion, generosity, filial love and affection to be found in Satyavana?" Narada answered, "Satyavana is Súrya's (sun's) equal in matchless glory, is wise as Vrihashpati himself, brave and warlike as Indra, mild and forgiving as Earth." The king asked: "Is the prince a sincere worshipper of God, walking in the path of righteousness? Is he beautiful, amiable and high-minded?" Narada replied, "O king, like Ratideva, the son of Sankriti, the beautiful Satyavana, is generous; like Sibi, the son of Usinara, he is a lover of God and Truth; and is as high-minded as Yayáti; all the pious old Rishis and other good men believe that Satyavana is brave, mild, meek, truthful, faithful to his friends, magnanimous, pious, and sincere in devotion and earnestness." The king again asked: "O venerable sage, you have named all the good qualities that can ennoble humanity; be kind enough to inform me in what he is wanting." "He has one great disqualification," said Narada, "which is enough to outweigh all his virtues, his life upon earth is very short, he is fated to live exactly one year from this day."

Hearing the fearful prophecy of Narada, the king tried his best to dissuade his daughter from the fatal alliance, but all his efforts proved unavailing. Sabitri, firm and constant in her plighted faith, fearlessly replied that, despite the ominious prediction which is suggestive of the appalling horrors of premature widowhood to the mind of a Hindoo female, she could not retract her pledge and surrender her heart to any other being upon earth.

Narada then exclaimed ; "O king, I see your daughter is true to her promise, firm in her faith and constant in her love and attachment to Satyavana. No one will be able to lead her astray from the path of righteousness. Let the unrivalled pair, therefore, be united in the sacred bond of wedlock." The king replied, "O great Rishi, unalterable are your words; what you have now said is just and right. As you are my *Gooroo* (spiritual guide) I will do what you have ordered me to do." "Heaven's choicest blessings be upon you all," said Narada, and departed.

The king now directed his attention to the solemnisation of the nuptials of his beloved daughter with becoming pomp and éclat.

The fair daughter of Aswapati was thus married in due form to Satyavana, the son of the blind old king, Dyumutsen. For a while the happy pair continued to enjoy all the blessings of conjugal life in their blissful and retired cottage, remote from the busy throng of men and quite congenial to religious meditation, though Sabitri knew full well, as predestined by Bidhátá, that this short and transient happiness would be soon followed by long and painful suffering which would very nigh destroy them both.

Thus week after week and month after month rolled away, when at length the prophetic day on which the terrible doom was to be pronounced upon Satyavana drew nearer and nearer, and when Sabitri saw that there remained only four days to complete the terrible year, perhaps the last year of Satyavana's life, at the end of which the fatal torch of *Yama* would appear before her beloved husband, her heart recoiled at the idea. To avert the dreadful doom she undertook the performance of an austere vow, which strictly enjoined three days of continuous fasting and prayer, pouring forth at the feet of the Almighty all the fervours of a devotional heart. Her father-in-law, Dyumutsen, though overwhelmed by the surging wave of grief, endeavoured to dissuade her from undertaking so trying a vow, but his admonition was quite ineffectual. She persistently adhered to her resolution and calmly resigned herself to the dispensations of a wise. and merciful Providence.

Mental conflict, internal perturbation, and continuous fasting made her weak and emaciated, and the prophetic words of Narada incessantly haunted her mind like some fatal vision. It is quite impossible to describe the violent struggles that passed within her when that terrible day at last arrived, and when the inevitable decree of fate by which her dear husband should for ever cease to live would be fulfilled. After bathing in the sacred stream she made burnt offerings to the gods and prostrated herself on the ground, as a mark of profound homage to the honoured feet of the old Rishis, and those of her revered father-in-law and mother-in-law, who in return heartily pronounced their sincere benedictions upon her When the hour for dinner came, she was desired to partake of some refreshment, especially after three days' continuous fastings, but animated by a fervent spirit of devotion she declined to take any food before sunset.

Presently she saw her husband going to the forest with his axe and a bag, to procure fruits and dry wood. Sabitri begged to accompany him, but from the prescience of imminent danger as well as from the warmth of affection he would fain keep her at home, being assured that her tender feet were not fittted to wander in the "brambly wilderness" in her present enfeebled state of body ; but regardless of all admonition she thus exclaimed : "O my beloved Lord, I am not at all weary with fasting, your very presence is my strongest support. I can never be happy without you, so do not turn a deaf ear to the earnest entreaty of an already disconsolate wife, whose fate is bound with yours in a gordian knot which no earthly force can break or cut." Satyavana was at last constrained to yield to her solicitations, and bade her take his father and mother's permission before her departure. It was with the greatest reluctance that their permission was given. Obtaining their benedictions and being armed with the panoply of divine grace, the unhappy pair quitted their sweet home for the dreary forest. On the way, Satyavana, half conscious of what would soon befall him, addressed his loving wife in the following affectionate words: "O dear Sabitri, behold how nature smiles in all her beauty, how the fields are adorned with fragrant flowers, shady groves, and a wide expanse of living verdure, how slowly and smoothly runs the murmuring brook with soothing melody, how the warblers of the forest pour forth their wild but sweet notes without fear of molestation, how merrily the peacock is dancing, how cheerfully the stag is frisking about, and above all, how the stillness of the scene invites the mind to contemplation."

While Sabitri was attentively listening to her husband's descriptive illustration of nature, her heart swelled in her throat, but her eyes were not sullied with even one tear-drop. She continued to follow her husband as a faithful, obedient wife.

At length they entered the forest, and Satyavana after having filled his bag with various kinds of fruits began to cut with his axe the withered branches of the trees. The effort soon overpowered him and he felt some uneasy sensation about his head. He slowly walked down to his dear wife and observed: "O much beloved Sabitri, suddenly I feel an acute headache which, becoming more and more painful, makes me quite insensible and almost breaks my heart. I cannot stand here any longer, but I trust by the aid of balmy sleep, soon to regain my health and strength."

On hearing her husband's heart-rending words, she sat down upon the ground and placed Satyavana's head upon her lap. But as fate had ordained he soon became perfectly insensible. When Sabitri saw this, her wonted presence of mind did not fail her; trusting, however, in the boundless mercy of an overruling Providence, she calmly and composedly waited for the ill-fated hour, when the shadow of death would hide for ever her beloved Satyavana—a doom she was herself prepared to share. Suddenly, after a short while, she believed she saw a grim figure, clothed in red and resplendent with lustre like the sun, slowly approaching her with a chain in his hand. This was not a figment of her imagination. The veritable *Yama* stood beside Satyavana and looked steadfastly upon him.

No sooner did Sabitri see him than she, taking her husband's head from her lap and placing it upon the ground, with trembling heart thus addressed him. "God-like person, your heavenly form and majestic appearance bespeak unmistakably that you are a god among gods. Vouchsafe to unfold yourself and break your mind to me."

Yama replied; "O Sabitri, thou art chaste and constant in thy devotion and meditation, I, therefore, feel no delicacy in satisfying your eager inquiry. I am Yama (Pluto), I am come here for the purpose of carrying away thy dead husband, as his days upon earth are numbered." To this, Sabitri said, "O king, I have heard that your imps carry away the dead bodies from the earth; why are you then come yourself?"

Yama replied, "O amiable Sabitri, while living, your excellent husband possessed many good qualities and was justly remarkable for his righteousness. It was improper, herefore, to have sent my imps to carry him away. With this view I am come myself." So saying Yama forcibly drew out the finger-shaped soul from Satyavana's body. Being deprived of the vital spirit, the dead body became motionless, pale and pallid; and Yama went towards the South. The chaste Sabitri, in order to obtain the fruit of her vow, followed him with sad looks and a heavy heart. Seeing this, Yama remonstrated with her and ordered her to return home and perform the funcral obsequics of her husband. Sabitri said she would go wherever her husband was carried, and that by her unceasing prayer to the Almighty, by her firm faith in her spiritual guide, by the solemn fulfilment of her sacred vow, and by his (Yama's) grace, her course would be free and unrestrained. "O king of the infernal regions," said she, "kindly deign to lend a listening ear to a suppliant's prayer. He that has not obtained a complete mastery over his senses should not come to the forest to lead there either a domestic life, or a student's life, or the life of a devotee. Those who have effectually controlled their passions are fit to fulfil the necessary conditions of the four different modes of life. Of these four modes, the domestic life is decidedly the best, being most favourable to the acquisition of knowledge and wisdom, and to the cultivation of piety and virtue. Persons like myself do not desire to lead any other than a domestic life."

"Now return home, O fair Sabitri; I am much pleased with your wise observations; I am willing to grant you any boon save the life of your husband," exclaimed Yama. Sabitri replied, "O king, be graciously pleased to restore eyesight to my blind father-in-law, and make him powerful as the Sun or the Fire, that he may be enabled to regain his kingdom and rule it with vigour." Yama granted the boon, and directed her to return home after the fatiguing journey. Sabitri answering said, "O virtuous king, I feel no trouble or fatigue while I am with my husband, for a husband is the strength and stay of his wife, and the wife is the sharer of her husband's weal or woe:

> The wife, where danger or dishonor lurks,
> Safest and seemliest by her husband stays,
> Who guards her, or with her the worst endures.

Wherever, therefore, you carry my husband, my foot-steps will dog you thither. Our very first intercourse with the good and the righteous leads to the growth of confidence and kindly feeling, which is always productive of the most beneficial results." Whereupon Yama replied, "O thoughtful lady, thy words are agreeable to my heart; they are fraught with meaning and good sense. I shall willingly grant you another boon save the life of your husband." "Allow me, then, O virtuous king, to ask for a hundred be-gotten sons to my father, who has no son," said Sabitri.

"I grant the boon," said Yama, "now that all your wishes have been consummated, do not continue to follow me any longer. You are far away from your father-in-law's cottage; return home at once."

Sabitri replied, "O virtuous king, we are apt to repose more confidence in the righteous than in ourselves; their kindness amply requites our love and regard." Yama said, "I am very much satisfied with your edifying speech, and am disposed to grant you another boon." Sabitri feeling grateful for the several boons granted unto her, presumed this time to ask for the resurrection of her husband as well as for the birth from them of a hundred powerful, wise and virtuous sons, to be the glory of the country and the ornament of society.

"Be it so," said Yama cheerfully and disappeared.

It is obvious that the fertile imagination of the hereditary priests of Hindoosthan, who, from their traditional mental abstraction, delighted more in the concoction of legendary lore than of the solid, sober realities of life, invented the above Brata or vow, mainly for the consolation of ignorant females, to avert the hardships of widowhood, than which a more unmitigated evil is not to be found in the domestic economy of the Hindoos. The unhallowed institution of the immolation of widows alive, was primarily traceable to the dread of this terrible calamity, which preyed, as it were, on the vitals of humanity. Hence the performance of this Brata is the culminating point of meritorious work in popular estimation, promising to the performer the perpetual enjoyment of connubial happiness, which is more valued by a Hindoo female than all the riches of Golconda.

It is annually celebrated in the Bengalee month of Joysto both by widows and by women whose husbands are alive, by the former, in the hope of averting the evil in another life, by the latter, in the expectation of continuing to enjoy conjugal bliss both in this world and the next.

On the celebration of this Brata on the fourteenth night of the decrease of the moon, the husband, being dressed in clean new clothes, is made to sit on a carpet, the wife, previously washing and drying his feet, puts round his neck a garland of flowers and worships him with sandal and flowers, wrestling hard in prayer for his prolonged life. This being done, she provides for him a good dinner, consisting of different kinds of fruits, sweetmeats, sweet and sour milk and ghee-fried *loochees*, &c. It should be mentioned here that a widowed lady offers the same homage to the god, Naraian, in the place of a husband.

The usual incantation is read by the priest, and she repeats it inaudibly, the substance being in harmony with her cherished desire. He gets his usual fee of two or four rupees and all the offerings in rice, fruits, sweetmeats, clothes, brass utensils, &c. If not dead, a woman has to perform this Brata regularly for fourteen long years, at the end of which the expense is tenfold more, in clothes, beddings, brass utensils, and an entertainment to Brahmins, friends and neighbours, than in the ordinary previous years.

Besides the Bratas described above, there are many others of more or less note, which are annually observed by vast numbers of females, who, from their early religious tendencies, seem to enjoy a monopoly of them. It is, however, a singular fact that the primary object of all these religious vows is the possession of all sorts of worldly happiness, seldom supplemented by a desire of endless blessedness hereafter. This is unquestionably a lamentable desideratum in the original conception and design of the popular Hindoo Shastras, clearly demonstrating its superficiality and poverty.

APPENDIX.

NOTE A.

OBSERVANCES AND RITES DURING PREGNANCY.

From the period of conception a woman is enjoined by way of precaution, to live under certain rules and restrictions, the observance of which is to ensure a safe delivery as well as the safety of the offspring. She is not allowed to put on clothes over which birds of the air have flown, lest their return might prolong the period of her delivery. She fastens a knot to one end of the *Achal* of her *Saree** and keeps it tied about her waist, and spits on her breast once a day before washing her body, and is not allowed to sit or walk in the open compound in order to avoid evil spirits; as a safeguard against their inroads, she constantly wears in the knot of her hair a slender reed five inches long.

When in a state of pregnancy, a Hindoo female is treated with peculiar care, tenderness and affection. She is generally brought from her father-in-law's house to that of her father, where all the members of the family shew her the greatest love lest she should not survive the throes of childbirth. Indeed the first childbirth of a young Hindoo girl is justly considered a struggle between life and death. As a religious safeguard and guarantee for safe delivery, she is made to wear rouud her neck a small *Madoolee* (a very small casket made of gold, silver, or copper), containing some flowers previously consecrated to *Baba Thacoor*† and to drink daily until her delivery a few drops of holy water after touching it with the *Madoolee.*

It is perhaps generally known that a Hindoo girl is married between 9 and 12 years of age—an age when her European sister would not even dream of being united in the bonds of wedlock; and the natural consequence is, she becomes a mother at thirteen or fourteen years. An eminent writer who had studied the subject carefully thus remarks: "Till their thirteenth year, they are stout and vigorous; but after that period, they alter much faster than the women in any of the nations of Europe." Her tender age, her sedentary life, her ignorance of the laws of hygiene, the common dread of childbirth, the want of proper midwives as well as of timely medical aid (should any be necessary), conspire

* A Saree is a piece of cloth, 5 yards long with colored borders.

† A Hindoo god generally kept by the lower orders of the people, such as *Domes*, *Chandals* and *Bagthees.*

sometimes to cause an untimely death. She must continue to observe many precautions until her accouchement is completed.

In the fifth month of her pregnancy takes place her *Kacha Shád.** The day must be an auspicious one according to Hindoo astrologers, and she is treated that day with special indulgence, inasmuch as all the delicacies of the season are given to her without restriction. In the seventh month she is treated with *Bhájá Shád*, when she eats with a few other females (whose husbands and children are all alive) all sorts of parched peas and rice as well as *Methais* and other sweetmeats; in the ninth month, the *Paunchámrita*† ceremony is held, when she is made to wear a red-bordered *Akhanda* Saree (a piece of cloth ten cubits long with the edges uncut), which is preserved with the greatest care lest any jealous and mischievous woman who has lost her children, should clandestinely cut and take away a portion of the same, which is considered a very portentous omen for the preservation of the new born babe.

On the celebration of *Paunchámrita* above mentioned the officiating priest, after repeating the usual incantation, pours into her mouth a little of the delicacies, without the same coming in contact with her teeth. She is forbidden to eat anything else that day except fruits and sweetmeats; and then a good day is appointed for the celebration of the grand final *Shád*, when all the female relatives and connections of the family are invited. In Calcutta, Hindoo females of respectability are not permitted to be seen, much less to walk in the streets; they live in a state of perfect seclusion, entirely apart from the male members of the family, it being considered a very great disgrace should a respectable female be in any way exposed to public gaze. The very construction of a Hindoo family dwelling house clearly indicates the prevalence of the close zenana system; the inmates must have an inner and an outer apartment, there must be an inclosed court-yard reached by tortuous passages, closed by low constructed doors, through which one has to wriggle rather than to walk; the sun seldom shines into it; small contracted staircases, foul confined air, no circulation or ventilation are the result: the noxious effluvia evaporating from this or that side of the house, especially from the lower floor, is a nuisance which the inmates put up with,

---

* *Kacha* means raw; the term *Shád* is synonymous with desire. The ceremony is so called from the female being allowed that day to eat all kinds of native pickles, preserves, sweetmeats, confectionery, several kinds of fruits then in season, sweet and sour milk, &c., but not rice or any sort of food grains. Her desire is gratified, lest the girl should not survive the childbirth. should be mentioned here that from the second month of her preganancy, she feels a great longing to eat Páthkholá (a sort of half burnt very thin earthen cake) which pregnant girls relish very much on account of its peculiar *sodha* flavour.

Paunchámrita means five kinds of delicacies, the food of the gods, consisting of milk ghee (clarified butter), dhahie (curded milk), cowdung and honey.

with scarcely any complaint. The drainage and water works have certainly effected considerable improvement towards the promotion of cleanliness, but still the dirty and filthy state of most of the family dwelling houses is a notorious fact. By a small door only there exists a communication between the inner and outer apartment; should the house be a small one, say from three to four *cottahs,* which is generally the case in such a crowded city as Calcutta, and should the women talk loud enough to be heard by men outside, they are not only instantly checked but severely reprimanded for the liberty. The great privacy of the close zenana system is, however, broken by females being obliged to travel in a Railway carriage: though Hindoos of rank, whenever they have occasion to go on pilgrimage by Rail, generally engage a reserved compartment for the females, yet they cannot manage to preserve absolute privacy when going into or coming out of the carriage at the Railway Stations.

To return to the grand final *Shád*, on the day appointed an awning is put up over the court-yard of the house. *Palkees* are sent to each of the families invited; and the guests (nearest female relatives) begin to come in from ten in the morning; a general spirit of hilarity prevails on all sides, noise and bustle ensue, the women are busy in receiving their guests, preparations are being made for the grand feast, the men outside direct the *Palkee* bearers where next to go, the little children have their own share of juvenile frolic, the young damsels and the aged matrons are seen speaking to their respective friends with mutual love, affection and confidence; and signs of joviality and conviviality are seen every where. It is on such occasions that women unbosom themselves to each other, and freely and unreservedly communicate their feelings, their thoughts, their wishes, nay their secrets to friends of congenial spirit and temper; their conversation knows no end, their amiable loveliness almost spontaneously developes itself; they unburden their minds of the heavy load of accumulated thoughts; their joys and sorrows, their happiness and misery, their sympathy and emotion, pleasurable or painful, have their full scope. If they are naturally garrulous they become more so at such a jovial assemblage, so that one can dive deepest down into their hearts on such an occasion. Many a matrimonial match is proposed and matured at such meetings, and to crown the whole, sisters of kindred spirit embrace each other with all the warmth of genuine love and affection. If their minds are contracted by reason of scanty culture, their hearts are full of affection, sympathy and susceptibility, which cannot fail to exercise a beneficial influence on human nature.

On such occasions, females are allowed to have some amusement or *támáshá*, according to their liking, (but of course not such as betrays a vitiated taste, overstepping the bounds of decorum, which was the case some years back). Dancing girls and *Panchálleys* are entertained, who contribute not a little to the amusement of the assembled guests. Immured within the walls of a close zenana they are seldom suffered to enjoy such unrestrained liberty. Otto of roses, rose water out of gold or silver pots, nosegays, and *paun* or betel are freely distributed among them. They sit on benches or chairs, or squat down barefooted on *forash bichana* (a clean white sheet), and enjoy the *támáshá* to their hearts' content. These amusements continue till evening, entertaining the guests with songs on gods and goddesses (Doorga, Krishna and his mistress, Rádhá): those relating to Doorga have a reference to the ill treatment she experienced at the hands of her parents, but those pertaining to Krishna and Rádhá tell of his juvenile frolics with his mother and the milkmaids, and amorous songs on disappointed love, which, though they may appear harmless to their worshippers, have nevertheless a partial tendency to debase the minds of females. By way of encouragement, the singing and dancing girls receive, besides their hire, presents of money, clothes and shawls, according to the circumstances of the parties retaining them. To do our women justice, however, it is pleasing to reflect that the progress of enlightenment has of late years wrought a salutary change in their minds. Instead of the former *Kabees* (songs) which were shamefully characterised by the worst species of obscenity and immorality, they have imbibed a taste for more sober and refined entertainments. Moral and intellectual improvement amongst perfectly secluded females is a sure harbinger of national regeneration. The young and the sprightly, as is naturally to be expected, enjoy these amusements most; but the more elderly and thoughtful females make the best of the opportunity in conversation about domestic affairs with those of their own age and kinship. They have certainly no distaste for these frivolous entertainments, but the thoughts and cares of home press more heavily on their minds. Age and experience have taught them to regard the enjoyment of unalloyed domestic felicity as the chief end of life. A good Hindoo housewife is a model of moral excellence.

About four o'clock in the afternoon, when almost all the guests are assembled together, long parallel rows of *pirays*, or wooden seats, the one quite apart from the other—are arranged in straight lines in the courtyard, in the midst of which is placed the seat of the pregnant girl, which, by way of distinction, is painted white with rice paste *(âlpând)* with appropriate devices. Adorned with ornaments of glittering gold, bedecked with precious stones, and dressed in an embroidered Benares *Saree*, she walks gracefully towards her particular seat, which is a signal for others (widows excepted) to follow; they all squat down on the wooden seats, before which are placed small pieces of green plantain leaves and a few little earthen plates and a cup, which are intended to serve the purposes of plates and glasses. Before her stands a light, a *conch* is sounded, and a rupee with which her forehead is touched is kept for the gods, for safe delivery. Fruits of different kinds, about fifteen or sixteen sorts of sweetmeats, *loochee*, *kachoory*, *papur* (flour fried with ghee) in the shape of *châppâtees*, vegetable curries of several kinds, sweet and sour milk, are provided for the guests, the female relatives of the girl serving as stewards. No adult male member of the family is allowed to assist in the feast, because Hindoo females blush to eat before men. Being most pre-eminent in point of caste, Brahmin women are served *first*. Here the rules of caste are strictly observed, and no departure therefrom is tolerated. It is not uncommon that uninvited females, or more properly speaking, intruders contrive by some means or other, to mix with the company; but they are soon singled out by the more shrewd and experienced, and to their chagrin and disappointment, instantly removed from their seats. They do not, however, go away with curses on their lips, but receive a few things and are ordered to leave the house without a *Palkee*.*

After the feast is over, the women, washing their hands and mouths, express their good wishes for the safe delivery of the girl, and make preparations for returning home. Here confusion and bustle ensue consequent on the simultaneous desire of all to return home *first*, and as the sun begins to set, their anxiety becomes more intense to see the faces of their absent children; laying aside their wonted modesty, some of them almost unblushingly make a rush and enter the *first Palkee* that comes in their way, regardless alike of their sex and the rules of

---

* A rather contemptible practice still lurks in the Hindoo community at the time of dining on such public occasions. The females for the most part place a portion of the dinner aside for the sake of carrying it home for their absent children; even a rich woman feels no hesitation or humiliation in following the example of her less fortunate sisters. We can only account for this unseemly practice on the supposition that the Hindoo ladies do not like to partake of good things without sharing them with their beloved children at home. The wish is not an unnatural one but the practice most unquestionably *is*. In making provision for a grand feast, the Hindoos are obliged to treble the quantity of food for the number of guests invited, specially when it is a *pucca jalpan*, consisting of *loochees* and *sundeshes* (sweetmeats). If they invite 100 families they must provide for about 300 persons, for the reasons specified above. It is a pity that in a matter of public entertainment both males and females cannot resist the temptation of appropriating a portion of the food to other than the legitimate purpose. Here feminine modesty is violated by infringing the ordinary rules of etiquette.

decorum. If 100 families are invited, about ten *Palkees* are retained. Hackney carriages are sometimes substituted in place of *Palkees*, but whatever arrangements are made it is next to impossible to satisfy at least 200 people at one and the same time. The guests are never expected to find their own conveyances. Before coming, some of them keep the Palanquin waiting for an hour or so, while they are engaged at their toilet and adorning their persons with divers ornaments. It is not unfrequently the case on such occasions that females in poor circumstances borrow ornaments from their more prosperous friends, in order to appear in society to the best advantage. In the absence of mental accomplishments, Hindoo ladies necessarily set a high value on the jewels about their persons. Some twenty years back, massive articles of gold were considered the most *recherché* ornaments, so much so that some rich ladies were adorned with gold articles alone to the weight of 6 or 7 lbs.; to an English lady, this might appear incredible, but it is a fact which does not admit of any contradiction. Hindoo females are religiously forbidden to wear gold ornaments about their feet, it being considered a mark of disrespect to *Lukxmee* (goddess of prosperity,) hence they put on pairs of solid massive silver *malls* or anklets, weighing sometimes about 3lbs.; though such massive articles are a great incumbrance to the free motion of the limbs, they are nevertheless used with great pleasure. Indeed it has been sarcastically remarked that were a Hindoo lady offered a gold *grindstone* to wear round her neck, weighing some 20lbs. she would gladly accept the offer and go through the ordeal. But as the spread of English education has improved the minds of the people, it has likewise improved their taste; instead of massive gold ornaments, ladies of the present day prefer those of delicate diamond cut workmanship, set with pearls and precious stones such as *chick*, *sittahaur*, *tárâhâur*, *seetee*, *tabij*, *bajoo*, *jasum*, *nabaruttun taga*, bracelets of six or seven patterns, and ear-rings of three or four kinds, for which girls in very early youth perforate their ears in 8 or 10 places, as also their noses in two places. By their choice of the modern ornaments they shew their preference for elegance to mere weight. Brilliant Pearl necklaces* of from seven to nine rows, and costly

---

* That the Hindoos have, for a long time, manifested a strong passion for ornaments, is a historical fact. Even so far back as the Mahratta dynasty, it was said of Dowlut Rao Sindhia that "his necklaces were gorgeous, consisting of many rows of Pearls, as large as small marbles, strung alternately with emeralds. The Pearl *(moti)* was his passion and the necklace was constantly undergoing change whenever a finer bead was found; the title of "Lord of a hundred Provinces" was far less esteemed by him than that of *motiwalla* the "Man of Pearls," by which he was commonly designated in his Camp. It was perhaps a sight of this description that led Macaulay to say—"Our plain English coats command more respect than all the gorgeous orient pearl of the East," indicating thereby the involuntary awe of savage for civilized life.

bijouteries of modern style, have superseded the old-fashioned solid gold *Bhawootees* and *Taurs*. A rich lady is sometimes seen with jewellery worth 15,000 to 20,000 Rupees and upwards; as a matter of course, such a lady is the cynosure of all eyes, and the rest of the company move as satellites round the primary planet. Conscious of her superiority in this respect and puffed up with vanity she disdains to hold converse with her less fortunate sisters. She is tramping, as it were, "to the tinkling sound of the ornaments of gold and gems on her person." As the grand centre of attraction, her gait, her gestures, her movements form the subject of general criticism, and as an object of envy she continues to be talked of even after the return of the guests to their homes.

In the villages, however, silver ornaments are more in vogue than gold ones, simply because the rural population have neither the taste nor the means of the people of the city. As a rule, the Hindoos invest their savings in gold and silver which is turned to good account in times of need and distress. Throughout Hindoosthan, the people have so great a *penchant* for gold and silver ornaments that not only women but men also adorn their persons with solid articles of sterling gold. I have seen Setts (shroffs) and Malgoozars go about with ornaments of considerable value; their dress, however, is generally exceedingly tawdry, and bears no correspondence to the worth of the articles of gold they carry about. I once weighed a solid pure gold chain worn by a Sett round his waist, which the natives call *Gote*, weighing over 4 lbs., worth about 3,000 Rupees.

In Bengal little children are seen with gold ornaments on their persons* till they are 6 years of age, but adults are entirely free from this passion. When a male child is born to a respectable Hindoo, the heart of the mother irresistibly yearns to adorn its person with ornaments, especially at the time of *vath* (christening), *i. e.*, at 6 months of age for a male and 7 months for a female child.

When the females return home after the entertainment, it is truly a scene of "sorry to part, happy to meet again." It is seldom that such opportunities are afforded them to give free vent to their feelings, thoughts and wishes;—a human being always feels unhappy at living in a perfectly isolated state; he or she naturally longs for society, and this longing is alike manifest in both sexes. The greater the restraint, as

* Such as *Bore*, *Komurpatta*, *Nimfull*, *Neyboofull*, *Ghoomur* round the waist, *Tabrej*, *Bajoo*, *Balla*, *Jasum*, *Taga*, &c. on the hands, pearl and gold necklaces of various sorts and gold mohurs or sovereigns strung together in the shape of a necklace.

in the case of Hindoo ladies, the stronger the desire for social intercourse. Can a zenana Hindoo lady with her veiled modesty suppress the impulse to look about through the shutters of a closed Palkee, with guards on both sides, in the light of day? The impulse is by no means a criminal one but is prompted by the irresistible influence of nature. The parting exclamation on such occasions is, "Sister, when shall I have the good fortune to see you again?" "Why, not before long," is the common reply. The consummation of the desire, if long deferred, naturally produces feelings of discontent. A few days after the feast the families that were invited, give a tangible proof of their regard for the pregnant girl by making her presents of clothes and sweetmeats according to their respective circumstances, as a matter of course the nearest relatives making the richest presents.

Note B.

THE GODDESS SOOBACHINEE.

The following is the story of this goddess:—In a certain village there lived a poor Brahmin boy, whose poverty was well-known throughout the neighbourhood. One day a fisherman came to sell some fish, on seeing which the boy began to cry for them. His mother, a poor aged widow, though very desirous to satisfy the craving of her son, had unfortunately no means to buy them, whereupon the fisherwoman affected by the cries of the boy, offered to give her credit and said she would come for the price on her way home. Meantime the mother cooked the fish; but before her son had time to eat them, the fisherwoman, according to her promise, returned for the price. The old woman being still unable to pay, the fish vendor demanded the return of the fish, which, though cooked, she was willing to take back. This being done, the boy, however, had the advantage of tasting the soup made of the fishes and was so much pleased with the taste of animal food that he could not resist the temptation of stealing one day a *lame* duck belonging to the king, and eating it privately. Investigation being made, the theft was traced to the poor Brahmin boy, who being summoned before the king, was tried, convicted and sentenced to be imprisoned, at which the mother became inconsolable. Seeing her distress and despondency, the goddess Doorga, in the form of *Soobachinee*, appeared to her in a dream, and, giving her hopes of consolation and better luck for the future, eventually advised her to perform the worship of the goddess *Soobachinee.* In obedience to the above injunction, she did as she was directed. Seventeen ducks made of rice-paste (sixteen with two perfect legs and one with a lame leg) formed a part of the ceremony. After the performance of the worship and the expiatory rite of *homa* (burnt offering) which expiates all sin, the holy water being sprinkled on the feathers of the stolen *lame* duck, that were concealed under the ashes, the devoured duck was at once restored to life and sent back to the king's poultry-yard. The miraculous resuscitation of the duck was brought to the notice of the king, who immediately sent for the poor old woman and questioned her how the dead *lame* duck was made alive again; the old woman, trembling through fear, related all the particulars about the appearance of the goddess in a dream. The king, being satisfied as to the truth of the tale, ordered the captive boy to be released at once and brought to his presence, concluding that the goddess must have been very propitious to the old woman and her son Consulting his ministers on the subject, he said within himself he could. not have a better match for his daughter, who was of marriageable age, than the late delinquent. So the nuptials were duly solemnized with becoming pomp, and the poor Brahman family lived ever after in a state of great affluence and happiness. Hindoo ladies of the orthodox school learn this tale almost in their nursery, and feel a peculiar delight in reciting it on certain occasions.

NOTE C.

The writings of the ancient Hindoo sages, as handed down to us by history and tradition, incontestably prove that they were chiefly theists; but as their religious ideas were supremely transcendental, ill suited to the comprehension of the great mass of the people, and consequently not adapted to bring joy, peace and rest to the mind, their descendants learnt to modify those ideas and practically reduce them to the level of the popular understanding. They gradually created a Trinity, *i. e.*, the Creator, the Preserver, and the Destroyer. But as this triad was not sufficiently attractive or intelligible to the unlettered mass, who wanted something in the shape of real, tangible personification of the deity, in place of indistinct, invisible supernatural beings, a designing priesthood subsequently attempted to satisfy their wishes by foisting upon them a whole rabble of gods and goddesses, which are almost as innumerable as the pebbles on the sea shore. In numerical strength the Pantheon of the Hindoos far surpasses that of the Egyptians, Greeks, and the Romans. What ancient system of mythology contained so many as 330 million gods and goddesses? As in mythology, so in chronology, the Hindoos stand unrivalled. Their pantheon is as capacious and extensive as their antiquity* is unfathomable and prehistoric. The origin of the Puranic mythology is to be attributed to this national predilection; and the worship of the female deities with bloody sacrifices is intended to terrify the ignorant populace into superstitious beliefs still grosser than were habitual to them.

The antiquity of the Brahminical creed and of the religious systems incorporated into, and engrafted on it, has long been a subject of interesting inquiry. It is not my intention to go into the subject more deeply than merely to affirm that it is still a debatable point among the most distinguished orientalists, whether or not the Egyptians and Greeks borrowed their system of mythology from that of the Hindoos, and afterwards improved on it by divesting it of the grosser excrescences. The character of the Hindoo deities is more or less puerile, impure and ungodly, not possessing any of the cardinal virtues, such as become the living and true God. Desiring to steer clear of such deformities and impurities, the Greeks and Romans consecrated separate temples to "Virtue, Truth, Piety, Chastity, Clemency, Mercy, Justice, Faith, Hope and Liberty."

It is a remarkable fact, says Ward, that "the sceptical part of mankind have always been partial to heathenism. Voltaire, Gibbon, Hume &c. have been often charged with a strong partiality for the Grecian and Roman idolatries; and many Europeans in India are suspected of having made large strides towards heathenism. Even Sir William Jones, whose recommendation of the Holy Scripture (found in his Bible after his death,) has been so often and so deservedly quoted, it is said, to

---

* It is curious to relate that Mr. Halhed, when he wrote his "Code of Gentoo Laws," hesitated to believe the Bible because it was outdone in chronology by the histories of the Chinese and Hindoos. With sacred reverence he exclaims, at the close of his account of the four *yagas*, "To such antiquity the Mosaic Creation is but as yesterday, and to such ages the life of Methuselah is no more than a span?" He says in another page. "The conscientious scruples of Brydone will always be of some weight in the scale of philosophy." If the age or reign of Brahma, *viz.*, 55,987,200,000,000 years, excited such sacred awe in the mind of this gentleman, what would have been his sensations, and how strong his faith in the holy writ of the Hindoos, if he had happened to read in the Ramayana the account of Rama's army, which this holy writ says, amounted to 1,000,000,000,000,000,000,000 soldiers, or rather monkeys? Again, two thousand times the four yagas, or 8,460,000,000 years is the age of the sage, *Markanda*. What; in the name of Mr. Halhed, is the life of Methuselah to this? This unbeliever in Moses became at last, it is said, a firm believer in *Richard Brothers*."

please his Pundit, was accustomed to study the Shastras with the image of a Hindoo god placed on his table; and his fine metrical translations of idolatrous hymns are known to every lover of verse. In the same spirit, we observe, that figures and allusions to the ancient idolatries are retained in almost all modern poetical compositions and even in some Christian writings."

It has been very wisely remarked by a philosophical traveller, Dr. Clarke, that "by a proper attention to the vestiges of ancient superstition, we are sometimes enabled to refer a whole people to their original ancestors, with as much, if not more certainty, than by observations made upon their language; because the superstition is engrafted on the stock, but the language is liable to change." Writing on the same subject, Sir William Jones remarks, "if the festivals of the old Greeks, Persians, Romans, Egyptians and Goths, could be arranged with exactness in the same form with the Indian, there would be found a striking resemblance among them; and an attentive comparison of them all, might throw great light on the religion, and perhaps on the history, of the primitive world."

The Egyptians described the source of the Nile as flowing from Osiris; so the Hindoos represent the holy stream of the Ganges as flowing from the head of Iswara, which Sir William Jones so beautifully describes in his hymn to Ganga:

> "Above the reach of mortal ken,
> On blest Coelasa's top, where every stem
> Flowed with a vegetable gem,
> Mahasa stood, the dread and joy of men;
> While Párvati, to gain a boon,
> Fixed on his locks a beamy moon,
> And hid his frontal eye in jocund play,
> With reluctant sweet delay;
> All nature straight was locked in dim eclipse,
> Till Brahmins pure, with hallowed lips
> And warbled prayers restored the day,
> When Ganga from his brow, with heavenly fingers free,
> Sprang radiant, and descending, graced the caverns of the west."

For composing such fine metrical translations of idolatrous hymns, Mr. Foster finds fault with the conduct of Sir William Jones: he writes, "I could not help feeling a degree of regret, in reading lately the Memoirs of the admirable and estimable Sir William Jones. Some of his researches in Asia have no doubt incidentally served the cause of religion; but did he think the least possible direct service had been rendered to Christianity, that his accomplished mind was left at leisure for hymns to the Hindoo gods? Was not this a violation even of neutrality, and an offence, not only against the gospel, but against theism itself? I know what may be said about personification, license of poetry, and so on, but should not a worshipper of God hold himself under a solemn obligation to abjure all tolerance of even poetical figures that can seriously seem, in any way whatever, to recognise the pagan divinities or abominations, as the prophets of Jehovah would have called them? What would Elijah have said to such an employment of talents? It would have availed little to have told him, that these divinities were only personifications (with their appropriate representative idols) of objects in nature, of elements, or of abstractions. He would have sternly replied—'And was not Baal, whose prophets I destroyed, the same?'"

Dr. Stiles, President of Yale College in North America, was so highly impressed with the amazing antiquity of the Hindoo Shastras that he wrote to Sir William Jones, asking him to make a search among the Hindoos for the Adamic books. Had he not been a sincere Christian, he would have asked Sir William to send him a translation of a book written some two or three millions of years ago.

General Stewart, who lived in Wood Street, Calcutta, was said to have made a large collection of Hindoo idols, which he arranged in the portico of his house. He was so fond of them that, it was said, a Brahmin was engaged to perform the daily worship, while he himself led the life of a Hindoo *rishi* or saint, inasmuch as he totally abstained from the use of either wine or meat.

Such instances of partiality on the part of enlightened Christians towards heathenism, we do not see in the present day. In the early times of the British settlement in India, there was a strong mania for exploring the untrodden field of Braminical learning, and the unfathomable antiquity in which it was imbedded. The philosophical theories of the *Munees* and *Rishis*, their sublime conceptions concerning the origin of the world and the unity of God, their utter indifference to worldly concerns and sensual gratifications, their living in sequestered *âshrums*, the practice of religious austerities, the subjugation of passions, and above all, their pure, devotional spirit, lent an enchantment to their teachings, which was, in the highest degree, fascinating. It was not an ordinary phenomenon in the annals of the human intellect that Europeans, possessing all the advantages of modern civilization, should go so far as to entertain a sort of religious veneration for a system of polytheism, which even the natives of the country now-a-days denounce as puerile and absurd. Deeper researches have, however, subsequently dissipated the delusion, and thrown on the subject a great body of light, which the progress of Western knowledge is daily increasing.

NOTE D.

THE BÁMÁCHÁREE FOLLOWERS OF KALI.

In some parts of Bengal and Assam, there still exists a sect of Hindoos, known by the name of *Bámácháreees*, or the followers of the female energy, who practise a series of *Poornabishaka* orgies in the name of this celestial goddess which are nothing less than abominable. The following is a rough programme of the rite. The Brahmin who is to perform the ceremony sits upon a sham image of the goddess in a private room, having beside him at the same time a quantity of flowers, red sandal paste, holy water, copper pans, plantain and other fruits, green plantain leaves, parched peas, cooked fish and flesh, and a certain quantity of spirituous liquor. When night approaches he takes the disciple who is to be initiated into the room, with nine females and nine males of different castes, with one female for himself and another for the disciple, and makes them all sit down on the floor. Taking up a small copper pan and a little of the holy water, he sprinkles it on all present and then proceeds with closed eyes to repeat a solemn incantation to the following effect: "O goddess, descend and vouchsafe thy blessings to Horomohun (the name of the devotee) who has hitherto groped in the dark, not knowing what thou art; these offerings are all at thy service"; saying this, he whispers in his ear the root of the *mantra*. From that time the goddess becomes his guardian deity. The Brahmin Gooroo then goes through divers other formulas, pausing for a while to serve and distribute liquor in a human skull or cocoanut shell to all the devotees, himself setting the example first. He next desires the females to lay aside their clothes, and bids his new disciple adore them as the living personifications of the goddess. Eating and drinking now go on freely, the males taking what is left by the females. Towards the close of the ceremony, the disciple, baptised in liquor, makes presents of clothes and money to the priest and all the men and women present. It is easy to conceive what sort of devotional spirit is evoked by the performance of these abominable orgies. Happily for the interests of morality in this country, the sect is nearly extinct, except in the most obscure parts of Assam and Bengal.